PRAISE FOR

Country Matters

"A prose stylist of surpassing wit and grace." —*Talk* magazine

"Korda's search for a rural paradise is easy, often hilarious, reading."
—Maxine Kumin, *New York Times Book Review*

"In *Country Matters,* Korda addresses a hackneyed theme and gives it a fresh flip. His nostalgia and affection for country life make his reminiscence a pleasure to read." —*Richmond Times-Dispatch*

"If you own a country house or dream of owning one, you'll enjoy this wise and amusing account of the foibles and rewards of giving up busy big city living for the simplicity of an ailing eighteenth-century farmhouse located in a dairy community in upstate New York."
—A. E. Hotchner

"The New York population growth will certainly diminish after Michael Korda's new book appears in bookstores. But despite the love/hate transplanted New Yorkers feel for the countryside, after a short time love wins out. [*Country Matters*] will become a much-loved American classic for everyone." —Bill Blass, designer

"Korda brings a foreigner's eye to his surroundings. . . . The overall effect is charming and ofttimes witty." —*Publishers Weekly*

"Why travel to Provence when smart pigs and charming eccentrics abound right here in rural America? Michael Korda, that sly anthropologist, serves up the humor and the humanity he's found living in the country, and reveals himself and his Margaret to be charming eccentrics themselves (not that that's news to his friends)."

—Richard Rhodes

"Brilliantly mapping the territory between fantasy and reality, Michael Korda's hilariously funny book is a guide to everything from weighing a pig and mollifying a plumber to dealing with unpredictable weather and breathtaking, surprising beauty."

—Susan Cheever, author of *As Good as I Could Be*

"Anyone who lives in a fast-changing rural area outside a big city will resonate to Michael's hilarious and sometimes exasperating experiences. Frankly, our best friends are the Fire Department!"

—Barbara Tober, owner of a horse farm in Dutchess County

About the Author

Michael Korda is the editor in chief of Simon & Schuster, as well as the author of *Charmed Lives*; *Another Life: A Memoir of Other People*; *Man to Man: Surviving Prostate Cancer*; the number-one bestseller *Power!*; and several bestselling novels, including *Queenie*, *The Fortune*, and *The Immortals*. He lives with his wife, Margaret, in New York City and in Dutchess County, New York.

ALSO BY MICHAEL KORDA

Another Life

Man to Man

The Immortals

Curtain

The Fortune

Queenie

Worldly Goods

Charmed Lives

Success!

Power!

Male Chauvinism!

COUNTRY MATTERS

The Pleasures and Tribulations

OF

Moving from a Big City

TO AN

Old Country Farmhouse

Michael Korda

ILLUSTRATIONS BY THE AUTHOR

Perennial
An Imprint of HarperCollins*Publishers*

A hardcover edition of this book was published in 2001 by HarperCollins Publishers.

First Perennial edition published 2002.

Illustrations by the author

Designed by Amy Hill

Map copyright © 2001 by David Cain

The Library of Congress has catalogued the hardcover edition as follows:

Korda, Michael.

Country matters: the pleasures and tribulations of moving from a big city to an old country farmhouse / Michael Korda; illustrations by the author.

p. cm.

ISBN 0-06-019772-2 (acid-free paper)

1. Korda, Michael. 2. Pleasant Valley (N.Y.)—Biography. 3. Pleasant Valley (N.Y.)—Social life and customs. 4. Country life—New York (State)—Pleasant Valley. 5. City dwellers—New York (State)—New York—Biography. 6. Dutchess County (N.Y.)—Social life and customs. I. Title.

F129.P72K67 2001

974.7'33—dc21

2001016670

ISBN 0-06-095748-4 (pbk.)

02 03 04 05 06 ❖/RRD 10 9 8 7 6 5 4 3 2 1

For Margaret—

and in memory of her father

Paul Mogford

farmer, gentleman

Contents

Cela est bien dit, répondit Candide, mais il faut cultiver notre jardin.

—Voltaire, *Candide*

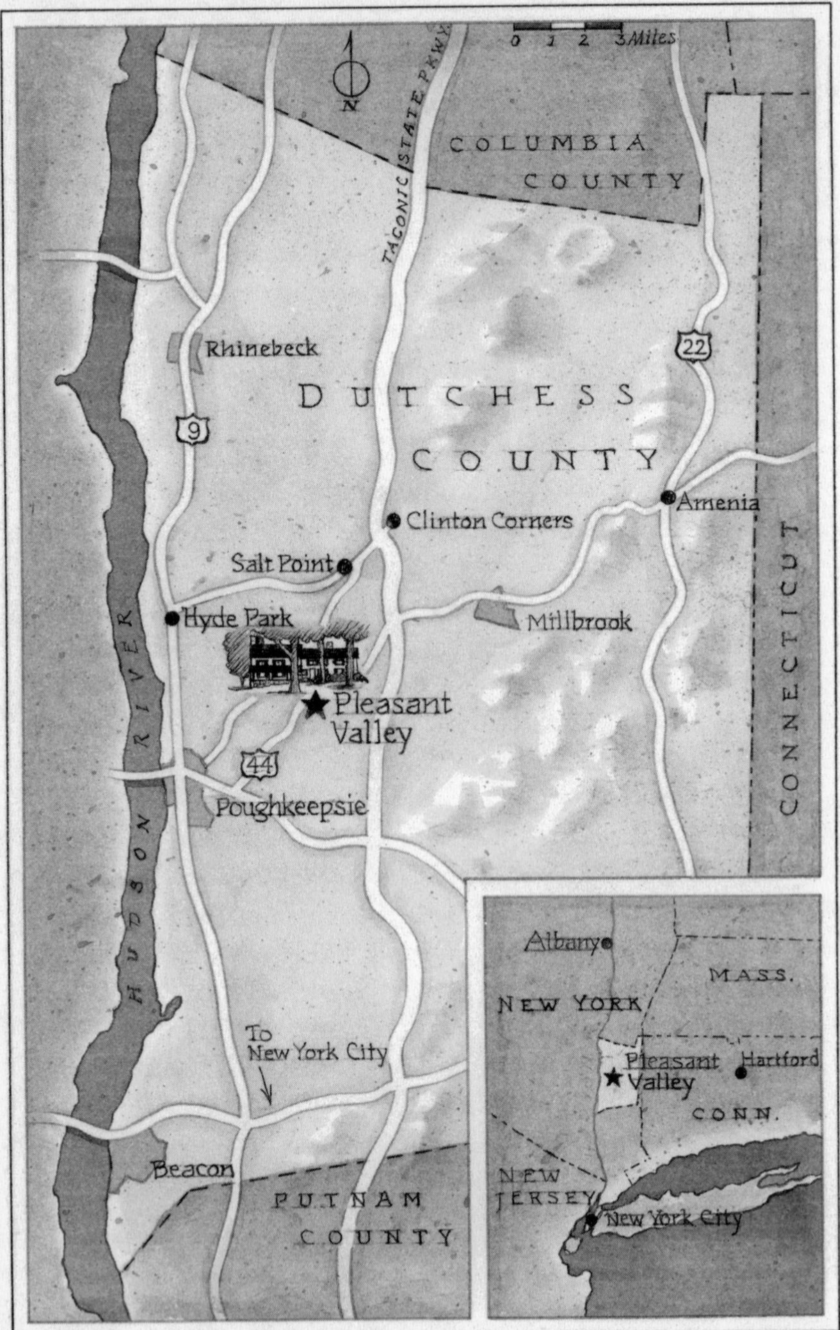
0 1 2 3 Miles
N
TACONIC STATE PKWY.
COLUMBIA
COUNTY
Rhinebeck
22
DUTCHESS
COUNTY
9
Armenia
Clinton Corners
Salt Point
Hyde Park
Millbrook
Pleasant
Valley
44
Poughkeepsie
HUDSON RIVER
CONNECTICUT
To
New York City
Beacon
PUTNAM
COUNTY
Albany
MASS.
NEW YORK
Pleasant
Valley
Hartford
CONN.
NEW
JERSEY
New York City

The Six "Golden Rules"

OF

Owning an Old House

1. Every change, however small and insignificant it may appear, will bring about a whole host of unexpected problems and expenses.

2. Behind every change, however small, lies the threat of "structural problems."

3. What the eye doesn't see, the heart doesn't grieve for.

4. Leave well enough alone.

5. Never sit down to lunch, because the moment you do, somebody will appear at the door with a problem.

6. If something will last ten years before it collapses or self-destructs, *leave it alone!*

CHAPTER ONE

"He Don't Know Shit About Septics"

"The Old Hubner Place"

TWENTY-ONE YEARS AGO, when my wife, Margaret, and I first moved up to the country from New York City and bought an eighteenth-century farmhouse in Pleasant Valley, New York, not far from Poughkeepsie, we didn't give much thought to our new neighbors, who were mostly hardworking dairy farmers of seventeenth-century Dutch or English stock and, while not exactly unfriendly, were reluctant to enter into conversation with people who didn't raise Holsteins and weren't interested in the price of milk.

Along with the house, we acquired (or were acquired by) a bluff, jovial, pink-cheeked old man in his late sixties named Harold Roe, a local who mowed lawns and was reputedly handy with a backhoe, a bush hog, a York rake, and a dozer blade—all objects that were soon to loom larger in our lives than we had supposed.

Harold turned up in the driveway the day we took possession of our new home and announced that everything was running to rack and ruin. A bulky, muscular man, despite his age, he waved around him to indicate how widespread our problems were. More than slightly deaf, Harold had a voice to wake the dead. Our trees needed pruning, wiring, fertilizing, our lawns needed emergency care, our shrubs wanted "whacking back"—a favorite phrase of his, as we were soon to discover, and by which he meant a kind of scorched earth policy; he didn't like the look of our cedar-shingled roof or our wooden gutters either, into one of which he contemptuously drove the blade of his folding penknife and announced with great satisfaction: "Dry rot."

Although the previous owners were still within earshot of normal speech, let alone Harold's roar, and were going through a small emotional moment together as they gave up their home of thirty years, he pointed to them as the source of our troubles. "They was do-it-themselves-ers," he shouted. "Did all the work without knowing how." He voiced his contempt: "Too tight with the dollar to hire help."

Harold was part of a numerous local clan of canny countrymen—there were a good many mailboxes around us that bore the name Roe—and one of his daughters had married into the Daley clan, which was almost as canny and widespread, and included the local highway superintendent and his brother "Turk" Daley, Harold's son-in-law, who dealt in sand, gravel, and septic system installation.

Harold himself, we soon learned, was one of those vanishing Americans who could set his hand to pretty much anything, from welding to fencing, and who put in an uncomplaining fourteen or fifteen hours a day of hard manual labor, for which he insisted on being paid in cash—the offer of a check had roughly the same effect on him as that of a cross when presented to a vampire. His only hobby was snowmobiling, a sport that had not hitherto played any part in our lives; in fact, he was the president of the local snowmobilers' club, and we had hardly shaken hands before he asked us to open up our land to them. This, as we soon discovered, was the first thing most of our neighbors wanted to know about us. Would we keep our land open to the Rombout Hunt, for foxhunting? Would we continue to let our neighbor to the south hay our fields? Would we open our land at the appropriate season to pheasant shooters, bird-watchers, cross-country skiers, and deer hunters, not to speak of one neighbor who trapped animals for their fur? Most of these people took rejection badly. Our home might be our castle, but our land appeared to be community property.

Shortly after we had settled in, on a hot summer day, we gave a dinner party to celebrate our new home, and as I was greeting guests in the driveway, I noticed an unfamiliar and unpleasant smell. I traced it to its source, and found the unmistakable signs of sewage rising in the garden, just in front of the dining room windows. Clearly, the situation was not going to get any better, so even though it was a Saturday evening, I called Harold, who soon appeared with son-in-law Turk in a pickup truck. Together, they sniffed the aroma, agreed on what it was, then proceeded to dig up the garden Harold had only just planted for us at considerable expense.

Since I felt obliged to show a certain amount of interest, I abandoned our guests from time to time to see how the work was getting on and bring Harold and Turk iced tea. Soon they had uprooted Margaret's favorite hedge and dug deep into the lawn, in search of the septic tank. On my next visit I brought them a couple of beers and asked a few questions, if only to show that I was interested and no citified snob. When they finally found the tank, would it have to be replaced? How much of our precious lawn would have to be backhoed if there was a problem with our leach field? Could the broken pipe to the tank—the prime source of the trouble, though not, as it was turning out, the sum total of it—be repaired, or would it have to be replaced?

Neither Harold nor Turk was eager to answer questions. Like surgeons, they refused to make guesses. "We'll have to see," or "It depends," was about as much as I was able to get out of them, and that was that. In the end, they went away as darkness fell, promising to return the next day with a backhoe and a bulldozer, leaving me with the task of telling Margaret that her lawn was about to be transformed into the equivalent of the testing grounds of the Royal Tank Corps at Chobam, and would she please not flush the toilet.

Eventually, in a saga that involved huge pieces of diesel-powered machinery and many, many hours of labor, the problem was solved. A few days later, I was having a cup of coffee in the Great Little Restaurant in Pleasant Valley, where the locals then met at or before dawn for breakfast, and the owner's wife asked if I was the Mr. Korda who owned the old Hewlett farm (for years locals continued to refer to it as "the old Hewlett farm," even though no Hewletts have lived in it since the 1940s, or as "the old Hubner place," after the family that owned it since then). I said I was. She brushed the hair out of her eyes with her hand and gave me a slightly embarrassed smile. "I figured," she said. "Harold Roe and Turk Daley was talking about you this morning, over breakfast."

What did they have to say? I asked her.

She screwed up her face. "Well," she said, "they said you seemed like a real smart guy, but then Turk said to Harold, 'I'll tell you one thing, though—*he don't know shit about septics.*' "

MOST OF MY LIFE I've had a hard time telling people where I was from, whenever the subject came up.

I know where I was *born* all right (Marylebone Parish in London—it says so on my birth certificate), but I've lived in so many places since then that it seems inappropriate to call myself a Londoner, and I don't.

As a child I lived in England and France until the war (we lived in France so much that for a while I thought I *was* French, until my English nanny sternly put me straight), then we moved to Beverly Hills, California, after the Blitz, during which our house near Hampstead Heath in London was blown up by the Luftwaffe. After Beverly Hills, I went to New York City with my mother when she and my father separated, then back to England, boarding school in Switzerland, the Royal Air Force, Oxford, and eventually back to New York City again.

I lived on and off for years—decades—in New York City, but I don't think of myself as a New Yorker any more than I think of myself as Swiss because I lived for several years in Switzerland. For a time I lived in New Mexico, but I'm not "from" there either.

Of course none of this mattered much really until I took up residence in the United States for good, and—eventually—became a citizen. Almost the first question anybody asks you in America is, Where are you from? (The other one is, What do you do? which I've always found it fairly simple to deal with—I edit books.) Most people can answer the question of where they come from easily enough. They say "L.A.," "Chicago," "Wichita Falls," or "Shaker Heights," or they name a state or a region—wherever it was that they grew up, and where, still, by implication, they have family, ties, *roots*.

I'm one of those people whose roots have wandered or withered away over the years. It's not that I have a gypsy soul or that I'm a rover by nature, not at all—in fact, mine is a distinctly sedentary nature; I'm immune to wanderlust, and once I've arrived somewhere, my first instinct is to stay put—it's just that in my formative years my family was so busy and so often on the move that such roots as there might have been never got put down. Wandering stones, they gathered no moss, and had no regrets on the subject.

Perhaps a Freudian might say that this gave me an unconscious need to put down roots of my own, some need that went deeper than owning a cooperative apartment on Central Park West or buying a vacation condominium with a pool in Florida. Roots, at some basic psychological level, in my case at any rate, require *land*, trees, a place in a community with some sort of history. The suburbs won't do, nor will a summer vacation place, however many summers one spends there, since the year-round residents who look after the summer places have a monopoly on the local roots. At the back of my mind, however dimly, I perceived that putting down roots was something that would have to be done in "the country," out beyond the suburbs, where there are farms and feed stores and old cemeteries and a Masonic lodge on Main

Street, a world in which, as it happened, I had never lived, and had only seen briefly from time to time through the windshield of a car when for some reason I had been obliged to get off the thruway or parkway in search of gas or directions.

It was not a sudden thing, nothing like Saul's vision on the road to Damascus—I didn't wake up one morning with a need to smell silage or live on a dirt road with a Rural Route address, nothing like that; it was a more gradual thing, a growing feeling that something was wrong about my life.

About *our* life, I should say, for my wife, Margaret, despite having been a model and a world traveler and living a conspicuously sophisticated life in New York, already had roots galore, firmly planted in the English countryside, where she had grown up as a farmer's daughter. Although a woman of considerable glamour, she never thought of herself as a city girl, and she was just as much at home among sheep, cattle, and horses as she was in midtown Manhattan, though one would never have guessed it at first sight.

*A*s it happened, it was a mutual love of horses and riding that brought us together in the first place, and that would eventually place us in the country. For years I kept a horse in Manhattan's last surviving livery stable, on West Eighty-ninth Street, and rode every morning on the bridlepaths in Central Park before going to work. I had learned to ride as a child, in England and in California, and it was something I kept up, like riding a motorcycle, which I still do to this day. Owning a horse in New York City was neither cheap nor easy, and made one a member of a fiercely embattled minority (consisting then of about twelve people). Most of my fellow Manhattan horse owners rode later than I did, so I had the park pretty much to myself in the early morning, until one day I saw a stunning blond woman riding around the reservoir in the opposite direction to mine. Her expression did not encourage conversation, so for many weeks we continued to ride in opposite directions, nodding to each other as we passed. Eventually, as if by unspoken consent, we found ourselves riding in the same direction one morning, and after that things accelerated.

Margaret had ridden since childhood—she was one of those typical English country girls who received her first pony (Snowy) at four and never got over it—but she had only recently taken it up again, and so had rented her horse. By the time we were married, however, she had bought a horse of her own, a big, flashy Thoroughbred gelding named Tabasco, so although we lived in Manhattan in a small apartment at the time, we were a one-car, one-cat, two-horse family. When Tabasco developed a back problem, Margaret wanted to send him to the country to recover from it. I had sent my own horse, Malplaquet,* to a farm in Dutchess County one summer, but I made all the arrangements for his vacation by telephone, with Katherine Boyer, who owned the farm and who had been recommended to me by a friend, so I never visited the place. The horse was collected in a trailer and brought back not only in one piece but so fit that it was a job to stay on him, and better groomed than I had ever seen him before, so I felt safe in recommending the same place for Tabasco's recuperation, which turned out to be an extended one.

Margaret is not the kind of person who would send an animal away without visiting it, and since Dutchess County is about two hours away from New York, she drove up several times, and came back each time tired from the drive there and back but aglow with enthusiasm about the countryside, the farm, and Tabasco's health, which soon improved to the point where Margaret could hack him lightly.

Had I listened with more attention, I might have realized that Mar-

*Don't ask. Well, all right, my former wife had developed an idea, somewhere between Shaker Heights High School and Bennington, during the course of her education, that cats should be named after generals, and horses after great battles, so I named my horse after one of Marlborough's greatest victories over the French. It wasn't an easy name to pronounce, and Frank, the groom at Claremont Stables in New York, usually referred to him either as "Malpuddle" or, more safely, "Mister Korda's horse." I never had the opportunity to learn her system for naming dogs, since, perhaps fortunately, we didn't have one.

garet was being drawn back to the transatlantic version of her roots, and that after nearly two decades of haute couture, glamorous parties, and first-class hotels, she was reaching out to embrace the country—or perhaps it was reaching out to embrace *her*. She returned in the evenings with mud on her boots, her hair tousled, her clothes smelling ever so faintly of horses and dogs, and was exuberantly happy. The only thing that would complete her happiness, it soon appeared, would be if I came up to see how wonderful it was myself. Katherine would provide me with a horse, and we could go out on the hunt trails, and have dinner at a country inn somewhere on the way home.

This sounded like a pleasant enough day to me, so I shortly found myself driving north up the Taconic State Parkway to visit the farm where Malplaquet had once spent the summer, at considerable expense, and where Tabasco was now living the life of Reilly.

After that, it was all over but the shouting. Dutchess County, at any rate seen from the Taconic and the saddle of a horse, looked like exactly the kind of place in which it would be possible to put down roots, and indeed where Margaret, whose ability to put down roots almost instantly is something of a miracle, had already done so—she could already find her way over the trails, knew the shortcuts to the farm, and even had the names of several local real-estate agents who specialized in "country properties." She was not a country girl for nothing.

Still, I hesitated to take the plunge—or, at any rate, I tried to put a toe in the water first. I suggested that we shouldn't restrict our search to Dutchess County. I drew a half circle on the map of New York State, to indicate places that were within a maximum of two and a half hours' driving time from Manhattan, and on weekends over the next few months we explored them, ranging into Connecticut and Westchester and driving a small army of realtors mad. Actually, distance from Manhattan, while important to me, was less important to Margaret than distance from Tarrytown, for we had finally given in to the inevitable, as the park became more dangerous and the stables more decrepit, and moved our horses from the city to the Sleepy Hollow

Country Club stables, right next door to the Rockefeller estate at Pocantico, the trails of which were open to us. We wanted to be able to drive down to Tarrytown to ride on the weekends, and an hour-and-a-half journey seemed about the most we were willing to undertake.

We soon learned the first and most important thing about the real-estate business, which is: *nobody listens to a word you say!* No matter how many times we explained that we were looking for a nice old farm with a barn and a modest amount of land, we were either shown brand-new houses on one-acre lots, collapsing shacks straight out of *Tobacco Road*, or vast great houses in the style of Gatsby's mansion, with tennis courts and pools, built by people who went broke in the Crash. We rejected a twee little rose-covered cottage in Westchester; a vast, baronial, crenellated, and uninhabitable Gothic castle near the Hudson, more suitable perhaps for Count Dracula; a house in the style of Marie Antoinette, like a miniature Versailles, complete with an orangery, in Dutchess County—an endless tribute to the fantasies and improvidence of people who had made enough money to build their dream house at one time or another, then gone bust. The only old farmhouse we saw that matched our idea of what we wanted had walls that were crumbling with damp rot and was surrounded by decrepit trailers on half-acre lots, with abandoned pickup trucks on cement blocks as lawn decorations and angry dogs chained to their rusty bumpers.

More by accident than by design, we finally stumbled upon an eighteenth-century farmhouse in Millbrook, Dutchess County, that seemed to fit the bill. It required considerable work, but not a total rebuild, and retained much of its original interior. More out of exhaustion than enthusiasm, we decided, rather tentatively, to make an offer. I comforted myself with the thought that it would take weeks or months to negotiate for it, and many, many months to make the house livable.

No sooner had I called the realtor, however, than I received an urgent call from Margaret, who had gone up to Dutchess County for the day. I was to drop everything, and forget all about the house in

Millbrook. Margaret had found just the house we were looking for, in nearby Pleasant Valley, not ten minutes from where our horses were.

She came back to New York full of excitement this time. Here was a house with not one, but *two*, barns, with twenty acres of land and no visible neighbors; built in 1785, it was surrounded on all sides by apple orchards and dairy farms—in brief, a country paradise, just what we were looking for. Lovingly kept by an elderly couple who had lived there for thirty years, it was in the process of being restored by a local builder, who had nearly finished the job. Nothing more needed doing; we could move in tomorrow—all we needed was a bed, a couple of chairs, and about $250,000.

The next Saturday, we drove up to Dutchess County, about ninety miles north of New York City, to look at it. The day could hardly have been less promising. Sheets of rain poured down, hammering the car, the Sawmill Parkway was flooded, heavy fog blanketed the Taconic State Parkway, gale-force winds sent leaves and branches flying. Pleasant Valley, when we passed through it, looked small, sodden, and lifeless, a bunch of vinyl-sided houses straddling Route 44, dominated by a red-brick Grand Union supermarket and an abandoned mill. The one traffic light was swinging back and forth in the wind like a pendulum.

The house, when we got to it, was hard to see, being surrounded by huge old maple trees looming out of the fog. There was so much water that it was erupting out of the culverts like Old Faithful, and cascading over the sides of the gutters. It was not, in any case, clear to me how Margaret was going to make her way to the house, or up and down stairs, since she was on crutches, having suffered a compound fracture of the leg when my horse had kicked her one day when we were riding together. I glimpsed two barns, which looked as if they might need a good bit of work, a well house—which set off a mild sense of alarm in someone whose previous experience with water supply had always consisted of turning on the tap—some run-down outbuildings that might be anything. The path to the house was made of huge stones, unevenly laid, that looked as if they had been placed there by careless giants.

Once we had made our way to the porch with great difficulty over the stones, which were lethally slippery with rain and moss, and were inside the front door, I could see in an instant that Margaret had exaggerated nothing. Every detail was as she had described it, from the original wide-plank floors, darkened by age and newly sanded and polyurethaned to a fine glow, to the delicate Greek Revival moldings, the rough-hewn overhead beams, and the four fireplaces (two of them vast brick-and-stone ones, big enough to roast a sheep in). Many of the windows still retained the original eighteenth-century windowpanes, the glass streaked, full of bubbles, slightly greenish, and everywhere there were the kind of details that no modern house can provide, from wrought-iron hinges, the work, no doubt, of some local blacksmith, to strangely placed wall cupboards and warming ovens—in short, the whole house had character, a sense of history, the feeling that it was old without being either quaint or precious.

The house, as we were soon to discover, had once been a tavern on the road between Poughkeepsie and Hudson, New York, where a ferry then took travelers across the Hudson River to Albany back in the eighteenth century for a three-day journey then, if you were lucky. The dining room still showed traces of having once been the main room of a tavern—the enormous fireplace, the warming ovens, the ancient beams darkened by smoke and cooking. Early in the nineteenth century, the tavern must have gone out of business—perhaps a victim of the first steamboats—and it once again became a farmhouse, which soon proved to be too small for the family that lived in it, at which point, rather than building an extension, they bought the house across the road and had it moved a quarter of a mile on rollers and joined on to the original house. Although by the twentieth century the join looked seamless, as if the house had originally been built that way, the fact was that if you looked carefully you could actually see where the two met, since the floors were at different levels, necessitating a lot of otherwise inexplicable stairs and steps, remarkably well calculated to send the unwary plummeting to the floor, as well as several rooms with ceilings that seemed low even by eighteenth-century standards. Sometime in the early twentieth century, porches had been added, as well as indoor plumbing and, eventually, electricity, but everywhere were reminders that our house had been built before George Washington was president of the United States, some of them pleasant, others inconvenient and likely to demand expensive repairs at some point in the future. Though something of a hodgepodge, it managed to look reasonably harmonious, though without even the slightest hint of ostentation—this was clearly a farmhouse or onetime tavern, not by any stretch of the imagination a manor house. As a result of joining two houses together—and perhaps also because a tavern needed one entrance for guests and another for the owner's family and the help, the house ended up with no fewer than five front doors, a curiosity that was to cause great inconvenience to Federal Express and the UPS until they got to know us, and so many windows that privacy was almost impossible on the ground floor, so that any moment one was likely to look up from one's work to find somebody looking right back, trying to figure out which was the front door. These were minor matters, things that gave the house *character*, we convinced ourselves, nothing compared to the view through the kitchen windows across a broad sweep of lawn to the woods—*our* woods—or the giant maples and sycamores that surrounded the house (and which, we were soon to learn, would require heroic pruning and miles of expensive stainless-steel cable if they weren't going to come right down on our heads at the first severe windstorm).

Our house *did* have a newly installed modern kitchen and reasonably up-to-date bathrooms—nothing fancy, no Jacuzzis or anything like that, but at least here at last was the first house we had seen about which the realtor hadn't said, "Of course it will need a new kitchen and modern bathrooms." In this case, the builder, Tom Kirchhoff, who lived just down the road, was also the realtor. His wife, Betty, he explained, as he showed us over the house, had actually decorated it herself. His men had started to put up the wallpapers she had chosen, but if we wanted to make a change, it wasn't too late. But we didn't want to change a thing, in fact—it was all fine. Less than an hour after we got there we had shaken hands on a deal. It would take time to draw up the contract, get a mortgage, arrange for a closing, Kirchhoff said genially, but in the meantime if we wanted to move some furniture in and start using the house on weekends, it was okay with him. So far as he was concerned, it was our house now.

As a bonus, he gave me the bulky ledgers that he had found in the attic while rebuilding the house, some of them going back to the mid-eighteenth century. It was an odd but not unpleasant feeling, this sense that we owned not only a house of our own—and land, however impossible it might be to actually see as the rain poured down in sheets—but one with a history of its own. It was not spectacular history—George Washington had never slept here, though he did inspect the local militia, drawn up for his benefit, at Rhinebeck, not twenty miles away—but it was nevertheless real. We might not have roots of our own here, but our house certainly did.

I drove back to New York, in part relieved that the search was over, in part feeling a leaden weight of responsibility on my shoulders, not just in the sense that the house would have to be paid for, but with the dawning realization that if the house was now as good as mine, so were the many mysteries and problems that it no doubt concealed. I had neglected to do any of the things neophytes are advised to do when buying a country house. I had no idea how the heating system operated, where the water came from, or who would look after it during the week while we were in New York. A glimpse of the cellar, the door of which Tom Kirchhoff had briefly opened for me, had revealed a low, dark, damp cavern, lit by a single overhead bulb and apparently carved out of bedrock, filled with twisting pipes and ducts like something out of a Rube Goldberg drawing, behind which an ancient furnace hunkered down in a corner on its haunches like some primitive, angry beast. "We didn't do too much down there," Kirchhoff said quickly, closing the door. I said it looked a little old-fashioned. It was that, he conceded, but all good, solid workmanship, the like of which you couldn't duplicate today, real copper pipes, not plastic like everyone uses these days. . . . Anyway, if it ain't broke, don't fix it, was his motto.

I agreed that made sense to me too, but somewhere deep inside my mind was a picture of myself, hunched over, flashlight in hand, groping through that maze of plumbing in the middle of the night to find the furnace, or the hot water heater, or whatever other vital organs the cellar contained, and fix it—how?

Honesty, had I been challenged on the subject, would have obliged me to admit that I had never developed any of the skills of a handyman. Most of my adult life had been spent in apartments, where the solution to almost any problem—leaking faucets, blocked drains or toilets, failure of the heating system or the air-conditioning, blown fuses—was to call the superintendent and have a twenty-dollar bill handy. I had the average man's obstinate and unrealistic pride in my mechanical abilities—what real man will admit to his wife that he doesn't know one end of a screwdriver from another, or that he can't hang a picture without making a hole in the wall like that caused by a twenty-millimeter cannon shell?—but I knew my own limitations when it came to anything much more difficult than changing a lightbulb.

"Did you ask whether the water was hard or soft?" Margaret said.

Not only had I not asked this question, I wasn't even sure what it *meant*. Up to now I had always turned on the tap and water came out, tasting slightly of chlorine, but otherwise perfectly adequate. Hard water, it transpired, would be difficult for Margaret to wash her hair in, among other things.

I promised to add this to the ever-growing list of questions I had for Tom Kirchhoff.

MOST OF THE FRIENDS with whom I shared the news that we had become the owners of a home in the country seemed delighted, though I noted a certain Schadenfreude among those who already owned a country home, along with a pronounced tendency to ask questions to which I didn't know the answers. Was the house cedar-shingled, and had I checked the shingles? Was the heating system zoned, so we could shut off the heat in part of the house? Had the house been rewired to code? Had it been inspected for termites, dry rot, fire ants, rodents? Had we tested for radon in the basement? I added all these questions (and many more) to my list, reassuring myself with the thought that since it had been standing since 1785, there was a pretty good chance it would go on standing for a while.

When I happened to mention that we had a bought a country home to my old friend Irving Paul ("Swifty") Lazar, the Hollywood super-agent, he paused to digest the news. Was it centrally air-conditioned? he wanted to know.

Here, at last, was a question I could answer. Not only was it not centrally air-conditioned, the previous owners didn't even have a window unit in their bedroom. I had asked Tom Kirchhoff about this, but he told me not to worry. This was the country, not the city; up here there was always a pleasant breeze—I would probably be needing an extra blanket in the summer, not an air conditioner.

Lazar snorted with contempt when I repeated this. "It's the Hudson Valley, kiddo," he said. "It's the same there in the summer as it is in New York City, only more humid." He paused. "I'm going to give you a piece of advice you'll thank me for. Tear the whole house down and build one with central air-conditioning."

I pointed out that it was almost two hundred years old—a piece of history. The Pleasant Valley Historical Society had actually placed an engraved brass plaque on the side of the porch attesting to its age.

Lazar was not impressed. "Tear it down, put up a new one with central air-conditioning, then reassemble the old house around it," he said. "That's what Paul Mellon did when he bought an historic house in Virginia. Trust me. Come June, you'll see I was right."

Time would tell, I said. Goddamn right it would, Lazar snapped back. "And while you're at it, kiddo," he added, "make sure to test the water. Some of those places, the water is so hard you can't even brush your teeth with it."

Kirchhoff, when I questioned him about all this, was calm. The shingles were cedar, and in good shape, the new wiring was up to code (about the *old* wiring he was less forthcoming), the house would be checked for everything before the closing, there would be a structural engineer's inspection, the whole nine yards, I was not to worry. As for the water, his house was just down the road—he and Betty and their children had been drinking it and washing in it for nearly twenty years with no ill effects.

Kirchhoff was as good as his word. I found myself a local lawyer, and paperwork soon flooded my desk attesting to the soundness of our house, the absence of termites, even the quality of the water, which was free from any contaminants. Within a month of having first seen the house, we were seated around our lawyer's conference table in Poughkeepsie on a cold, rainy day in 1979, as I passed out checks like confetti, made out to people I had never met and whose functions seemed mysterious. At the end of the session, we all shook hands solemnly, Kirchhoff handed me the key, and Margaret and I drove back to the house—*our* house now—where we first met Harold Roe.

CHAPTER TWO

Asleep at the Switch

AS THE NEWEST RESIDENTS of Pleasant Valley (population then around 8,000), Margaret and I were lamentably ignorant of the place where we were henceforth to live and vote. Except for a couple of visits to the supermarket on the way back and forth to New York, we had hardly set foot there, in fact.

At first sight, on a bleak day in March, it did not in any case appear to be the kind of place that caused tourists to stop and reach for their cameras. The Hudson Valley, as it happens, *is* a tourist attraction, particularly in the autumn, when the parkways are crowded with people driving up from the city to look at the leaves turning and buy apples and pumpkins from the local farm stands, but nobody wandering off the Taconic State Parkway onto Route 44 in search of gas or a bathroom would mistake Pleasant Valley for a picturesque village. There *are* picturesque villages aplenty nearby—Millbrook and Rhinebeck are both well-known tourist attractions and not twenty minutes away in different directions—but Pleasant Valley is not among them.

There is nothing "quaint" about Pleasant Valley. On the contrary, at first sight it presents itself as almost defiantly ordinary. This, it seems to be saying, is not one of your effete, precious New England or Connecticut postcard villages, in which every house around the meticulously kept village green is a perfectly preserved eighteenth-century landmark, and where Washington, or at least one of his lieutenants, spent the night in the inn. So far as is known, neither General Washington nor any of his lieutenants ever spent the night in Pleasant Valley.

In fact, the chief monument of Pleasant Valley, when we first started to take stock of it, was the Grand Union supermarket and its parking lot. The main street had long since given up its white picket fences and stately trees to become a state highway, along which were to be found three gas stations, an automobile parts store, several bars and pizza parlors, a small department store (selling work clothes, bait, ammunition, and notions), a feed store—the one throwback to the rural past—a hardware store, three churches with cemeteries, a fire house, a liquor store, and a Masonic lodge. The local building material of choice was vinyl siding, and any exploration of the town soon revealed rather more trailers and small trailer parks hidden away than most tourists would have wanted to see. Here, clearly, was the typical American small town that pollsters are always looking for in the Midwest, with no pretensions and a decided blue-collar atmosphere.

As it happens, Pleasant Valley's identity had been more or less fixed after the Second World War by the simple fact of its proximity to Poughkeepsie, situated about ten miles to the west on the Hudson River. With a population of over one hundred thousand people, Poughkeepsie was hardly a glittering or scenic metropolis—even in the nineteenth century it was widely caricatured by New Yorkers as a place full of comic country bumpkins with Dutch names (it was no accident that the action of the Broadway musical *Hello, Dolly!* not only takes place in Poughkeepsie but parts of the movie version were actually filmed there)—but it was big enough to turn Pleasant Valley into a predominantly white suburb of the nearby (and increasingly poor black) big, bad city, thus swamping its modest rural roots.

These roots went way back, however, and there were still traces of them to be seen, despite the postwar effort to cover everything in sight with blacktop and franchise fast-food restaurants. Originally consisting of three tiny hamlets settled largely by Presbyterians fleeing the intense dislike of their neighbors in Connecticut, a few no doubt equally unpopular Quakers and Baptists, and a leavening of the original Dutch settlers, Pleasant Valley had been founded in the first half of the eighteenth century as the humble site of a gristmill for local farmers, and prospered mildly because it was along its main street that herders drove their cattle to the Poughkeepsie slaughterhouse. (The nearby village of Salt Point was named thus because it was here that the cattle were fed as much salt as possible by their canny owners, then watered in the local stream so as to increase their weight before they reached the slaughterhouse, and the few picket fences that still remain derived from the need to keep the cattle from browsing in people's gardens as they made their way slowly down the muddy road to Poughkeepsie.)

By the beginning of the nineteenth century, thanks to water power, Wappingers Creek had spawned several thriving mills, of that "dark, satanic" appearance memorialized by the poet William Blake, and Pleasant Valley became a mill town, like those of New England—basically a cluster of small houses and churches for the mill workers, surrounding the gray, grim mill with its smoking stack, the whole set among the farms that sent milk, cattle, and produce down to feed New York City by boat or rail via Poughkeepsie.

It was not until 1821 that Pleasant Valley was finally incorporated as a town, taking as its symbol on the town seal the famous two-lane wooden covered bridge that was its center, and which, with an early and typical act of unsentimentality, was torn down and replaced with an ugly modern one at the dawn of the automobile age. A singular lack of zeal for the preservation of the past was then, as now, the spirit that separated Pleasant Valley from its more scenic rivals. In Millbrook, on the other side of the Taconic, every remnant of the past is still lovingly protected; in Rhinebeck, only twenty minutes to the north, old houses are zealously preserved and even the slightest suggestion of change or—God forbid!—"commercialization" is furiously opposed at the meetings of the town planning board, but Pleasant Valley has never looked toward the past with a sentimental eye, whether it came to the old covered bridge or, in the days after our arrival, its last surviving old hotel, the 1830 Inn, which was replaced by a parking lot for the new A&P, and the last old mill building, which was torn down unceremoniously and without regret to make room for a McDonald's.

Unbeknownst to us, Margaret and I had chosen the "wrong" side of the Taconic to live in. The "gentry," with their rolling farms and great estates, lived on the other side of the Taconic, around Millbrook, and referred to Pleasant Valley as "Peasant Valley," when they mentioned it at all. Pleasant Valley's place in Dutchess County history was perhaps best symbolized by the fact that it was the site of a famous train wreck in 1902, when one of the locals, Everett (Sok) Kellerhouse, fell sound asleep at the switch and allowed two trains of the now defunct P&E (the Poughkeepsie & Eastern Line, nicknamed the "Perverse & Eccentric") to run head-on into each other, with calamitous results.

I suppose if all this had been clear to us before we bought our house, we might have hesitated, perhaps even have opted for a place among the polo-playing, foxhunting gentry on the "right" side of the Taconic, with their acres of pasture and beautifully fenced fields, but perhaps fortunately for us, the idea never crossed our minds. A careful drive down our road, for instance, might have revealed that our next-door neighbors to the north consisted of a commune of young people living in a rusty trailer on cinder blocks on a one-acre plot hidden away in the trees, right on our property line, or that our immediate neighbors to the south, also mercifully hidden, were a huge family with many snarling dogs and no-neck teenage children, living in the middle of a kind of mini wrecking yard of worn-out snowmobiles and pickup trucks in a ramshackle house from which the toilet emptied onto the lawn without the benefit of a septic system. From the trailer to the north there came the sound of loud rock music and wild late-night parties; from the south there came the noise of revving chain saws, chained dogs barking, and the occasional gunshot.

That this was not Walden Pond did not dismay us, even as we discovered the fact bit by bit. After all, we told ourselves, it was a weekend house, not a full-time home, and for people who had been living on Central Park West, it was still plenty quiet and bucolic, with our nearest neighbors at least half a mile away, as opposed to the other side of the wall. At first, however, we found it curiously difficult to sleep. The house was big, as well as old—four bedrooms, five bathrooms, a dining room, a living room, a library, and some kind of studio or family room, with many narrow staircases and doors that led God knows where. Late at night it was easy to convince oneself, lying in bed, that there was an intruder creeping around somewhere in the dark as the house creaked and moaned like a sailing ship in heavy seas, for all the world as if it had a life of its own, while from below the ancient furnace in the basement roared, rumbled, and sent up a sound like heavy breathing through the heating vents, punctuated by the occasional muffled explosion, not to speak of the sound of tiny clawed feet running up and down behind the walls as our resident colony of mice went about their business. It took a while before we got used to it, what with the hoot of the owls, the creaking of the floorboards, and the faraway barking of dogs. Perhaps too, we missed the familiar background noise of traffic, police sirens, quarrelsome neighbors, and garbage cans being picked up at five in the morning—the night sounds of New York City.

Throughout that spring, as Margaret's leg healed and she progressed from crutches to a cane, we got used to our new routine—late Friday afternoon we left the city, with Margaret's cat Irving (a retired world traveler, who in his younger days had journeyed to Beverly Hills, the Okefenokee Swamp, and Cuernavaca) in his box on the backseat, and late Sunday night the three of us made the return journey. We didn't shop much in Pleasant Valley—we brought along with us full shopping bags from the local West Side food stores, as if we were setting out every weekend on safari.

We did not really feel that we *lived* in the country—the house remained largely unfurnished, pretty much as it had been the day it changed hands. Most of the rooms were empty, and looked like staying so for some time—indeed, when Margaret's parents came over from England to visit, it was so uncomfortable by their standards that they fled back to our apartment in the city, though they were country dwellers themselves. Her father, Paul, a Gloucestershire farmer, was polite enough about our new house, but clearly felt that we had bitten off more than we could chew, and cast a jaundiced professional eye on our twenty acres of land, which seemed to him rocky, poorly drained, and infested with cedars, weeds, and second growth. "You won't do much with this lot," he told me glumly after a walk to the end of our property line.

I didn't have the heart to tell him I wasn't *planning* to do anything with it. Once upon a time, over thirty years ago, it had been part of a farm that went back to the eighteenth century, "the old Hewlett farm," as it became known and as locals still referred to it, but the Hewletts had long since fallen on hard times, either through improvidence or bad farming, sold off their land in bits and pieces until there was nothing left, and now lived in trailers scattered all over the local countryside. Here and there, buried in the undergrowth, were traces of their labors, or lack thereof—an abandoned chicken house, rusty farm machinery and cattle troughs, a derelict old barn in which sheep had once been kept, rotted fence posts, rusty barbed wire, and crumbling stone walls that marked the borders of what must once have been fields. It was amazing how quickly and completely the second growth had obliterated the farm and turned the field into impenetrable thickets of thorn and scrub—clearly nature here was almost as quick to reclaim her own as in the Amazonian rain forests. "You'll have to cut all this back," Paul said grimly. "Cost you a packet."

CHAPTER THREE

"Whack It All Back!"

PAUL'S OPINION was shared by Harold Roe.

"Whack it all back!" he shouted at me every time he appeared in the driveway in his pickup truck, towing a flatbed with a small tractor, and waving toward the horizon as if he intended to clear the land from here to Albany or the Canadian border.

Everything, Harold told us, needed whacking back, and he was just the man to do it. The forsythia and lilacs that surrounded the house (and were part of its charm) needed pruning and thinning out, our hedges needed trimming; even the old mulberry tree by the porch, one of the things that had sold Margaret on the house, needed attention.

As we were soon to discover, Harold's approach to pruning and thinning was drastic, and his favored instrument was a chain saw rather than a pair of pruning shears. His first attack on our foliage left Margaret in tears—tears of anger, as it happened—but Harold was not a man to be swayed from his task by tears of any kind. He grumbled, argued, pretended to complete deafness, then, since we were only there on weekends, went right back to doing whatever he wanted to do the moment our backs were turned.

No plant, brush, shrub, or tree was safe from his assault. Only once he had reduced whatever it was to a stump of its former self was he satisfied. "All that dead stuff needed whacking back," he would say proudly, admiring a lilac that had been cut back to bare, leafless stalks. "She'll grow back in no time."

But nothing Harold took his chain saw to grew back, not in a hurry anyway. He had the reverse of a green thumb, a black thumb, perhaps—except for lawns, where his touch was surer. He wasn't much interested in planting things, either. He liked machinery, the noisier and more destructive the better—a day with the backhoe or the bulldozer, sending up clouds of diesel smoke and reconfiguring the landscape, was Harold's idea of a day well spent. Gardens he held in genial contempt—he just didn't see the point of things like flowers or herbaceous borders, it was all just "pretty" stuff. In any case such gardening as couldn't be accomplished with a backhoe, a dozer blade, or a chain saw Harold dismissed as beneath him, and performed only under duress.

The notion of dismissing Harold never occurred to us—or occurred to us only on those occasions when he went too far and cut down something to which Margaret had become specially attached, like the tiger lilies by the driveway. For one thing, he seemed to be as much a part of the house as the hand-hewed beams, and for another he was the only person who understood the intricate drainage system. Besides, cantankerous, opinionated, and stubborn as he was, we liked him. He and Margaret fought like cat and dog over every leaf, branch, and tree limb, but he was the only person in Pleasant Valley—the only person we knew, at any rate—who fit her idea of a real countryman, such as might be found in her native Cotswolds, able to put his hand, however hard, to anything from building a fence to cleaning up the debris after a storm.

Something of a perfectionist in his own way, Harold was a workaholic, happy, even eager, to turn up every day at seven in the morning, rain, shine, or hail, and work until long after the sun had gone down, as he mowed and bush-hogged by the lights of his tractor. On one occasion Margaret called his wife—"Birdie" Roe—late one evening to say that Harold was still out somewhere in the fields bush-hogging and ask if she would like us to send him home. "Nope," Mrs. Roe replied firmly, and that was that.

Harold's bills were firmly presented to me—he didn't believe in presenting bills to womenfolk—once a week, usually just as we were eating lunch. They were meticulously made out by Birdie Roe, in the kind of clear penmanship that hasn't been taught in this country for fifty years, and listed in great detail every minute that Harold had spent on our place during the week. Confusingly, Harold had a different rate for every possible variety of work—mowing was different from bush-hogging, pruning was different from weed-whacking, cleaning up was different from leaf-blowing. The one thing that *wasn't* confusing was the fact that Harold expected to be paid in cash, and to get his money then and there on the spot—he made it clear that the idea of settling up tomorrow or next week was not an option. Once the money was in his hands, he placed it in a well-used wallet, bound up with a stout rubber band, in which it was possible to see a thick wad of bills.

He was not poor—at one time he and a partner had installed underground tanks for gas stations, and he owned a large number of rentable properties (some said half the village, if you excluded the church and the firehouse) in Salt Point, where he lived—he simply liked working and earning money. Whether he kept all his cash in his mattress or not, I don't know—he didn't like banks, so anything is possible—but he kept a deliberately low profile. Birdie sent him out every day with a thin bologna sandwich wrapped in wax paper for his lunch, and his favorite meal, when he finally got home, was fried bologna with mashed potatoes. Once a week the Roes ate out at the local diner, and Harold always had a well-done steak, with ketchup. He seemed to feel the same way about vegetables as he did about checks. On hot days, Harold could be persuaded to drink a beer, but one was his limit. His sole extravagance was snowmobiling, which is the motorized equivalent of ice fishing, testing the ability of the hands, feet, and nose to resist subzero temperatures and windchill factors in the double digits. He was the only man I had ever met who was absolutely indifferent to weather—Harold never took shelter in a rainstorm, never had sunstroke, and never complained about the cold. Nothing stood in the way of his determination to uproot everything in his path, or to whack back whatever he had been told not to touch.

Even boulders were no match for him. Huge lumps of stone that still lay buried where they had been inconveniently placed by the Ice Age, Harold regarded as a challenge. He dug a trench around the boulder, heaved away at it with a long steel crowbar until its hold in the ground was loosened, then gave it the coup de grâce with his bulldozer, leaving a hole like that caused by a heavy artillery shell, which had to be filled in, graded, rolled flat, and seeded with grass. "She'd have broke a mower blade on me one day," he would say with intense satisfaction, to explain why he had spent two days doing something that we hadn't asked him to. "Save you money, in the long run."

The idea of leaving well enough alone seemed never to have occurred to Harold. When he was not occupied in rearranging nature around our house, he prowled around looking for problems closer to hand to bring to our attention, pushing his penknife deep into beams and windowsills to show us that the wood was rotten, peeling off chips of paint to demonstrate that the previous owners had used the wrong kind ("Latex!" he would shout cheerfully. "They didn't know what they was doing!"), stabbing at the edges of our windowpanes to show that the putty needed replacing, prying up shingles from the roof so that he could show us how easily he could crumble them between his fingers, and in general intimating with considerable satisfaction that the house was about to fall down around our ears if we didn't turn him loose on it.

Fortunately, he took no umbrage when we ignored his advice. At least three times a week, sometimes more, he came rattling down the driveway with his equipment in tow, shouting out to us, "Have no fear, Roe is here!" Margaret made an effort to supervise what he was doing at first and keep his mind on our garden, but Harold was crafty—as soon as her back was turned, he would go chugging off on his tractor and vanish into the woods, from which there would soon emerge the scream of a chain saw. Early on in our relationship, I discovered that the local Cornell Cooperative Agricultural Extension, just down the road from Pleasant Valley, was actually giving away pine tree seedlings to anyone who would plant them, in an effort to reforest the area.

Thinking that it might be nice to put more trees between us and the road, I ordered a couple of hundred seedlings and borrowed a truck to pick them up with, only to discover to my disappointment that they were so small—each about the size of a thumb—that I could carry them all home in a couple of buckets.

It had been my thought that Harold would play the Johnny Appleseed role with my seedlings, but he was deeply resistant to the idea, and did his best to nip it in the bud by not refilling the water in the buckets. In the end, despite his grumbling and many delays, Margaret persuaded him to join the project—Harold was stubborn, but faced with a determined woman, he eventually gave in, as no doubt he did to Birdie at home. Though disgusted by a job that required him to get off the seat of his tractor, Harold went off reluctantly to the Cornell Cooperative Agricultural Extension for exact instructions on planting the seedlings and, claiming that he was following these to the letter, planted most of them in careful, exact rows, too far away from the house to be watered and wherever possible in the shade of large trees, so they would be sure to die. The few that I planted are now sizable, if scrawny, specimens, and not always placed where I would have wanted them, in hindsight, but of Harold's there remains not a trace—which is probably just as he intended.

He was not above saying "I told you so," especially after any trip Margaret took to the local nursery to bring back flats of plants and flowers. "Money down the drain," Harold would say as we unpacked them, and mostly he was proved right, particularly if they were left in his care for more than an hour or so. On the other hand, in an emergency—of which country living provided plenty—Harold could be counted on to appear right away, often without our having phoned him, apparently alerted by the country grapevine. We attributed supernatural powers to him at first, but as we were later to discover, Harold's main recreational activity, as with a lot of people in Dutchess County, was listening to the police channel on the CB radio in his truck and his workshop, so he knew everything that was going on, from a murder to a downed tree limb. He had very little interest in world affairs, unless you include a passion for Joan Collins in *Dynasty*, but he could fill you in on every domestic disagreement, automobile accident, lost dog, and break-in for twenty miles around. What's more, Harold was at his best in an emergency—doggedly, uncomplainingly, with astonishing strength for a man of his age, he put things right somehow, digging into the camper bed of his truck for whatever he might need—lengths of chain, an ax, jumper cables, a winch, a scavenger pump, a portable generator—there seemed no limit to what he carried there in anticipation, apparently, of Armageddon. Besides, he was our point of contact with our new neighbors, the man who knew everybody (and everything about them). When someone crashed head-on into our fence in the middle of the night, Harold was there, unbidden, in minutes, and everybody in the road—the state trooper, the deputy sheriff, the EMT people, the flatbed man, even the unfortunate accident victim himself, albeit feebly—waved a hand or a flashlight at him and said, "Hi there, Harold, how's it going?" and stood by as he told them what to do and how to do it, and that they had been doing it all wrong.

With Harold on our side, we had a connection to all those people whose services are vital, but who never seem to answer the phone ("He isn't here now, but I'll get him to call you. . . . No, I don't rightly know when he'll be back. . . ."), from the plumber to the tree surgeon. They might not know who I was, beyond the fact that I lived in the old Hubner place (or, if they were older, the old Hewlett farm), but Harold Roe they knew. When *he* called, their wives said, "Hi, Harold, he's down at the Agway, I'll call him in his truck." One call from Harold, and they were on the way. Anyway, without Harold's help, we could never have sorted things out about our land.

CHAPTER FOUR

A Man's Home Is His Castle

BEING ENGLISH, I've believed that a man's home is his castle, though it was academic, since so far my homes had always consisted of apartments. The concept of trespassing doesn't count for much when it comes to an apartment. Except for the people who have a key, after all, anybody else is breaking in—it's burglary you worry about with an apartment, not trespassing.

But land is a whole different ball game, as we shortly discovered. You may *own* your land, but short of surrounding it with concertina barbed wire and having it patrolled night and day by the Eighty-second Airborne, it's hard to keep your neighbors off it, especially if they've been using it for generations. And that's not even counting the people who stop on the road to dump their garbage on your property at three in the morning!

When it comes to land, of course, the more you have, the harder it is to defend, as many a Russian czar has learned, and although we started off with a modest twenty acres, we might as well have been defending Byelarus. Every day there was some new incursion. Refrigerators, bedsteads, stacks of worn-out tires, appeared overnight, as if by spontaneous generation.

More to the point, we almost immediately began to meet our neighbors. Some of them came to the front door, usually accompanied by a large dog of one of the more sporting breeds, to ask for permission to continue doing whatever they had been doing on our land since time immemorial, if they were to be believed. Others we met on the land itself, when we went for a walk, like the man setting traps. It was all right, he assured us after we had introduced ourselves, he had a New York State trapper's license (we hadn't even known such a thing existed, or that trapping as such was still going on—I assumed it had gone by the way along with Jim Bridger and the last of the beavers). The trapper wasn't the Jim Bridger type—he was slight, dressed in blue jeans and a plaid wool shirt, and didn't have a full, bushy beard—but he was armed with a bowie knife and a pistol. The previous owners, and the ones before them, had let him put out his traps, he said, so he figured it was okay with us. As gently as possible, we informed him that it wasn't okay with us, that in fact Margaret had a soft spot for exactly the kind of small, furry, cuddly animals that would get caught in his traps, and thought of those on our land as *hers*, and somehow under her protection.

He gathered up his traps and went, but he did not leave a happy man. We would discover, he told us darkly, that without trapping nature would get out of balance—we would soon be overrun with varmints, rabbits, raccoons, skunk, possum, woodchucks, you name it. They would breed and feed until our land was reduced to a desert. Although this sounded like one of the plagues of Egypt, we stood firm, and nothing terrible happened. We seemed to have about the same number of small furry creatures as everybody else, and provided that the garbage cans were kept firmly closed, they presented us with no problems—far fewer, in fact, than our neighbors did. A family of raccoons took up residence under our front porch but made no trouble, though if we made too much noise on the porch during the day, when they were sleeping, they made known their displeasure by thumping on the board above their heads as hard as they could, like angry downstairs neighbors in an apartment building calling for silence. Margaret took to feeding them under the kitchen window at night, by the light of a red floodlight like those in the nocturnal animal building at the Bronx Zoo, and it was hard to imagine that our lives would have been made better by having them trapped and made into fur collars. Every so often, if I was up early, I would meet them coming home in the morning from our woods, in a straight line, by order of seniority; far from being frightened by my presence, they walked past with great dignity and squeezed themselves under the porch one by one, apparently secure in their rights as tenants. Very occasionally they made a fearsome noise over some family quarrel, or showed up on the porch roof, staring in through the bedroom windows, but for the most part they were no trouble, and we became fond of them. Of our two cats, one, Irving, who had accompanied Margaret on her many travels as a model, was too old to bother them, and the other, Queenie, having been born with a deformed front leg, was kept strictly indoors, but even had they been younger and fiercer it would take more than a cat or two to frighten the raccoons.

Trapping was, in any case, a no-brainer. Neither of us wanted to see animals caught in traps on our land (or on anyone else's, given a choice)—besides, the trapper himself was more of a vanishing species than his quarries. Practically nobody does trapping anymore, and our neighbor may have been the last of his kind in our neck of the woods. Deer hunting is another story, of course. Almost everybody around us hunts deer, and those few who don't have plenty of relatives who do. Down at the local pub, as the leaves turn and the air becomes crisp, the number of people wearing Happiness Is a Pile of Warm Guts T-shirts and busily stocking up on hand warmers and deer slugs at the Pleasant Valley Department Store (which sells ammo and bait as well as work clothes) far outnumbers those who believe that every deer is Bambi.

Of course the deer are hardly a vanishing species. They come by the dozens in the winter to feed on our shrubs and bushes; they are so bold that I have actually looked up from my word processor to find one peering in at me through the window, its moist nose pressed up against the glass, and they are second only to drunk drivers as a menace on the roads. I am not a sentimentalist about deer; still, even at their most intrusive, they don't do much in the way of damage, compared, say, to a couple of teenage trespassers on dirt bikes, and there's no question that they by far exceed in grace and beauty most, if not all, of the people who want to shoot them. Half a dozen deer grazing on the lawn are a more attractive sight than half a dozen hunters, or even a single hunter, particularly since deer hunting is mostly carried out in much the same bulky clothing as ice fishing.

Deer hunters, in our neck of the woods, come in three categories, those who hunt deer with a shotgun (rifles are illegal), those who hunt them with a bow, and those who hunt them with old-fashioned muzzle-loading weapons. During the shotgun season, the deer hunters tend to stand or sit, nursing a Thermos flask, waiting for the deer to pass within range, or to perch in the trees, like ungainly birds, on deer stands reached by a homemade ladder. In the bow season, the hunters tend to hide in the brush, heavily camouflaged, and often fire at the snap of a twig. These are the *legal* deer hunters, of course—they do not include poachers, people who hunt deer out of season, and those who hunt them at night, blinding them with the headlights of a truck or a powerful flashlight.

Given the total firepower arrayed against the deer, it is a wonder that any of them survive, but the days of Leatherstocking have long since passed, and the standard of marksmanship among deer hunters seems to have decreased in direct proportion to the efficiency of their weapons. To put it simply, while at dusk and at dawn during shotgun season it sounds like the opening day of the Battle of the Somme, not many deer actually appear to get killed (some are wounded, and die an awful death by the sides of the roads, but that's another story).

Most of the bad stories about deer hunting, we were assured by everyone, were about hunters from the city, not locals—the strangest being that of a man who was found by a state trooper by the side of the road, cheerfully butchering a Great Dane he had just shot, convinced that it was a deer. Tales of livestock shot by outsiders were rife—the locals, we were given to understand, were a different story, men born and bred to the hunt like James Fenimore Cooper's hero, though when we got the chance to observe them in action they seemed more interested in keeping warm than in shooting anything, and so far as sporting instincts are concerned, might just as well have been going after deer with land mines.

We didn't give much thought to deer hunting until the early autumn, when people started turning up at the door to ask if it was still okay to hunt on our land. Being English, we had a tendency to think of deer as decorative—picturesque, even aristocratic ornaments to the landscape. In England, deer are in fact much prized for their decorative properties, and my Oxford college, Magdalen, is famous for its deer park—it is only in the Highlands of Scotland, generally regarded by the English as a savage, barbarous place, that deer are stalked and shot. Deerstalking is, in any case, an expensive and aristocratic blood sport, rather like grouse shooting. People like the Prince of Wales stalk and shoot deer (usually togged out in an outfit consisting of a kilt, a tailored tweed jacket, and a variety of strange-looking hats), to the dismay of most of middle-class Great Britain, so nothing prepared us for the fact that deer hunting in Dutchess County is basically a blue-collar pursuit, and that the hunters are more likely to be the local plumber or the supermarket manager than the gentry, such as it is. *Autres pays, autres moeurs.*

It's hard to say no to the man who has just unplugged your sink or sold you a roll of paper towels, but there was simply no way we wanted deer hunted on our land, even by people we knew and liked. On the other hand, when it comes to deer hunting, a "no" is hard to enforce, short of patrolling your own land night and day armed to the teeth. For a while we went through a period of mild paranoia, in which we did just that, and I actually managed to perform a citizen's arrest on a group of trespassers hunting deer on our land (unsuccessfully), who fortunately turned out to be not only outsiders but foreigners, who didn't speak a word of English and had the look of Serb irregulars. The sight of four heavily armed men draped in bandoliers, with bowie knives and shotguns, was enough to make me think twice about playing game warden, however—in the long run it seemed likely that I would meet up with somebody who wasn't going to put down his shotgun without an argument—and although I had no objection to carrying a pistol on my own land, having carried one for years during my service in the Royal Air Force, I didn't see myself as the weekend Wyatt Earp.

As usual, Harold Roe had a solution. Harold himself was no deer hunter, perhaps because there was no money to be made out of it, more likely because he disliked venison, which he would only have eaten if it had been made into something resembling supermarket bologna, but most of the men in his extended family were hunters. The trick was, Harold told us, to let the local rod and gun club post our land. They would keep trespassers off on our behalf, and if we let them shoot pheasant, say, they would enforce a ban on deer hunting in return. "Give and take," Harold said, "give and take"—that was the way to get things done in the country.

And so it proved. The Pleasant Valley Gun Club—represented by two very polite men in camouflage suits, built like Mack trucks—was delighted to have the right to shoot pheasant in season on our land, and in return, their "marshals" would post our land and enforce it. I had a few qualms about the pheasant, but bird shooting has never offended me, and I've enjoyed the occasional day in the field or the duck blind myself—besides, the pheasant breed rapidly, and don't stand around the house in the late afternoon looking soulfully at us while we have our tea.

The gun club marshal, when he turned up in a four-wheel-drive pickup truck to post our land, was something of a surprise. I'm not sure what we had expected, but what we got was a soft-spoken giant of a man, dressed in the same uniform as a deputy sheriff, wearing the kind of sunglasses favored by state troopers, and carrying an immense .357 revolver and two speed-loaders on his gun belt. Despite his martial, even fearsome, appearance—Bob was definitely not somebody a trespasser or a poacher would argue with—he turned out, like so many of our Dutchess County neighbors, to be an "ex-IBMer." At one time IBM had been the largest employer in the county (the state prisons and insane asylums had run IBM a close second). Working for IBM was thought of as a lifetime job, like being a correction officer or looking after the insane, with a decent pension at the end, but when IBM ran into trouble in the 1970s, the first thing it did was to drop its paternalist image in a hurry; tens of thousands of Dutchess County residents were fired or plunged into premature retirement, with the result that a lot of local blue-collar workers once used to be white-collar IBM lifers, and that a burning resentment against Big Blue is perhaps the one thing most of the county's residents have in common.

The local car detailer is a former IBM executive, as is the trainer at the health club, a taxidermist, and the owner of at least one local bar. So, it turned out, was Bob, the gun club marshal, who had gone from some desk job involved with building mainframe computers to game management. Though bulky and heavily armed, he spoke like the white-collar corporate man he had once been, in a low, soft voice, the voice of compromise and years of management training. Once our land was posted, he explained, he would have powers of arrest on it. We had only to call him day or night, and he, or one of his subordinates (a kind of paramilitary corps of ex-IBMers, it appeared), would come running. All of the club members would carry a membership card, which they must show on demand, and their vehicles would have special windshield stickers so we could identify them. If any of the members violated safety rules, or hesitated to show their card, we should call him at once—he was responsible for maintaining good order and discipline among the members, as well as for keeping trespassers out. "Don't hesitate," Bob warned us sternly, and he was as good as his word. At the slightest sign of trespassing, poaching, or lack of compliance from the club membership, he was there, ready to deal with it firmly and to call in the deputy sheriffs if it was more than he could handle—though it was hard to imagine what kind of trouble Bob couldn't handle himself. He gave the impression of a man who was dying for the chance to bring down a poacher with his revolver.

When I told Harold Roe how grateful I was for his recommendation, he nodded gravely. Bob was good folks, he said. I asked whether Bob had ever had occasion to draw his weapon. Not to his knowledge, Harold said, then he thought for a moment. "I'll tell you what, though," he said, with a grin. "I sure wouldn't want to be a senior IBM executive caught hunting on posted land off season by Bob!"

Perhaps fortunately, this never happened. Bob kept peace on our land during the deer-hunting season, when people from Millbrook to Rhinebeck were complaining about horses, children's ponies, and prize cattle being shot by overeager or inexperienced hunters, and kept his pheasant shooters in line—a politer group of armed men has seldom taken the field. On the other hand, it opened us up to demands from other "sportsmen" around us.

Harold was the first to exploit this leverage. If it was all right for the gun club to hunt pheasant, he said, how about snowmobiling? Here, after all, was a sport in which nothing got killed (except for the occasional accident in which a snowmobiler broke his own neck), and which would take place far from the house, where the snowmobile club, of which Harold was apparently president for life, would clear the trails. In the spring, summer, and autumn, we could ride on the trails—it was a no-lose proposition. More importantly, Harold pointed out, the snowmobile club would keep illegal, irresponsible snowmobilers—the snowmobile hoi polloi, as it were—out. We promised to think about it, but one snowfall was enough to convince us. From all over our land there was the scream and roar of snowmobiles, driven by unknown strangers in bulky suits with face masks, apparently unable to read our many No Trespassing signs. Once Harold's members had our permission to use the land, they swiftly put an end to other people's using it. When I asked Harold how he had accomplished that, he simply said, "I put the word around," and that was that.

THE ONE GROUP OF PEOPLE over whom Harold had no influence at all was our local hunt. Foxhunting was still looked on as the prerogative of the gentry, although the Rombout Hunt, like most of the nearby hunts, was no longer anything near exclusive as it had been before the war, or even for a few decades after it, when Franklin Delano Roosevelt Jr. had been the hunt master, and when the membership was still largely drawn from those families who owned big estates and great, historic houses. Since then, the foxhunters had fallen on hard times. Taxes had broken up most of the big estates in the Hudson Valley, local land developers had spread trailer parks, mini-malls, and housing estates across what had once been farmland open to the hunt, and the people who had moved into the area from the suburbs and the cities did not necessarily see the point of foxhunting, nor were they inclined to play the role of the humble peasantry, baring their heads and tugging their forelocks, when the hunt, clad in splendid livery, pursued the fox across their backyards, to the terror of their children and pets.

Dutchess County used to be about as feudal as America can get, back in the days when the big employers were those who owned the large estates and when the county was rock-ribbed Republican and proud of it (it is surely no accident that the county voted against its most famous native son, FDR, in every one of his gubernatorial and presidential elections, despite the fact that his home in Hyde Park was something of a national shrine), but those days were gone after World War II—the Great Depression and high taxes did the old landowners in—and had always been something of an illusion. The real wealth was in the dairy farms and small businesses and growing industrial base of the Hudson Valley, not in the hundred-room mansions along the Hudson River, and foxhunting, with its unmistakable whiff of the ancien régime, was, along with polo, the symbol of reckless, wasteful wealth and social snobbery.

The gentry might have been looked up to, albeit with a certain skepticism, during the days of FDR's father, but the real power had long since slipped from their hands, along with most of their own estates, and not much remained to separate them from locals—who were often very much richer than they—but the right to put on a scarlet coat and a white stock twice a week during the foxhunting season, and play at being the lord of the manor.

Here, however, was a sport with which we were at least familiar, unlike snowmobiling. Margaret, an exquisite, daredevil horsewoman, had hunted in England as a child and then as a much-admired young woman, and I at one time in my life had flown down regularly to Virginia to ride with the Middleburg Hunt. My feelings about foxhunting were (and remain) deeply ambivalent. On the one hand, I like foxes and, since I don't keep chickens, have never regarded them as any particular threat, while at the same time I don't much like most of the people who hunt foxes. On the other hand, riding full tilt over unfamiliar stone walls has a certain appeal to me, as do all the ancient traditions of dress and behavior that go with foxhunting, and in fact constitute its chief attraction. Either you enjoy getting dressed up in what amounts to costume to risk your neck on a horse, or you don't, is what it amounts to. No great moral issue has ever seemed to me at stake, one way or the other.

The Rombout Hunt had always ridden over our land, and there didn't seem any reason to stop them, especially since their joint master was one of our neighbors; so was our electrical contractor (the hunt was no longer in any position to look down its nose at tradesmen); one of Harold's best friends, old Stanley Money, was one of the "hunt servants," a formidable figure in his scarlet coat on a horse, and something of Harold's equivalent in the local horse world. Besides, we were immediately made "landowner members" and invited to the opening meet, which was held just down the road from us. Neither of us wished the local foxes any harm, but it seemed like a question of noblesse oblige—to withdraw the hunt's permission to use our land would, it was clear, be taken as a clear sign that we were enemies of our own class, or the kind of city folk who just didn't understand the social obligations of landowning—in short, not gentry. This, as it was to turn out, was something of a mistake, but we didn't know it at the time.

What with the local gun club people shooting pheasant, the Rombout hunt chasing after foxes in the fall and winter (and cubbing in the summer), and Harold's white-haired snowmobile seniors, dressed like the Michelin Man, buzzing back and forth after every snowfall at breakneck speed, our land was not quite the quiet country idyll we had anticipated—and that's without even including poachers jacking deer by the lights of a truck at night, or trespassers on four-wheelers, or kids on dirt bikes, or the ballooners whose huge, brightly colored balloon came down on our land, or the elderly pilot who ran out of gas and crash-landed his airplane on it.

Nor, of course, had we given much thought to the fact that deer and pheasant are not the only things people hunt in our part of the country. There was hardly any time of the year, it transpired, when it wasn't the legal season for *something*, or when our neighbors weren't letting off shots from what seemed to be directly below our bedroom windows. Our county sheriff (who billed himself as "the Sportsman's Friend," which tells you what side of the hunting issue *he* was on, since "sportsman," outside New York City, is the recognized code word for hunter or gun owner) handed out useful little cards at election time with the year's hunting calendar printed on one side. It made for enlivening reading.

September 1 is the beginning of squirrel season (six per day), then October brings ruffled grouse season (four per day), cottontail rabbit (six per day), "varying hare" (two per day), woodcock (three per day), and wild turkey fall season (two birds, either sex).

Mid-October ushers in duck season (six per day, including no more than four mallards, one pintail, one canvasback, two wood ducks, or two red heads), black duck (one per day), brant (two per day), and snow goose (*fifteen* per day). For those who, like myself, have read as children Paul Gallico's *The Snow Goose,* that seems like a lot of snow geese, quite apart from the fact that shooting at a snow goose is a little like shooting at a Boeing 747 as it lands—a large, slow-moving target that's very hard to miss.

November brings raccoon season (no limit), red and gray fox (no limit, to the fury of mounted foxhunters, to whom shooting foxes is anathema), coyote (no limit), and deer archery season. Mid-November and December bring deer shotgun season (when the big guns come out and sensible people dress in blaze orange to pick up their mail and keep their pets and children indoors), deer muzzle-loading season, as well as another duck season and a second deer archery season.

From February through March there is a second snow goose season (still fifteen per day), for those who haven't had their fill of killing snow geese. Crows (*crows?*) can be shot from September 15 through March 31 (no limit, but only on Fridays, Saturdays, Sundays, and Mondays, for some reason), then for those who still have any ammunition left, there is a second wild turkey season (two bearded, one per day) from May 1 through May 31.

Thus, from September through May there is hardly a day when *something* furry or feathered isn't in season. The period from June through August is spent target shooting and sighting in your weapons for the fall, so there's still plenty of gunshots in the woods.

Cubbing keeps the mounted foxhunters (as opposed to the lower-class wretches who shoot foxes) busy in the summer, the general idea being to train young hounds to go after the fox's scent and to accustom young foxes to run in a straight line from the hounds (though one would have thought they were born with that instinct), so there's still a pretty good chance of finding the hunt crashing through your woods in the early morning in midsummer, though they don't put on formal hunting clothes for cubbing, just a hacking coat, shirt and tie, and a velvet hunt cap—not that it matters to the foxes, one imagines.

I had pretty much forgotten about the hunt, in fact, until I woke up one Saturday morning to the sound of hunting horns and hounds from our woods. I ran downstairs in my bathrobe to see what was going on, and almost bumped into a fierce-looking woman of a certain age, mounted on a big chestnut horse, at the bottom of our garden. Both she and the horse were fidgeting with impatience. "A couple of the hounds have gone missing," she said loudly and sternly, as if I were at fault. "Have you seen 'em?" I was about to reply that I was hardly likely to have seen them in my bedroom, but it's not easy to come up with a snappy to retort to somebody on horseback when you're barefoot and wearing a bathrobe, so I indicated that I hadn't. "If they turn up, call the kennels and somebody will come and pick 'em up," she snapped, in a tone that sounded more like a command than a request, and trotted off across our lawn back into the woods, leaving hoof marks in the expensive turf.

In fact, the two missing hounds turned up shortly afterward. We found them tearing up one of the few flower beds that Harold hadn't managed to kill. They were nice, gentle animals, and we put them in one of the stalls in the barn with a bowl of water and some table scraps until the huntsman came by as promised and picked them up with his van.

I liked the hounds a lot more than I liked the huntsman or the members of the hunt, who didn't seem to care where they rode their horses and assumed that as a fellow member of the gentry I would be pleased to see them galloping across my property in pursuit of a fox. "Good fences make good neighbors," they like to say out west, but while that may be true, it doesn't take into account twenty or thirty of your neighbors on horseback jumping over your fences, while the hounds in full cry scramble over or under them.

By the end of our first year in the country, it seemed to me that we had given permission to so many people to use our land that it might as well have been Central Park. Some of them seemed harmless enough—a couple who wanted to go on bird-watching walks, some cross-country skiers, a mushroom gatherer—but still, every time we went beyond the immediate vicinity of the house we were likely to meet somebody who was doing *something*, whether lethal or not.

Those of our neighbors who were working farmers didn't seem to suffer much from this kind of problem. That, as we worked out, was because they *used* their land (it didn't hurt that their family had been on it for several generations, of course). As nature is said to abhor a vacuum, country people are drawn to land that isn't being used in some visible way. Put cows on it, or use it to grow alfalfa, or plant it with apple trees, and trespassing drops to near zero, but since we didn't seem to have a use for our land, it was fair game. The general feeling was that if we said no to anything, we were being selfish, as well as standoffish—typical city people.

I discussed this with Harold, who agreed. Land that wasn't in use was a temptation, it was a well-known fact. He himself lived on a half-acre plot—he believed in putting money in buildings, not land—but the idea of doing something useful with our land brought a gleam to his eyes. He could only put in so many hours a week rearranging the landscape around our house, but once we turned him loose to farm our fields, the sky would be the limit, as we both knew. Visions of cutting down the woods and brush to make pastures, of bulldozing terraces to plant with apple trees, of large drainage projects involving the use of his beloved backhoe, danced like sugarplum fairies before his eyes.

These ideas I discouraged as firmly as I could. Turning Harold loose on our twenty acres to turn them into a working farm was a direct path to bankruptcy—besides, I had no illusions about my ability to run a farm, even had I wanted to. My paternal grandfather had been a farmer, in Hungary, at the turn of the century, but photographs of him do not suggest that he was happy about it. In any event, all three of his sons had fled to Budapest as soon as they were old enough to hitch a ride, and never expressed any nostalgia for the farming life. Our land had once been a farm, of course—or part of one—and the endless stone walls and piles of rocks remained as mute evidence of just what hard and unrewarding work farming had been here. The ground was not just rocky—at the first sign of frost it actually *grew* rocks! You could pick a field clear of stones (if you wanted to break your back doing it), but on the first cold day new ones rose to the surface, even bigger and more numerous than the ones before.

Among our neighbors, the Vandenkamps (two shy, silent, elderly brothers and their sister, Gertrude), ran a model farm—it was (and remains) one of the most photographed farms in Dutchess County, a veritable tourist attraction with its neat white fences, its fields full of Holstein dairy cattle, and its rolling acres of corn, pastureland, and alfalfa—but the Vandenkamps rose in the middle of the night and worked nonstop seven days a week. They had done nothing to encourage tourists—on the contrary, they fled from the approach of strangers like Transylvanian peasants from a vampire. Even Margaret was unable to make eye contact with them, and she was a farmer's daughter—they did everything but cross themselves when she appeared in their driveway, and remained firmly hidden in their barn, behind large piles of hay bales.

Our first personal encounter took place when a large, friendly dog appeared at our house. A look at its collar identified it as the Vandenkamp dog—in fact, now that we thought about it, we had seen it from time to time, sitting beside one or the other of the Vandenkamp brothers (they were indistinguishable) on a tractor, as whichever one it was chugged up and down a field. Since we didn't want the dog to go home by way of the road, where a car might hit it, I put in a call to the Vandenkamps and explained the situation to Gertrude, who sounded as if this was the first telephone call she had ever received. Cornelius would be along in a few minutes, she said, and would take care of it.

A couple of minutes later Cornelius Vandenkamp turned up in a pickup truck. He drove slowly, and got out of the cab even more slowly. The Vandenkamps never did anything quickly—Haste Makes Waste might have been their motto. Cornelius was a big man, probably in his seventies, but solid as a brick wall, wearing overalls over a plaid wool shirt and a dark green tractor cap, the bill pulled low over thick bifocals. The Vandenkamps, I had been told—and found no difficulty in believing—neither drank nor smoked, and had never married. Their only known entertainment was that once a week one of them drove Gertrude to the Grand Union in Pleasant Valley to shop, in a well-looked-after elderly station wagon, driven at about the same cautious speed as their tractor. Cornelius, I noticed, was carrying a thick rope, like somebody on his way to a lynching, and a shotgun.

He shook hands with us formally, trying to keep his eyes from Margaret's direction. "I'm sorry Buddy's been a trouble to you," he said, speaking very slowly, like somebody who doesn't often get the chance to speak. His manner was polite but glum. Buddy seemed pleased to see him, though I had the impression that Buddy was such a friendly dog that he would have been pleased to see anyone.

No, no, we protested, Buddy had been a perfect gentleman and we had enjoyed his company. He had arrived the back way, over the fields and through the woods, but we were just afraid he might try to go home the short way, down the road, and get hurt.

"He ought not to be running off like that," Cornelius said, giving Buddy a reproachful look. "He's old enough to know better." Cornelius was still not making eye contact, except with Buddy. He stared off into the middle distance and sighed. "I can't have him being a nuisance to you folks," he said. "I can take him home and shoot him, if you like."

No, no, we cried in horror, Buddy had done nothing wrong, that was the *last* thing we wanted. It was only Buddy's safety that had prompted our call. We *liked* Buddy.

"I like him too," Cornelius said, as Buddy looked up at him soulfully. "I just want to do the neighborly thing."

In the end we persuaded Cornelius—to his visible relief—to lift Buddy's death sentence. He fastened the rope to Buddy's collar and put him in the passenger seat of the truck, said good-bye courteously to us, and drove off.

"Do you think he would really have shot Buddy?" Margaret asked, as we watched him go.

"Absolutely," I said. And I was pretty sure I was right.

Harold Roe confirmed it when I told him the story. The Vandenkamps took things seriously, he said. They said what they meant, and meant what they said. Neighborliness was high up on their list of values (maybe a notch or two below hard work and thrift), and if we'd said that Buddy was a nuisance, he would certainly have felt obliged to shoot the dog. Harold shook his head—the Vandenkamps' ways were mysterious, even to him, and he'd been to school with them. "I'll tell you what, though," he said, "they're real farmers."

That alone would have been enough to convince me that farming, in however indirect and gentlemanly a fashion, was not for me.

Fortunately, a different way of using our land was about to emerge, thanks to Margaret.

CHAPTER FIVE

A Barn of One's Own

AT FIRST we continued to keep our horses down at the stables of the Sleepy Hollow Country Club in Westchester, about an hour and a half away, in good weather (and traffic), and drove down there on Saturday and Sunday mornings to ride—no great hardship, but perhaps inevitably, it began to dawn on Margaret that there was no need to drive three hours there and back to ride on the Rockefeller family's trails when we were surrounded by country, with miles of riding trails made by the local hunt.

Up to this point I had paid very little attention to our barn, except to note with a certain dismay that it had once upon a time been used to contain sheep, and that nobody had cleaned it out since those far-off days. It was dark, dilapidated, and run-down, though the structure was certainly sound. I was more concerned with the adjoining studio barn/garage, in which the previous owner's wife, in the remote past, had taught art to children, and which seemed to have accumulated the debris of decades. Since I wanted a place to keep our car, this outbuilding was my first priority, and I did my best to encourage Harold Roe's efforts toward it, though his view was that it would make more sense to tear it down and build a new one. "Cheaper too," he prophesied (correctly, as it turned out), but then nothing was more likely to please Harold than the opportunity of tearing down a solid eighteenth-century structure and replacing it with something that had vinyl siding and garage doors you could open without getting out of your car. Harold was no sentimentalist when it came to buildings, nor to anything else.

Since the horse farm where Tabasco had recuperated was a twenty-minute drive from our house, it did not take long until our horses and all their gear had made the journey from Tarrytown to nearby Staatsburg. We could ride them there without having to drive all the way down to Tarrytown and back, and Margaret could go over to see them whenever she wanted to, which was often.

There were, of course, a few disadvantages, not all of them instantly apparent. The major one was that while Katherine Boyer loved having the horses, which could hardly have been better cared for, she did not much like having owners underfoot, come to ride their horses. She was a purist—her "boarders" were cared for, carefully exercised by riders who knew what they were doing, and kept to a strict schedule. Their owners upset the routine, got in the way, and undid much of her good work.

Eventually, she came up with a masterly solution—one of the farm's grooms, Roxanne, was getting married, and there was no room for a married couple on the farm. We could let them live in the added-on part of our house—which was really a separate little house, with its own front door—we could then keep our horses in our own barn, at home. Roxie would look after them before she left for work and when she got home in the evening. A further benefit was that Richard Bacon, the young man who was marrying Roxie, was handy at almost anything we might need doing around the house. Though he worked in the control room of Central Hudson, our local utility, he was apparently good at plumbing, carpentry, electrical work, car repair—almost anything we might have in mind, in fact. Besides, since we were in the city all week, the presence of Richard and Roxie would add a considerable security factor.

While I had a slight premonition of many problems to come, I could see from Margaret's face that the prospect of having her horses at home was not one she could resist. Besides, it answered a growing concern of mine, as I struggled with leaking taps, burned-out fuses, and septic problems. What we needed was a caretaker, and it took only a few minutes with Richard to see that he was clearly the man for the job—there was almost nothing he didn't seem to know how to fix, and he was of a size and disposition to discourage any intruder. We brought back Tom Kirchhoff and his men to install a kitchen in the separate wing of the house, and do whatever else seemed necessary to make it a home for a young couple beginning married life.

I remembered that my lawyer and old friend Morton Janklow had once owned a weekend house in Westchester, with a barn in which he and his wife Linda kept a couple of horses, and over lunch I asked him what he thought of our plan. Normally ebullient, his expression turned sober. "My father," he said, "once told me: 'Mort, my boy, never own anything that eats or shits.' " He looked at me sternly. "My father was right," he added.

Despite this warning, we went ahead. Richard Bacon cleaned out the barn, whitewashed the walls, and got rid of the wire netting that had been used to enclose the sheep, along with whatever else remained from their stay in the barn, while Margaret paced the grounds around the barn to determine how many paddocks she could build.

This required a certain amount of imagination. The ground was level, with plenty of grass, but densely sprinkled with cedars. Cedars are not good for horses, and besides, they were in the way—the cedars would have to go, along with a hideous aboveground pool. Richard Bacon nodded when told this. The size of the job did not seem to dismay him. He knew where he could rent a backhoe. In his spare time, he would uproot the cedars. Of course it was a big job—it would be sped up if I took my turn at the backhoe too.

Until now, the backhoe had not played any part in my life. I had seen them lifting pavement and digging ditches in New York, without giving them much thought, big, noisy machines, with enormous tires and a roll cage to protect the operator. As soon as ours came roaring off the trailer in a cloud of diesel smoke, I was eager to try my hand. After all, I could drive a car, and had driven many large and improbable pieces of equipment during my military service without major disaster. Here at last, I felt, was something I could do! I had a picture of myself, cheerfully puffing on my pipe as I gracefully maneuvered the backhoe into position and pulled up cedar tree after cedar tree, a Jeffersonian gentleman farmer of the twentieth century, busily improving his property. What was it that Candide had learned after all his sad adventures in the world? "Il faut cultiver notre jardin," he told Dr. Pangloss, and surely uprooting cedars to create horse pastures was a form of cultivating our garden? Voltaire and Jefferson would have approved, I thought, as I pulled myself up onto the backhoe and sat down, surrounded by hydraulic tubing, levers, and cheerful red-on-yellow "danger of death" warning labels.

Richard took me quickly through the drill—position the backhoe so the blade is in the right position for digging up the cedar, put down the hydraulic arms that prevent the backhoe from going ass over tit, swivel the seat around so that you face the blade end, and using the small control levers, lower the blade into the ground until it has firmly engaged the cedar's root system; then haul the tree right out of the ground, roots and all, like a dentist pulling a bad tooth.

With Richard waving, pointing, and making hand gestures like a man bringing a fighter-bomber in to land on the deck of an aircraft carrier, I eventually managed to lumber forward to the nearest tree. Neither the steering nor the gear change seemed to bear any resemblance to those of a car, or even a large truck, and the clutch felt like a weight machine at the gym. I proceeded by fits and starts and wild lurches, leaving behind me deep (and unwanted) ruts, while the diesel motor behind roared, coughed, and sputtered. Expressionless as Richard's face was, I could sense his dismay, and admired the sangfroid with which he stayed close to the machine. In his shoes, I would have run for my life.

After many false starts and mistakes, coached patiently by Richard, whose face betrayed a certain amazement that any adult male could be such a butterfingers when it came to hydraulic controls, I finally managed to get it right. With a sense of triumph, I pulled up a cedar, moved it out of the way, dropped it on the ground, and filled in the hole with the 'dozer blade.

I cut the engine and looked at my watch. It had taken me just over two hours to deal with one cedar, by no means the largest of the bunch. If I did nothing else, I might uproot ten cedars in a full day. At that rate, it would take months, possibly years, to clear the ground for Margaret's paddocks. Backhoeing was clearly not my métier. With great reluctance—but a certain sense of relief, at the same time—I decided to leave it to Richard and Harold Roe, who operated the machine with the grace of ballet dancers, and before long we had enough acres clear of cedars to call in Eddie Macdonald, the fence man recommended by Harold, and start building fences.

Eddie, a genial part-time boilermaker and pig fancier, worked at a slow, steady pace, but unlike most people in our neck of the woods, at least he turned up every day, and before long we had enough paddocks for our horses, all made with Secretariat fencing, as it was called, after the famous Triple Crown winner—"the Cadillac of horse fencing," according to Eddie, with fine-meshed wire through which no horse was ever going to put a hoof and creosote pressure-treated fence posts that are still standing more than twenty years later. (They have stood the test of time, sadly, better than poor Eddie.)

The bills, when they came, seemed to me astronomical—I thought back to Mort Janklow's remark at lunch—but of course they were just the beginning. Regularly, Margaret and Roxie returned from trips to the tack shop at Rhinebeck, the car loaded down with supplies—pitchforks, rakes, shovels, manure buckets, mangers, grooming equipment, food supplements—the list went on endlessly as the barn slowly filled and began to look like a proper stable.

The next step—the big one—was to add the horses themselves. I had assumed that we would have them shipped from Katherine Boyer's farm, where they were boarded, to our own when the day came, but on reflection that seemed foolish—after all, it was a distance of less than ten miles, as the crow flies. So on the day, we simply had ourselves driven over, mounted the horses, and rode off to the south until we were on trails that were unknown to us, past homes and lakes I had never seen before, occasionally emerging onto hilltops from which it was just possible to make out familiar landmarks in the distance. I was to experience exactly the same feeling vicariously many years later when I watched Augustus McRae and his friend Woodrow Call ride off together from Lonesome Dove, on the start of their long journey, in the miniseries of Larry McMurtry's novel. We crossed a few familiar roads, then descended into thick woods that seemed totally deserted except by deer and wild turkey, until finally, a couple of hours later, we emerged suddenly from the woods in sight of our own barn—a tribute to Margaret's sense of direction—and dismounted.

The horses were home—they did not know it yet, of course—and suddenly our house had become an honest-to-God farm. People called in trucks to deliver hay and feed, a succession of blacksmiths appeared at regular intervals to shoe the horses, the vet came in his truck to give them their shots. The tenor of our life subtly changed; before we had lived in isolation, disturbed only by an occasional UPS delivery and Harold Roe, but now we found ourselves in the middle of a beehive of activity—a modest beehive as yet, but still buzzing—most of which centered around the horses, who remained calm at the center of it all. Besides, whereas it had been, before, just ourselves and the cat living in a huge house with five bedrooms, surrounded by twenty acres, on the weekends, it now included the Bacons, possibly the quietest tenants in the history of landlordship, but still *there*.

For two people like ourselves who had lived for many years in New York City apartments, where you seldom see or know your neighbors and look down at your feet in the elevator to avoid eye-to-eye contact, this was a big change, and took some getting used to. No doubt it took some getting used to for them too. The level of noise from their wing of the house was so eerily low that I wondered if they might be holding their breath, or creeping around on felt slippers, and was relieved to hear the occasional flush of the toilet.

All the same, the country house no longer seemed peripheral to our lives, something you could own and forget about for long periods of time, or think of as "seasonal" like a summer beach house, or a skiing cottage. We began to refer to it, at first facetiously, but then naturally, with perfect seriousness, as "the farm," which was curious, since it had been almost thirty years since it had last been run as a farm, and almost as many years since Margaret had last lived on one, back home in Gloucestershire, with her parents. With the horses there, and the Bacons in residence, with Harold Roe busying himself at our expense with ambitious projects of drainage and earth moving—and the addition to our household of his sister-in-law Dot Burnett as our housekeeper—the house on Gretna Road seemed to have taken on a life of its own. Like the country estates of people on both sides of the Atlantic in the eighteenth century—admittedly much grander than ours—it was something more than a house. The presence of the horses, and all that came with them, gave it a certain *poids*, gravitas, sense of purpose. It was a pleasure—more for Margaret than for me, but I had my moments of feeling it too—to arrive in the car on Friday evening and see them in their fields, perhaps fifty yards from the driveway, snorting softly as horses do when they see something going on, for as animals they have a highly developed sense of curiosity. It was a pleasure too to contemplate the house, the big trees around it, the fields, the woods, the broken-down stone walls that we would soon have to rebuild at great expense, the barn that was always full of activity now that Roxie was looking after it, and realize that it was *ours*—that these were *our* trees, fields, woods, walls, and barn, not necessarily better than anybody else's (in many cases not as good), but different because they belonged to us. I developed a proprietary interest in the trees, as Margaret had in her paddocks, and brought in a tree surgeon (the first of many) to correct decades of neglect, and when one of them, a huge old maple that must have been a good-size tree when the house was built in 1785, had to be cut down because it endangered the house, it was like losing a pet, or a child, or a tooth.

With the arrival of the horses we had, without altogether realizing it, put down roots at last. Years later, when we occasionally question just what the hell we are doing living here in this corner of Dutchess County—usually because something or other has gone wrong on a big scale, or because a day after we have cleaned up the garbage on the road somebody has tossed a new batch of it out of his car, or because yet one more ugly, vinyl-siding-clad development has crept closer to us, or at the news that the property next door has just been bought by people whose hobby is racing four-wheelers, snowmobiles, and two-stroke dirt bikes—I end up sighing and saying, "Yes, but this is where we live. This is *home*."

"Home" doesn't have to be perfect (it seldom is), and doesn't have to be on Walden Pond, but it does have to be where you have your roots, your history, your good times and bad times, where people know you, whatever they may think of you, and feel you belong, and all that started the day we rode our horses home to our own barn.

CHAPTER SIX

"Them's Nice Pigs, Them Pigs"

ONE THING ABOUT HORSES—you get a whole different view of the country from a horse than the one you get from a car. Things are closer up, seen from the back of a horse, and since you're moving more slowly, you have more of a chance to look at them. In a car, you tend to approach somebody's house or farm from the front, so you see what they want you to see, whereas on a horse you tend to emerge from the woods with a good look at the part of somebody's property that most people never see—the backdoor view, as it were, with the illegal garbage dumps, the discarded cars and trucks, the old outhouse, the killer dog on a chain, the muddy fenced-in enclosures with forlorn cattle or donkeys, the rotten, collapsing barns and outbuildings.

The thing is, horses have a friendly image. There are plenty of places in our neck of the woods where a stranger arriving in a car represents a threat, or at least an unwelcome intrusion—some meddler from child welfare or the parole office, a bill collector or somebody serving a summons, who knows? A stranger on a horse, on the other hand, is almost certain to be harmless.

We began to take long rides through the woods and over the trails around us, and discovered a world that was never shown in the glossy pages of *Dutchess Magazine*, which more resembled, in fact, something straight out of the movie *Deliverance*, though the local backwoods, white-trash way of earning a living was less likely to involve tending a still than getting paid by the state to keep a foster home, or a group residence for handicapped people who weren't able to live on their own.

A couple of miles from our farm you crossed under the power lines and over a two-lane highway, then plunged into steep woods where the houses were unfinished, or merely trailers with the wheels removed placed on a foundation of cinder blocks, and where every once in a while you came across some run-down nightmare place guarded by fierce dogs that housed mentally handicapped children, or adults who had been released from mental institutions and warehoused by the state in squalid private houses, away from prying eyes.

You couldn't make much of a living looking after them, of course, but for some people it was the best they could do, and as in most things, the way to make money was to concentrate on quantity and keep your costs down. The more people you could get the state to cram into your home, and the less you fed them, the more money you made; it was as simple as that, and whatever it cost the state, it was less than the cost of keeping the old institutions going, or, God forbid, modernizing them, so everybody in Albany was happy.

You could always tell when you saw a crumbling old house with a jerry-built fire escape tacked on behind or a crude wheelchair ramp that you were approaching one of these homes, even before you saw the hopeless, downcast boarders, usually standing around in the mud, staring down at their shoes, or sitting blankly on an unscreened porch, rocking back and forth. Very often the proprietor was a tough, more-than-middle-aged woman who would appear on the porch herself, pushing her charges out of the way, ready to repel boarders, but the fact that we were on horseback usually calmed things down, and we were waved on our way. Where the proprietor was a man, he was likely to have a big dog on a short chain, and to make no secret of wanting us to move on as quickly as possible, and not to come back. Still, the worst we got was scowls.

In other places, the woods concealed tiny farms where somebody was trying to carry out the Jeffersonian ideal of rural self-sufficiency in the wrong climate, with a log cabin, a couple of carefully tended fields, and very often a few pigs. More places than not we saw (or smelled) pigs, and when we did, Margaret always smiled. Pigs reminded her of her childhood.

I myself had never thought much about pigs. As a child of six my nanny once took me on a visit to her family in Yorkshire, and I vaguely remembered having been taken to see the pigsty and helped up to peer over the rough stone wall at a muddy enclosure full of pigs. Nanny's farmer brother, perhaps in an effort to keep me from wandering about on my own, told me an alarming story about a neighboring farmer who had returned home from the pub drunk one evening (" 'E'd 'ad a few too many, see?"), and having stopped to look at his pigs, fell into the pigsty, where his pigs promptly devoured him. "Don't you never forget it," Nanny's brother warned me mournfully, "pigs will eat anything." When I returned to London, my father concurred. He had been brought up on a farm in Hungary himself, and feeding the pigs had been one of his chores as a small child. He had had no fears of them, but they were the smartest animals on the farm, in his opinion.

Pigs as a subject then left my life and did not reenter it until shortly after the Bacons had settled in. Richard and Roxie, Margaret said, were thinking of buying a piglet, and keeping it down by the manure pile, a hundred yards or so away from the barn. All things considered, given a choice, I would not have wanted a pig on the place, but on the other hand I wanted to keep the Bacons happy, and God knows we had enough acreage so that a pig would hardly be noticeable. Besides, I could tell that Margaret wanted the pig as much as they did; she was not a farmer's daughter for nothing.

On the grounds of the Dutchess County Fair, in Rhinebeck, there was a livestock auction, it transpired, and it was here that we would go to give moral support to Richard and Roxie as they bid for a pig. This seemed a pretty harmless way of spending a Saturday afternoon, and might have remained so if we hadn't met our fence builder, Eddie McDonald, and his boy in one of the big sheds where the pigs were kept before being auctioned.

The pigs were mostly piglets, and had been marked by lot with some kind of mysterious code with a spray can of paint. They were restless and noisy, not surprisingly, and very lively. There was a certain surreal quality to the whole experience for me, perhaps triggered by the fact that there was a stand selling hot roast pork sandwiches right outside the barn where the pigs were kept—but that, I reflected, was the whole point. The large, bulky men in the hall, most of them carrying a good, solid expanse of belly over the belt of their blue jeans and wearing John Deere tractor caps, chewed on their roast pork sandwiches reflectively as they leaned on the railings looking down at the pigs—pigs were pork on the hoof, however cute they might be as piglets, and it was hard to look at them without thinking about the end product: ham, pork, bacon, sausages. The pigs seemed to know that too—they did not have the trusting look of small puppies or cats, for instance, as if they already knew what was in store for them once they reached the magic weight of two hundred pounds.

There were plenty of kids around—raising pigs is still viewed as a responsibility-producing task in rural America (as it had been in Hungary when my father was a child), as well as a good way for a kid to earn a few bucks of his own, and 4-H and Future Farmers of America members abound, for all of whom the pig plays a central role. Eddie, of course, was under the impression that the Bacons were buying a piglet to raise for slaughter, and so very probably was Richard, but once Roxie and Margaret saw the pigs, that plan went out the window for good—the Bacons's pig was coming home as a pet, not as future pork chops, and it was not coming alone, because, as Eddie explained the rules of the auction, you couldn't bid on a single animal, you had to bid on lots. If the lot contained more pigs than you wanted, you traded back and forth with other bidders until you had more or less what you wanted, but it was almost impossible to buy one piglet. As it happened, Margaret had discovered two piglets that she wanted, one of them a rather charming male Duroc (for those not familiar with pig breeds, the Duroc is a particularly handsome dark red, with ears that flop forward and fold over its eyes), the other a Hampshire-cross female who looked like trouble. Eddie and his boy approved our choices wisely, not yet aware that these pigs were destined to lead unnaturally long lives. "Them's nice pigs, them pigs," Eddie pronounced solemnly.

At this point a further difficulty emerged. The Bacons were showing signs of embarrassment that I found hard to understand, until Margaret had a whispered conversation with Roxie and explained it to me. Roxie feared that if they bid on their pig themselves, everybody would laugh when Richard called out their name. It had not occurred to me, but I could see that this might in fact be true, so I agreed to do the bidding as we filed into the auction hall and took our seats on plank benches around a good-size oval of wood shavings.

I'm not good at auctions, for some reason, and get nervous when I'm bidding—even more so when I'm bidding for somebody else, as was the case here with Margaret and the Bacons. Eddie McDonald had given me a friendly warning that things moved pretty fast in here, but nothing prepared me for the sight of the auctioneer, a tiny little man who looked exactly like my friend the diminutive superagent Irving Lazar, except that he was wearing a ten-gallon hat—like Lazar, he spoke at a machine-gun pace, very little of which I understood. From time to time a lot number was read out, a gate was opened, and a whole bunch of pigs ran squealing out into the ring, while the heavyset men all around us listened to the auctioneer's call. I couldn't tell who was bidding—part of the game was that the people made bids by signs that were almost invisible, to me at any rate; a wink, a forefinger to the nose, a nod—and found it even harder to understand the prices from the auctioneer's high-pitched gabble, which reminded of the tobacco auctioneers spiel that ended with the cry "Sold American!" in prewar Philip Morris radio ads. As our lot neared, Roxie, tears in her eyes, squeezed my hand and said, "Don't let us down, please," which made me more nervous still, with the result that when our pigs appeared in the ring I stood up, causing everybody in the room to turn and stare at me, and raised my hand firmly at frequent intervals, until after a few moments, the auctioneer stopped calling out prices and glared at me himself. "You want these pigs, son?" he asked. I nodded. "That's good," he said, "because you own 'em. You're bidding against yourself."

Very fortunately, the Bacons had brought their own car, so I did not have to take the pigs home in mine—the pigs' natural good manners being stressed by the forced separation from their siblings, no doubt—and by the end of the day they were installed in a pen by the vegetable garden and had made themselves at home. For reasons that I can no longer remember, the Bacons named their pig George. I had wanted to name ours Edward and Mrs. Simpson, in homage to the duke and duchess of Windsor, but Margaret decided on Winston for the male and Miss Piggy for the female.

The arrival of the pigs had unforeseen consequences. Even more than the horses—much more than the horses, in fact—the pigs anchored us firmly as country dwellers. True, we were English; true, Margaret, with her fashion model's blond good looks and dramatic clothes, did not exactly blend in with the crowd at the Grand Union; true, I was a writer and editor, and worked "in the city," as people upstate always call New York, as if there is no other; but despite all these and many other differences between ourselves and our neighbors, *we owned pigs*. Once word got around about our pigs, perfect strangers began to speak to us at the drugstore or the Great Little Restaurant, people waved at us from their cars, and the owner of the garage and gas station at the hub of Pleasant Valley began to greet us by our first names.

Owning horses and keeping them on our property didn't do the trick—plenty of people nobody ever called by their first names did that, and in fact horses had a slightly undemocratic feel to them, a whiff of the gentry, as it were—but pigs were "common, base and popular"; they stamped us as being, though perhaps not instantly or obviously, "real folks," not just another city couple with aspirations to play at being gentry with more money than was good for them, and not your typical city-bred weekenders, carpetbaggers, as it were, either, because people like that might own dogs, or even horses, but never pigs.

People who came to our house to deliver something, or do some job, would stand in our driveway for a moment, frowning and sticking their nose up in the air, catching the faint smell of a familiar odor, and say, "You people got pigs?" When we allowed as how we did, they would insist on seeing them. Pig watching is not something anybody does in a hurry, as we came to learn. You have to shift your trousers down a bit, loosen up your belt a notch or so, give your belly a little breathing room, light a cigarette if you're a smoker, and look at the pigs for a good long time. Then you sigh, nod your head, and say, "Them's nice pigs, them pigs." Then you look at them some more.

The pigs, once they were properly installed, didn't mind being looked at, either. They were cautiously interested in people, but generally speaking, visitors didn't slow them down from the more absorbing task of rooting the ground up with their snouts in search of something good to eat. They turned the earth over with the care of somebody looking for diamonds or gold, and when they reached the far end of their pen they came back and rooted it all up again—there was never a dull or boring day for the pigs, even when there were no visitors for them to look at, which was seldom the case, since almost everybody in the county had at one time raised pigs, or planned to at some point, and invariably had strong ideas about what they should be fed, and how they should be raised.

Ours, as it turned out, were fussier than we had figured. They liked the pig food in pellets that we bought from the local feed store well enough, but they were selective when it came to leftovers and garbage. Leftover salad they despised, particularly cucumbers, and showed their indignation by flinging it around their pen with their snouts. Things they liked a lot included pumpkins (they would chew their way deep into a pumpkin, then walk around with their head stuck in it until they could shake it loose), chocolate mints, beer, and—a discovery made after somebody gave us a bottle—Bailey's Irish Cream liqueur. They were a lot cleaner than they were generally given credit for, and just as smart as people said they were, or smarter. Their eyes, fringed with remarkably human eyelashes, showed a sometimes alarming intelligence and a certain joie de vivre too. Eventually, when they got a little older, Margaret would take them for walks, with Miss Piggy in a harness and the other following behind; she learned to take along a bag of marshmallows, since they would follow a trail of marshmallows just about anywhere.

The only creatures who didn't like the pigs were the horses. Pigs are noisy, low to the ground, smell funny, and make fast, unpredictable moves, which just about sums up most of the things that horses don't like—on the other hand, the pigs weren't afraid of the horses, or anything else. Not too many animals, even big dogs, want to tangle with three pigs. Visitors from the city were mostly on the same side as the horses. They often expressed a desire to see the pigs, but unlike the locals, they seldom wanted to stay, particularly at feeding time, since the pigs were not dainty eaters by any stretch of the imagination. A visit to Margaret's pigs became a kind of litmus test for weekend guests, and those who failed to make the grade were not invited back in a hurry.

Of course as it became apparent, as it very soon did, that George, Winston, and Miss Piggy were not going to be turned into sausage and bacon, locals became concerned—it was a definite plus in our favor that we had pigs, but very curious behavior on our part when they were still around (and growing) past the two-hundred-pound mark. On the balance, however, the pigs won us more friends than not and established our right to call our place a farm, even if most people did still continue to refer to it as "the old Hubner place," or in the case of older people, even "the old Hewlett farm." The Hubners had had sheep perhaps twenty years ago, but sheep hadn't done it for them. There was nothing wrong with sheep, and there were plenty of them around, but pigs were different, Jacksonian democracy on four feet (or trotters). The pigs were in some ways something of a mystery. Since very few people ever kept them alive past the weight of two hundred pounds, nobody seemed to have much idea how big they would get. Eddie Macdonald guessed they would get "damned big," and left it at that. A hint of what was in store for us came from beyond the far end of our property, where an old farmer named Joe Bellino lived. Joe was something of a local character, a wiry, toothless, grizzled, opinionated old man who lived in a bewildering ruin of old barns and outbuildings from which he had once operated a livery stable, surely before Margaret or myself was born.

Joe's proudest possession, as we learned from Harold Roe, was a locally famous boar named Buzzy, which Joe kept for breeding purposes, and which was reputed to be of fearsome size and disposition. Buzzy was also about as old as a pig can get, so it stood to reason that if we wanted to get a hang on what size a full-grown pig could get to, we should go see Buzzy.

Joe wasn't used to visitors, but once we had explained our purpose—no easy task since he was deaf—he became positively jovial. These days very few people came to see Buzzy—people just didn't appreciate pigs anymore, that was all. Joe guided us through a labyrinth of collapsing sheds to what looked like a very large outhouse. "There he is," he said with pride, pointing to a knothole in one of the boards at a convenient viewing height.

The presence of Buzzy was overpoweringly evident—a kind of dense, piggy funk filled the air, combined with a sharper male odor that our male pigs, which had been castrated very young, didn't have. I peeked through the hole into the gloom, but could see nothing that I could identify as a pig.

"Ain't he something?" Joe Bellino cackled from behind me, and I stared harder. Something moved—blinked, in fact—and I distinguished an eye looking back at me, very human in shape, as perfectly lashed as any fashion model's, and apparently filled with cunning and rage. Buzzy gave a couple of warning grunts, then slammed against the boards of his shed like a Sherman tank in first gear. The movement revealed Buzzy's outline in the gloom of his home, and I backed away in sheer amazement. Buzzy was *huge*, the size of a grizzly bear. Even when he was seated, his head was at my height—and what a head it was, massive, enormous, and heavy, like that of a rhinoceros—while the rest of his body seemed to fill the shed. I had been looking right at him and missed seeing him at first because he was so big.

"How much does he weigh?" I asked, a certain awe in my voice.

"Cain't say. Never tried to weigh him." Joe cackled at the thought of trying to coax Buzzy onto a scale.

"He must weigh a thousand pounds!"

Joe nodded sagely. "Could be," he said proudly. "Maybe more."

Margaret took her turn at watching Buzzy, but I had seen enough. If Buzzy was a good representative of a full-grown pig in its prime, then we were going to have a housing problem, and maybe a fencing problem as well.

"Come back anytime," Joe Bellino called out as we left. "Buzzy loves company."

Our pigs were pretty fond of company too. Margaret used to get into the pen with them—they were very neat, and carefully reserved only one corner of the pen as their bathroom—and scratch their ears, which they loved. In the summer, they suffered from the heat (pigs have no sweat glands), so Margaret and Roxie went down to the Kmart and bought them a child's inflatable plastic wading pool, with dolphins on it. The pigs loved it, though once they got in it they usually displaced all the water, or tipped it over in their sheer exuberance, which had the happy side effect of producing mud, which they loved wallowing in. They loved being cooled down with a garden hose too.

On the whole, they were easy to please. As they got bigger, you had to be a little more careful around them. They weren't dangerous—though Miss Piggy had a certain mean streak when it came to men she didn't like—but they packed a lot of weight, and it was compact, with a low center of gravity. If they bumped into you, they could knock you flat, but one never had the sense that they *wanted* to. Myself, I kept in mind what my nanny's brother had told me all those years ago in Yorkshire, whenever I was anywhere near them.

SOME PEOPLE found the pigs genuinely upsetting. During the time when my novel *Queenie* was being transformed into a seven-hour miniseries, we became friends with James Goldman, the screenwriter (and brother of William Goldman), and his wife Bobbie. The Goldmans were city folks right down to the soles of their Gucci loafers, but they often expressed a desire to visit us. We were at pains to explain that Pleasant Valley was not the Hamptons, or even New Hope, Pennsylvania—that it was the *country,* basically a rural small town in the process of being degraded to bedroom community. If the Goldmans wanted to go antiquing, or visit historic sites, they could certainly do so within twenty miles of us, and good luck to them, but not in Pleasant Valley itself, which was a black hole so far as such attractions were concerned. Besides, ours was a simple country house, basically a farm—we did not have a swimming pool, a tennis court, or chic neighbors whom they were likely to know from the red-eye back from Los Angeles. We did have pigs, however.

The Goldmans proclaimed themselves delighted to sample the simple, country life—it was just what they needed, in fact, and they looked forward to seeing the pigs. A date was made, and it soon arrived.

When they came down the driveway in their tobacco-brown Rolls-Royce Corniche convertible, one of the fruits of Jim's writing *The Lion in Winter,* I had an immediate foreboding that they were going to be disappointed. They were relieved to find that the house, once they were in it, was not altogether a rural hovel, but they looked edgy and uncomfortable, besides being burdened down with enough luggage for a year, rather than for the weekend. Bobbie always carried Jim's handsome leather cigar case—she shared his passion for fine cigars—while he, to my surprise, carried with him from the car a very large stuffed lion.

Lion, as the lion was named, I soon discovered, went everywhere with them. When they had lunch at the Four Seasons, Lion accompanied them and had a place of his own at the table. I thought Jim would be more comfortable without carrying Lion, so we all went upstairs, where Lion was placed on the bed in their room with the television set on, though we could not leave until Bobbie had placed the remote control of the television set in Lion's paw in case Lion wanted to switch channels. I had a faint sense that this was likely to be a more trying weekend than we had anticipated, though it was only just beginning.

Bobbie was equally concerned about the Rolls, which they called Baby. Baby, it seemed, was normally only used for trips from the garage in their apartment building to the garage at the Four Seasons and back. Baby had never been upstate, or in the country, or even parked in the street. Where, Bobbie wanted to know, was Baby going to spend the night? Margaret and I exchanged glances. Baby, I explained, like our car, would have to spend the night outside on the driveway, where she was unlikely to come to any harm.

Bobbie brooded about this. Baby wouldn't like that a bit, she said. She had never spent the night outdoors before. What if she didn't start the next day?

Margaret looked Bobbie firmly in the eye. If Baby didn't start, we would send for Harold Roe, and he would push Baby down the road with his tractor until she did. "Actually," Margaret went on, "that isn't what I'd worry about. I'd be more worried about what will happen if the pigs break out of their pen and decide to eat Baby's tires."

The Goldmans exchanged glances now, shot with sheer terror, I could not help noticing, as if they had inadvertently stumbled into Norman Bates's motel. We gave them a stiff drink, walked them down to the pigpen, and introduced them to the pigs—it was feeding time, and the pigs were in boisterously good spirits. The Goldmans had been keen enough to see the pigs when we talked about it over dinner in New York, but at the sight of them in the flesh, they clutched each other's hand for mutual support. I'm not sure that up until that moment the Goldmans had actually believed in the pigs. They may have imagined that the pigs were our fantasy, much in the way that Lion was theirs, but standing there at feeding time the pigs were only too clearly real, with nothing of the cuddly stuffed animal about them. Unlike Lion, you certainly would have thought twice about putting Winston or Miss Piggy in the Rolls for a trip to The Four Seasons.

The Goldmans were witty, voluble conversationalists, but the pigs left them speechless—not, in their case, a good sign. On their part, the pigs did their best to be friendly to strangers, but their mind was on their supper. Having seen the pigs, the Goldmans clearly thought anything was possible, and the idea that Margaret might in fact release them during the night to root at Baby's beautiful black Dunlop tires preyed on Bobbie's mind through dinner at the Beekman Arms Tavern, in Rhinebeck.

From time to time she asked if the pigs could break out of their pen. I reassured her. The pigs were much too smart to tangle with barbed wire. When they were first on the property, they had made a couple of attempts to burrow their way out—pigs are good at burrowing, and their snout is as close as Mother Nature gets to a bulldozer, even when they are small. They are also patient, hardworking, and smart. The trick, Richard soon learned, is that you have to put strands of barbed wire underground as well as above it. The pigs soon learn it's buried there and leave it alone—unlike cattle or horses, pigs are not dumb enough to hurt themselves twice, or in most cases, even once.

Bobbie was not greatly reassured by this lesson in natural history. The thought of Baby surrounded by the pigs must have kept the Goldmans awake most of the night—from time to time I could hear them getting up restlessly, no doubt to look out the window and make sure that Baby was safe—and they left early in the morning, alleging an important Sunday-morning appointment they had forgotten all about. Baby, to their undisguised relief, started without a problem.

"It's a pity," Margaret said, as Baby disappeared down the road. "They missed watching the pigs have breakfast." The pigs brought to their breakfast an even greater enthusiasm than they did to their supper, and loved an audience.

Somehow, after the visit, our friendship with the Goldmans was never quite the same, as if every time they looked at us they were reminded of the pigs. It occurred to me that they might have thought that the pigs were a complicated and monstrous practical joke arranged at their expense, but it seemed better not to pursue the matter. In any event, the Goldmans never came back for a second visit, despite many invitations.

They just didn't have the right country spirit, Margaret decided. How could you if you didn't like pigs?

OVER THE YEARS, plenty of guests got a glimpse of the pigs—in fact it was the high point of the weekend for many people, since we had neither a pool nor a tennis court.

This was a problem to which Margaret and I had given very little thought, perhaps because we're both busy people, and perhaps too because ours wasn't the kind of country house that only gets used on the weekend—that you go to, in short, looking for two days of relaxation and fun. We *lived* here—having guests in the house was just as difficult as having guests staying in the apartment, with the difference that in New York City they would have been out doing things by themselves, instead of sitting around from breakfast on asking what our plan for the day was.

Most of my day gets spent at my desk, editing or writing. Margaret is either in the barn, or exercising her horses, or away competing, or doing farmer's chores—dragging the fields, mowing the paddocks, weed whacking around the jumps. As we discovered early on, very few people actually seem to want to come up from the city and spend a country weekend picking rocks out of a paddock by the hundreds and carrying them out to the woods to dump. They have in mind visiting antique shops, a long leisurely lunch on the screened-in porch, a swim—none of which is in our game plan.

Perhaps as a result of this, we had very few repeat visitors. We took to explaining that while we welcomed guests, and indeed prided ourselves on our hospitality, they would have to make do with simple country living, and most important of all, find some way to amuse themselves. "Michael's going to be working," Margaret would explain, "and I'll be in the barn, but we'll see you at drink time, and be *dying* to hear how you spent the day."

This seldom put people off. "*Great!*" they would cry—"that's *exactly* what we're looking forward to, not another of those Hamptons weekends when every moment of the day is organized, and you don't get up from the lunch table until four in the afternoon." When reality set in, however—usually by Saturday morning, after a cordial Friday-night arrival and dinner—the very guests who has said how much they looked forward to being left alone were standing around the kitchen like lost souls, chewing glumly on a bagel and asking, with a certain amount of petulance, what there was to *do*, with some expectation that whatever it was, we'd all be doing it together. The fact that Margaret was in her riding breeches and already impatient to be off to the barn and that I was clutching a manuscript and glancing at my watch were taken as signs of indifference, at best, or sheer hostility, at worst.

Of course it almost goes without saying that whatever was going to go wrong would do so to coincide with the arrival of houseguests. Two friends of ours from California, deeply involved in nutrition and living a healthy life, were just getting their bags out of the car at the very moment when one of our neighbors, an apple grower, had chosen to have his orchards crop-dusted.

Here were people whose whole life revolved around eating the right organic foods, taking every possible exotic vitamin and mineral, and avoiding contaminating substances as much as possible, standing awestruck—and, unfortunately, mouths open—as the crop-dusting plane zoomed back and forth above our heads, not a hundred feet high, spewing a long cloud of pesticides, which the pilot never quite managed to switch off completely as he pulled up and turned around over our property to go back for another pass. Poison came floating down on us, dusting the car, the luggage, and ourselves.

I wasn't as alarmed as our guests—an early riser, I often caught the radio program put out at dawn by the local agricultural extension program, a chatty talk show having mostly to do with pesticides, in which callers reported in exactly what kind of bugs or fungus they had found on their apples and the host told them what to spray. It was a friendly, first-name-basis kind of deal, in which the host—a folksy agronomist and pesticide expert—would say things like, "Well, Vern, old Chester Vanvilkomen, out Esopus way, he called in yesterday with pretty much the same darned thing on *his* apples, and I told Chester to get out there and start spraying. . . . No, you don't want to use it half-strength, or anything like that, you got to get the jump on these little critters hard right now, so don't dilute it, whatever it says on the drum. . . . Hell, forget what the EPA says, I'd do it every day for the next week or so, Vern. . . . Of course if you've got dairy cattle you'd best keep them inside. . . . And now here's Walter, from Pleasant Valley, with a different pest problem."

By dinnertime our friends were coughing and complaining of chest pains and skin lesions. They were not hugely reassured by my telling them that the pigs seemed to be just fine—far from collapsing dead in their pen, they had enjoyed a hearty dinner and seemed in fine form—and by Saturday lunchtime our guests were on their way back to New York City in their rented car, probably to check themselves into a hospital, and have never returned.

The arrival of London literary agent Ed Victor and his wife Carol was another memorable moment in our experience over the years as hosts. Ed and Carol had expressed a desire to see our house in the country and escape from the luxury and social pressures of the Hamptons, where they had built a much-admired house using timber imported from England, from a medieval barn. When I cautiously pointed out that Pleasant Valley might, in fact, be rather more distant in tone from the Hamptons than they actually wanted, they pooh-poohed me—a couple of days of simple country living was exactly what they wanted.

I suggested that if they met me at my office late on Thursday afternoon, we could drive up together, but for complicated social reasons that wasn't possible. The Victors were going to be on the Island, and saw no reason to spend three hours or so to come into the city, only to drive another couple of hours more up to Dutchess County. Ed promised to explore alternative means of transportation and call me back.

When he did, he was buoyant and cheerful. "It's easy as pie," he said. "There's a flight from MacArthur Field on Long Island, just a hop, skip, and a jump away from our house, that goes straight to Poughkeepsie—actually, it may land in Danbury, Connecticut, first, but never mind."

"Are you *sure?*" I asked. I didn't know of any airport near Poughkeepsie, and had never heard of anybody flying there from anywhere.

"Absolutely. Dutchess County Airport. Regular flights go in and out of there. Bustling little place, apparently. How far is your house from it?"

I hadn't a clue. As it turned out, when I got to my car and looked at the map, there the airport was, perhaps twenty minutes at most from where we lived, though not particularly easy to find, I guessed, looking at the tangle of rural roads around it.

"I wonder if we're making a mistake," I said to Margaret as I told her all this. We had not done much to prepare for their arrival, unless you count removing the cat litter box from their bathroom.

"What kind of mistake?"

"Well, don't you think they might be bored? They might be a little grand for Pleasant Valley."

"They can borrow the car and go antiquing, surely? Hudson is full of antique shops. And see the pigs."

Prudently, I made plans for dinner in Rhinebeck—a small dinner party might, I thought, amuse the Victors more than the pigs, despite Margaret's touching faith in them as a tourist attraction.

On the appointed day, leaving myself plenty of time, I set off to the airport, which, as I had predicted to myself, was anything but easy to find. There were lots of road signs marking the way to the airport, which I had never noticed before, but following them merely led me in circles, deeper and deeper into the rural backwoods of Poughkeepsie, full of motorcycle repair shops and trailers on cinder blocks. At one point I thought I had found the airport, but it turned out to be a kind of burned-out ghost town used by the local firefighters to train recruits. I got out my map, retraced my steps, and eventually, by stopping at every gas station I saw and asking for directions, found myself in the parking lot of the airport.

It was not a busy, bustling scene. There were several hangars, outside of which were parked a few private planes and a couple of crop dusters, a tower of sorts, and perhaps half a dozen cars in the parking lot. I walked over to the runway in search of somebody in charge, but all I could find was a freckled, red-haired teenage boy in overalls, with ear protectors around his neck and a baseball cap worn backward—the Huck Finn of general aviation, it appeared. I asked him if the plane from Long Island was on time. He shrugged. "Nobody tells *me* anything," he said. "Where did you say it was coming from?"

"Long Island."

He shook his head, perhaps in wonder, as if I had said Kathmandu. "Don't know about that," he said. "There's a plane supposed to come in from Danbury this afternoon."

"That'll be the one. It originates from Long Island, you see. Is it on time?"

"Hard to say." He stared up at the sky. "Depends on the weather. They get some mighty funny weather over there in Danbury. It could still be sitting on the ground there, if there's a storm."

I reflected that Danbury was perhaps an hour and fifteen minutes away by motorcycle—it is the site of Marcus Dairy, the big Sunday-morning gathering place for bikers—hardly far enough for their weather to differ significantly from ours, which was crystal clear, without a cloud in the sky.

I sat down on the fender of my car, and waited, along with Huck Finn. After a while, a small twin-engine plane appeared on the horizon, landed, and taxied toward us. Huck Finn straightened his cap, grabbed a baggage cart, and pushed it briskly toward the plane. The door opened as the propellers came to a stop, and Ed Victor, a big, bearded man, appeared. He was dressed in a white suit, with pointed black-and-white correspondent's shoes, a black silk shirt, and a white foulard. On his head he wore a white Borsalino, at a rakish angle. Carol followed him, dressed in a glamorous, flowing gown, strappy high-heeled sandals, a big, floppy straw hat with a flowered ribbon, and the kind of long silk scarf that Isadora Duncan was wearing when it caught in the wheel of her Bugatti in the south of France and broke her neck. They formed a picture of elegance, glamour, and luxury seldom glimpsed in Dutchess County—they might have been arriving for the Venice Film Festival.

Huck Finn was virtually paralyzed by the sight, but he was swiftly brought back to life when confronted with the Victors' luggage—as he pulled it out of the hatch I marveled that the airplane had been able to leave the ground at all. Out came hatboxes, soft bags, suitcases, shopping bags, tennis rackets—the baggage cart was piled high with the Victors' weekend luggage, and I suddenly began to wonder if it would fit in the car.

Eventually Huck Finn and I got it stowed away in the car, leaving just enough room in the backseat for Carol to squeeze into—it wasn't a small car, either; in those days I was driving a Cadillac Seville—while Ed and Carol admired the countryside.

Margaret watched in horror as Ed and I unloaded the car at the other end and carried the luggage piece by piece up the narrow stairs to the Victors' bedroom, huffing and puffing with exertion. "How long are they *staying?*" Margaret whispered in a panicky voice as I maneuvered one particularly large piece through the door. "Till Sunday," I said, gasping.

"But what do they *need* all this for?" she asked.

The answer to this question was forthcoming. No sooner had the Victors arrived and expressed their admiration for the house than they went upstairs and changed out of their traveling clothes. Ed descended in a lightweight tweed jacket, a sports shirt, a pale lemon ascot, tailored gray flannels, elegant shoes—looking, except for his beard, as one imagines that Gatsby might have looked when he first visited Daisy's house. Carol was wearing a different flowing gown, in soft pastels, with another big picture hat, and many layers of silk scarves and foulards, carrying the kind of straw bag that Marie Antoinette might have picked for a walk in the garden at Versailles. Margaret was in her riding breeches, and I in my blue jeans, so we made an ill-matched foursome as we walked down to see the pigs—always a welcome moment in their day—then back to the house for lunch.

During the course of the day—and the next day—the Victors changed clothes at such frequent intervals that I was afraid they would come to the end of the outfits they had brought before they caught the plane back to Long Island on Sunday. They had outfits for lunch, outfits for tea, outfits for drinks before dinner, outfits for walking in the country, and probably for anything else that a weekend in Dutchess County could provide.

I was reminded of my father's experience as the guest of honor at a banquet given by the local sultan in the Andaman Islands, while filming *The Outcast of the Islands* on location there. He had been dismayed when an apparently endless succession of highly spiced dishes featuring fish and coconut was presented to him for hours on end, long past his bedtime and, from the looks of it, everybody else's. Politeness required him to taste each dish, however fiery, but eventually he noticed that his hosts were only picking at their food, and that some of the dishes from earlier in the meal were being presented to him a second time, though with less enthusiasm. He asked his host how long the banquet would go on. The sultan belched softly and sighed, then, with infinite politeness, pointed out that the banquet would continue until my father said no to a dish—until he did, protocol required that the banquet continue and new dishes be offered to him.

It occurred to me that the Victors might feel the same way—perhaps they felt obliged to keep putting on new outfits until we said we'd seen enough. In the end, as I drove them to the airport on Sunday afternoon—clad in new and different traveling outfits, and looking more as if they were about to board the *Mauretania* for an elegant prewar Atlantic crossing than about to fly by puddle-jumper to Danbury, Connecticut, and Long Island—I reflected that the Victors' idea of country life was surely very different from ours. In England, they lived in an Elizabethan cottage at Sissinghurst, the home of Sir Harold Nicholson, the author-diplomat, and his poet wife Vita Sackville-West, surrounded by what are universally acclaimed as the most beautiful gardens in England—a far cry from our crumbling stone walls and luxuriant beds of poison ivy.

Still, they seemed to have had a good time, I thought, and certainly enjoyed meeting the pigs.

*I*N THE BEGINNING we rather saw ourselves in the roles of host and hostess, and gave candlelit dinner parties for our weekend guests, even bringing our Hungarian housekeeper up from the city with her mother, a formidable cook, to prepare and serve the meal in style. One thing you could say for old Mrs. Böhm—nobody left the table hungry after a meal she had cooked. In fact some people were hardly able to leave the table at all. The Böhms favored rich, hearty soups, with sour cream, a roast duck per person, plus a couple of extra ducks in case anybody was *really* hungry, potato pancakes, and for dessert *palatschinke*, stacks of paper-thin pancakes covered with whipped heavy cream, preserves, and chopped nuts. The word "cholesterol," if its exists in Hungarian, was unknown to them—one evening I entered the kitchen (carrying my English-Hungarian phrase book) to ask them something and found the Böhms, mother and daughter, standing on either side of a huge stainless-steel mixing bowl. They were breaking eggs into it, chattering away in Hungarian as they did so, and as I stood there, I began to count—a dozen, *two*-dozen, *three*-dozen, and on they went, still breaking eggs into the bowl. On the table beside the bowl was enough heavy cream and butter to stop the hearts of a regiment, let alone a dinner party of ten. What, I asked, were they making? The young Mrs. Böhm, who spoke English and translated for her mother, smiled broadly. Mrs. Korda had asked them to make something light for dessert, she explained, so instead of *dobos-torte*—nut strudel with cream—they were making summer *palatschinke*. She blew into the air. "Light like a feather!" she said, while her mother cackled with laughter and unwrapped five or six sticks of butter.

With meals like these on a Saturday night, most of our guests never got a chance to complain of boredom the next day. Far from fretting about how they were going to amuse themselves on Sunday, they were happy to sit around on the porch fanning themselves feebly with the *Times Sunday Magazine* and listening to their digestive system complain—all the more so since the Böhms liked to prepare a good, solid Austro-Hungarian breakfast, featuring a lavish selection of fresh pastry, all of it, of course, "light like a feather."

Even after we lost the Böhms, once we gave up the big apartment in the city, we still gave ambitious dinner parties, with candlelight, Margaret's parents' gleaming silver, and a selection of vintage ports, but then, as it were, the impetus flickered out and eventually died. Margaret was riding full-time, a serious competitor in the eventing world, a national champion; I was working full-time and writing books; and without our realizing it the house, which had once seemed barely big enough to contain the number of people who wanted to spend the weekend with us, seemed to be only just big enough for the two of us, all our possessions, and four or five cats. We continued to have the occasional overnight guest, and once or twice a year the house filled up when Margaret gave her own event on our land, but the urge to fill the house up with guests, never overwhelmingly strong on our part in the first place, seemed to have ebbed. The days when there was a bowl of potpourri and fresh Penhaligon soap in every guest room were gone.

At first we felt guilty—having a big house in the country without guests seemed wrong somehow—but gradually we got over it. In fact, we discovered, everybody else went through the same progression, from filling the house up with people and giving elaborate dinner parties to living in the kitchen and the library, with meals on a tray in front of the television set. We simply got there sooner than other people.

We remembered our guests with fondness, and in some cases could still see traces of their stay with us years later—the downstairs ceiling cracked because Margaret's friend Mayo did her exercises on the floor of the bedroom above it (not a good idea in an eighteenth-century house), the headboard and the wall damaged by two guests who were, presumably, having violent sex one night, innumerable cigarette burns and rings from glasses put down without a coaster—but far from brooding when the house was empty except for ourselves, we came to rather like it that way, to the extent that the prospect of actually having a guest threw us into a state of alarm and panic. No, no, they can't use the pink room because the tub in that bathroom still leaks, and the plumber never showed up to fix it; they *could* have the blue bedroom, but there aren't any bulbs in the bedside lamps and one of the screens is missing; or how about the red bedroom, but there's a cat litter tray in the bathroom that will have to be moved, and there's always the danger of somebody falling on the stairs if they have one too many drinks after dinner. . . .

Somehow, at the last minute, we always manage to pull things together, often by removing things from one bedroom or bathroom and moving them into another, but it's not like the old days, when the house was often full up, and guests went on drinking long after we had said good night and gone to bed, and the smell of candles and Hungarian cooking was in the air. . . .

On the other hand, as everybody who lives in the country knows—it's nice to be alone.

The pigs missed guests a lot, though. They liked the company, and people often brought them snacks off the table as a way of saying hello. Still, they too were philosophical about it, and got on with life, as did we.

CHAPTER SEVEN

Lunch at Cady's

Cady's bar—lunchtime

ONE OF THE FIRST THINGS you learn about owning an old house is that even when things are running smoothly and everything looks fine, something, somewhere, is probably going wrong. We hadn't been in our house for more than a few months before a local, glancing at it from the driveway, said, "I guess you folks know your shutters are all on upside down?"

A quick look confirmed that he was right—nobody had noticed it, not the previous owners, not Tom Kirchhoff, not even Harold Roe, a born nitpicker, with an eagle eye for disaster. I thought it would be an easy task to take the shutters off and put them back on right side up, but no, of course not. They had been put on the way they were thirty or forty years ago; all the wrought-iron fittings would have to be changed, for a start, then the shutters would have to be sanded, the holes filled in and repainted—in short, a big job.

I assumed that it was a question of aesthetics, basically, but no such luck. With the louvers facing the wrong way, the shutters had funneled water in, against the side of the building, for three or four decades, with the result that a lot of rot had built up in the wood behind them. The boards would have to come off, there would have to be probing for any structural damage or unsoundness in the walls, which would need to be fixed, then everything would have to be put back and repainted before the shutters could be rehung the right way up. In other words, just the kind of nightmare that keeps sensible people living in city apartments, where this kind of thing is the landlord's problem, or the co-op board's.

Here the problem was mine, and I elected to follow Tom Kirchhoff's sensible advice—wait until the house needs repainting, and do it then. All the same, every time I looked at the shutters, I felt a headache coming on. What else was going on that we'd all missed?

With houses, as with people, hypochondria is a bad idea. Lying awake all night listening for the sound of the pipes gurgling and wondering whether they're leaking is no way to live, and besides, old houses are tricky—failure will almost certainly come from some part of the house you haven't been listening to, or looking at, or worrying about, out of the blue, at a moment when it will take you by surprise, and if possible on a national holiday, when nobody answers the telephone.

Thus, while we were looking at the shutters, and deciding for the moment to leave well enough alone, we were overtaken by a new problem: a pipe sprang a leak above the library. We had been having a drink there when I looked up and noticed—or thought I noticed—a slight change in the ceiling above me, neither a discoloration nor a bulge, just a fleeting sense that it was somehow different. I looked more closely, and saw nothing. A few minutes later, I felt what I took to be an imaginary drop of water on my head. I looked up and realized that the ceiling had suddenly developed a big bulge, about the size of a pillow. It appeared to be growing as I looked at it.

Soon we had moved the furniture out of the way, covered it with sheets of plastic, and placed a bucket beneath the bulge. The next morning the plumber arrived, cut through the ceiling, unleashing a small Niagara of dirty water, and began a careful examination of the pipes he found there. His diagnosis was gloomy—the pipes were old, going back to the early days of indoor plumbing, and the brazing was worn. He had cut out a section of pipe to show us—sediment had virtually blocked it off, leaving just a tiny hole for water to trickle through, and throwing intolerable pressure on the places where the pipe was brazed. I could not help noting that all of this exactly resembled a demonstration of arteriosclerosis in a human being, or a lecture on the dangers of high cholesterol. I said so. The plumber thought about this and nodded. Yup, he said, that was about the size of it, all right. These were old pipes, and just like an old person's arteries, they were a time bomb waiting to explode. What could we do about it? I asked.

The plumber rolled his eyes. Not much, unless we wanted to tear the house apart and renew all the plumbing. Failing that—and our expressions made it clear that was not an option—we should keep our eyes peeled for the first sign of a leak, and maybe learn how to shut off the valves to whatever part of the system seemed to be causing trouble—this with a dark look in my direction, because it had not occurred to me to do so, nor would I have known where to find the valve. Whenever there was trouble, we should use the opportunity to repair a section of pipe. In the meantime, quick action to turn off the right valve would at least save us a lot of redecorating expense.

The plumber glanced up, as if expecting water to appear from the ceiling at any moment. Of course, we should bear in mind that pipes and plumbing fittings weren't the only causes of leaks, no sir, not by a long shot. Water leaked in through the walls, and traveled who knew where (I thought of our upside-down shutters), and that's not even counting the roof. Those were old cedar shakes, very traditional, but a real pain in the butt, if we could excuse his French, and the house was surrounded by big old trees. . . . He shrugged. Well, need he say more?

The one thing we *could* do was to make sure where to find the valves in a hurry.

Richard Bacon and I undertook a reconnaissance of our pipes—those, at any rate, that could be reached—and he carefully tied a label to every valve, with its place in the system neatly written on the label (they are still there twenty-odd years later, like Christmas decorations that somebody has neglected to take down). The plumber's predictions have come true time and time again over the years, with the result that whole sections of pipe have been replaced after a leak, like an endless series of heart bypass operations, while the system itself labors on, wheezing and groaning and causing high anxiety on winter nights when the temperature drops below zero, and the pipes have to be cosseted like an invalid patient with heat tape, heat lamps, and electric hot-air blowers in the crawl spaces.

Still, a house that was built before George Washington's first term as president of the United States is never going to be trouble-free. The fact that each subsequent great leap forward in domestic technology—first indoor plumbing, then electricity—had been carried out as these innovations were in their infancy, and by not particularly talented hands, wrestling with the unknown and poorly understood, only made matters worse. The house was a museum piece all right—perhaps for a museum display labeled Common Mistakes in Domestic Architecture. But, it was ours, and we stuck to it stubbornly, feeling no envy (or not much) for those of our friends who built new country houses with state-of-the-art plumbing and electricity, and had Thermopane glass in their windows instead of eighteenth-century glass.

Electricity was less troublesome than plumbing, though more worrying. Who knew what was going on in all those wires placed between the walls when Theodore Roosevelt was president by some local guy who had learned how to wire a house by trial and error? On the whole, though, we could ignore the wiring, unless and until it burned the house down around our heads. The real problem with electricity, as we rapidly discovered, wasn't in our house anyway, but in the overhead cables of Central Hudson, our local utility. A bit of wind, a bad rainstorm, snow, ice, a tree that skidded into a utility pole, "birds on the line"—any incident, however small, was apt to lead to the power being out for hours or even days while the utility company's telephone "hot line" rang unanswered, and their crews sat around their trucks blowing on their coffee mugs and eating doughnuts.

Having come from England, where power outages were rare even in 1940 during the Blitz, it was hard to understand how the world's most advanced industrial power could limp along with an electricity system as fragile as antique stemware. Even when the weather was warm, sunny, and breezeless, the power was apt to go out for no apparent reason, nor was Central Hudson at pains to explain why, let alone put it right. Their customer relations team had apparently been trained at some utility behind the Iron Curtain, the Karl Marx Consumer Electric Cooperative in Tomsk, perhaps, or the Bulgarian People's Electricity Board. On a day when it was in the seventies and perfectly clear, and the power failed, I finally managed to get through after innumerable calls to a living human being at the Central Hudson office in Poughkeepsie, to ask what the matter was this time. "Bad weather," she snapped. "Why don't you look out the window?" She hung up, leaving me staring at the cloudless, clear blue sky.

I figured we could learn to live with power failures—at least they weren't my responsibility, whereas electrical problems in the house were. The thing was to stock up on every possible type and size of flashlight, stuff the pantry drawers full of batteries, and eventually install a propane-powered generator, while awaiting for the introduction of competition into the electric utility business (fat chance!).

More perplexing, however, was an electrical device that predated the lightbulb. The master bedroom, the living room, the library, and several other rooms in the house had an electric button set in the wall to signal to the help in the kitchen. This system—at the very heart of middle-class domestic life around the beginning of the twentieth century, when there were still people whose job it was to sit in the kitchen waiting for the buzzer to sound—had fallen into disrepair before World War II, but the wires were still buried deep in the house somewhere, and above the kitchen closet there remained a kind of signal board, with little metal flags behind glass windows that clacked up to indicate which room was signaling down for help. Many layers of wallpaper and paint now covered the buttons in a good many of the rooms, and those that weren't covered didn't work, so it was surprising, and even alarming, when from time to time the buzzer would sound in the kitchen and a ghostly clack as the little metal flag sprang up would signify that somebody was signaling from a bedroom that had been unoccupied since we bought the house, and probably for most of the thirty years the Hubners had lived here. I am no believer in ghosts myself, but I found these unexpected signals unsettling, and eventually persuaded Richard Bacon to remove the panel and cut the wires behind it. Even then, it still went off from time to time, as if the house had a life of its own.

But, of course, old houses *do* have a life of their own—many lives, in fact. And we were always turning up odd little traces from the past, buried away in the attic or in odd closets. There were initials carved on beams, labels on shelves in the cellar that might have gone back to the nineteenth century, odd and unrecognizable old tools. Every family that inhabits a house eventually stamps a part of itself into the fabric, and all the painting in the world won't entirely cover it up. We too, Margaret and I, will one day be a part of the house, as surely as if there were such a thing as ghosts.

In the meantime, we were obliged to deal with the house's nonspiritual problems. Very shortly the plumber's gloomy prognosis about the roof would prove correct; as Tom Kirchhoff had warned, the house would need repainting, during the course of which further problems would inevitably emerge that would make that of the upside-down shutters look like small potatoes; and all of this without counting the barn, or the slightly smaller "studio-barn" in which Mrs. Hubner had once taught art to the local children, which now served as our garage. All these buildings contained enough doubtful patches of roofing, leaky gutters, dry rot and wet rot, and suspect siding to keep a small army of craftsmen busy for months, or possibly even on a permanent basis.

My first thought, of course, was whether I could afford to keep a substantial part of the Dutchess County workforce employed, but since the alternative would be to let the house fall in wrack and ruin about our heads, doing nothing was not an option. That was made clear to me every time we made a new discovery and gathered to examine it like a hanging jury. Usually this group consisted of myself, Richard Bacon, Tom Kirchhoff, Harold Roe, and whatever specialist had been called in to give his opinion—plumber, or painter, or roofer, or gutter man. Everybody would stand and stare for a few minutes, each person shaking his head glumly, even the normally ebullient Harold Roe, while the specialist put his hands in the back pockets of his overalls and sighed. Nobody wanted to break the silence, but Tom was usually the first to speak. "What's it look like to you?" he would ask the specialist. That worthy would then screw up his face in deep thought and say, "It don't look good, Tom. 'Course we're not going to know how bad it is till we've gone through this wall and had a good look at what's in there. . . . Might not be too bad, of course. . . ." A shrug. "But with an old house like this . . ." Another bout of head-shaking on everybody's part, then Harold Roe would say, "Well, I'm sure glad it ain't *my* house," to which everybody but me would nod Amen. And with good reason—whatever lay behind a wall or ceiling in a two-hundred-year-old house was almost certain not to be good news for the owner.

The gutters, for example, to which none of us had given much thought ("If it ain't broke, don't fix it"), were a source of amazement to everyone who examined the house. Built in the age before zinc or stamped tin gutters, they were made of wood, each one a small masterpiece of carpentry, but also a guaranteed source of rot. It was possible—just barely possible—to maintain the gutters, by constant repair work and painting, and lavish applications of tar, but in the end they were going to have to be replaced with modern ones, offering a good opportunity for checking out what had been going on behind them for the past seventy-five or a hundred years or so.

Of course, as we soon discovered, it was one thing to learn that something needed doing, and quite another to get anybody to do it. Take the roof. We decided to start small by only redoing the worst sections, much against everybody's advice, and finally found a roofer who could deal with this. That it would be a big, messy, noisy job went almost without saying, but we knew there was nothing for it but to bite the bullet. For the first few days things went as predicted—at eight every morning the roofer and his guys arrived in their pickup trucks, with their mugs of coffee and their bags of doughnuts, and often with a dog in the front seat. We got to know their names, and those of the dogs, and much as we didn't enjoy having them on our roof banging away all day long and complaining about what they were finding once they ripped the old shakes off, we grew used to having them there. Then one morning they didn't turn up. Eight o'clock came, eight-thirty, *nada.* The weather was overcast, a light rain was forecast, but nothing the roofers hadn't dealt with before. I called the roofer's office number—no answer. I called his home. His wife had thought he was here, but if not he had probably had an emergency to deal with elsewhere, and would be at our place soon. I pointed out that there were holes in the roof and it looked like rain. She said it looked rain to her too, and promised to pass the message on to her husband if he called.

Nevertheless, the roofers didn't turn up for the next couple of days, despite a flurry of increasingly frenzied calls from me—these were the days before the cell phone, of course, when the best you could hope for was that somebody's wife just might reach him in his truck over the CB radio, or that you might catch him at home by calling before six in the morning or after seven at night.

The roofers were no more difficult than anybody else to reach. Plumbers would arrive, turn off the water, take apart a few pipes, then go off in their truck to pick up some tool they'd forgotten, never to reappear. You always knew that whenever a workman stood up, stretched his back, and said he'd have to go down to the hardware store for a left-handed clevis, that was it for the day. Hard as it was to get somebody to start a job, the real problem was to get them to finish it—or even to keep at it on a regular basis.

At first we found this hard to understand, but gradually it became clear that this stemmed from a kind of natural survival instinct. When it came to artisans, it was always either feast or famine—you either had more work than you could handle, compressed into the few months when it could be done, where outside work was concerned, or not enough to keep you in business. That being the case, nobody in their right mind ever turned down a job—the notion of finishing one job before beginning the next was simply impractical. Instead, everybody piled up as many jobs as they could, and as a result spent most of their day rushing back and forth across the county trying to keep up with them. The customer who yelled the loudest, or had the good sense to withhold a crucial payment, might get dealt with first, but sooner or later he too would be stamping his feet as he waited in his driveway for the workers to turn up in the morning—it was simply part of the system.

It was absolutely certain that once the men from our local oil heat company had taken apart the furnace (a major source of trouble) or the hot water heater (more reliable, but also given to mysterious problems involving jets, oil-feed pipes, and the like, which defied expert analysis and any number of attempts to put things right), then they would have to leave either to pick up a part or a tool or to respond to some other emergency, while the house cooled and the hot water turned icy. Everybody involved was nice enough—politeness was not an issue—but hardly anybody seemed to know what he was doing, or be willing to stick around until it was done. Somewhere just over the horizon were probably half a dozen other customers waiting impatiently for their heat and water to be restored.

As the years went by, this problem became more intense, first of all because more people were buying or building homes in Dutchess County as Westchester and Putnam Counties to the south of us filled up or became too expensive; secondly because the advent of the computer, and a certain level of prosperity, meant that fewer and fewer kids wanted to join their father in the roofing or the plumbing business. Kids who had spent ten years in school mastering the computer were not likely to want to go straight from school to apprenticeship as a chimney builder, say, however many chimneys there were to build in Dutchess County. Thus the craftsman—particularly if he was competent—became a precious commodity, much in demand, which made it even less likely that he would respond to your emergency calls or turn up for work on the day he said he would.

Newcomers to the country raged at this, as we once had, without realizing that the order of priorities was simply different here. In the city, it might depend on who you were, or what your job was, or how much money you had, but here, generally speaking, "locals" came first. A busy craftsman—a painter or a roofer in the summer months, a plumber at any time, a gutter installer before the autumn—would tend to look after his neighbors, his wife's relatives, his girlfriend, or the guys he went to high school with first, people he saw every day and couldn't avoid, as opposed, say, to somebody who could get a good table at the Grill Room of The Four Seasons in New York City, or reach Oprah by telephone. The fact that you were on the A list in New York did not necessarily mean that you would be on the plumber's A list, even if you paid your bills on time and listened to his jokes when he finally arrived.

We solved this problem early on, in a fit of inspiration. One day, having run out of food for some reason, we decided to drop in at Cady's Bar & Grill, in the same shopping mall as the Grand Union supermarket and the local liquor store, for a quick lunch. Our roofer and his men had vanished again, as well as the man who was working on our gutters, who had gone off to find some right-angle supports and never returned. Telephone calls to their work numbers and homes had produced no information—"I thought he was over to your place," was the usual comment—so we decided to go have lunch in town.

The word "unpretentious" leaps to mind when attempting to describe Cady's (which later changed hands and became Mackey's Pub, without any substantial alteration to the decor, the cuisine, or the clientele). Like the Roes and the Daleys, the Cadys were a local clan, and Cady's was run in the spirit of a club, in which outsiders were not exactly greeted with open arms. The front room, facing the Grand Union parking lot, contained a good-size bar, half a dozen tables, a jukebox, and a cigarette machine. A narrow corridor with the kitchen on one side and the bathrooms on the other led you into a larger back room, sparsely decorated (to put it kindly), with a moth-eaten wall-mounted deer's head as its principal ornament, where the overflow crowd from the front room could eat, or which could be used for private parties, like Harold Roe's anniversary party, to which we were invited, and which featured immense steaks, mashed potatoes, a complete absence of green vegetables, and the entire senior membership of his snowmobiling club, as well as some relatives of Harold's and Birdy's who looked old enough to have attended the mustering of the local militia before George Washington in front of what is now the post office building in Rhinebeck.

Cady's was not a place for haute cuisine, even by the standards of rural Dutchess County. At lunchtime it was pretty much a place for a burger or a tuna melt, but within those narrow limits, it was good, solid, substantial food, heavy on the cholesterol and low on the greens. The concept of health food hadn't made much headway in Dutchess County at that time, least of all at Cady's, but you certainly weren't likely to leave the table hungry.

Or thirsty. Beer and soft drinks at Cady's were served in giant glasses—big enough to make me wonder if the locals had cast-iron bladders. Cady's wasn't a hot spot at night necessarily—not that Pleasant

Valley's nightlife was by any stretch of the imagination a major attraction—but they did a pretty good luncheon business. It wasn't until we'd sat down and ordered lunch that the penny finally dropped.

Of course it took a moment for it to sink in. We were seated at a table, opposite the bar, waiting for our food, when Margaret commented on the size of the men at the bar. I glanced up and saw what she meant. Their backs turned toward us, the lunchtime regulars at Cady's bar were of an impressive width, size, and poundage—inferior, certainly, to Buzzy the boar, but big enough so that one feared for the bar stools that carried that kind of weight, and so that the men were wedged in against each other, hip to hip, like animals at the feeding trough. Most of them had the kind of bottoms that overflowed over their bar stool, and, this being summer, a gap between the T-shirt and the top of the blue jeans that exposed ample love handles. Those who wore the tools of their trade fixed to their belt exposed the top of the crack of their ass every time they leaned forward to grab the ketchup bottle. It was not a sight to invigorate the appetite, or remind one of the Mr. Universe contest, and I said so.

Margaret dismissed this comment impatiently. She had lost interest in their size. "Can't you *see?*" she asked. "*This* is where they are! Half the people who are supposed to be working at our house, or went off to get something and didn't come back, are right *here* at lunchtime!"

There was a big mirror behind the bar, so if I craned my neck I could catch a glimpse of the faces of the men at the bar, somewhat obscured by the fact that local custom is to keep your baseball cap on while eating. I saw at once that Margaret was right. Seen from behind, they merely presented a line of more or less identical large, blue-jeans-clad bottoms and broad waists, but many of the faces in the mirror were identifiable and familiar. I made out our roofer and three of his men, as well as the man who was working on our gutters—or would have been working on them if he hadn't been here.

"Yes, I see," I said. "But now what?" After all, we could hardly press-gang people straight out of Cady's.

But Margaret is not a woman for nothing. The moment there was room at the bar, she took her plate and went over there and sat down, me following behind her. In those days, women didn't sit at the bar much, if at all, at lunchtime. It was a kind of unwritten rule—women had lunch at the tables in front of the bar, from which it was okay for them to exchange ribald greetings and comments with the men at the bar, but never *at* the bar themselves.

When the men realized there was a woman sitting there, they shifted uneasily, like spooked cattle. It wasn't that they were telling each other dirty stories, or using profanity—that wasn't the issue at all—the bar was simply where working men sat at lunchtime. When they noticed who the woman was, they looked more uneasy still.

One by one, Margaret greeted those of them who were working on our house. She didn't ask them when they would be back at work—she didn't have to. By two o'clock, everybody was working again, even the gutter man, and from then on, whenever we could, we made it a habit to lunch at Cady's at least twice a week.

When eventually a Dunkin' Donuts opened in Pleasant Valley, I took to going there in the morning to pick up a cup of coffee for myself, and coffee and doughnuts for whoever was working in Margaret's barn. That too brought me face-to-face with most of the people I wanted to see—the plumber, who still hadn't come round to fix a leaking faucet, the oil heat service guys who were supposed to have cleaned the furnace but never showed up, the electrician, the painter, whoever. . . .

Since none of them was willing to lose his place in line, and inside the Dunkin' Donuts it was narrow and crowded, they had no means of escape, and it was usually possible, by good eye contact and a quick chat, to get them to fix a definite time by the time they were at the cash register. They usually showed up too, once it became clear that I was very likely to be in the Dunkin' Donuts the next morning, and the morning after. After all, it's a lot easier to avoid a telephone call than it is to avoid somebody who's standing right next to you in the flesh as you wait for your large regular with three sugars and your two maple-frosted doughnuts without sprinkles—or who plunks himself down next to you at lunch, just as you're about to bite into your tuna melt with double cheese.

Really, it was just part of becoming a local—a *neighbor* whom people see every day, instead of an outsider, because once you're thought of as a neighbor, your gutters are going to get fixed before the big rains, and, more important, before those of all the people from the city who have bought big places up here and haven't discovered about Cady's yet.

The trick is to become just plain folks somehow, however you manage it—and if it takes the occasional tuna melt, so be it.

CHAPTER EIGHT

Just Plain Folks

UP WHERE WE LIVE, however, it's hard to be taken for "just plain folks" if you work five days a week in the city, particularly at a relatively high-profile job. As the horses began to take up more of Margaret's attention, she began to spend more time in the country, driving down to New York City whenever we had a dinner date with somebody, or for the many obligatory social functions without which it is supposed to be impossible to publish books.

The truth was that without either of us having planned it that way, the house in Pleasant Valley was no longer just a weekend place. Some people with far larger establishments than ours came up late on Friday afternoon and went back on Sunday evening, and never thought twice about it—Millbrook was full of them—but we had somehow stopped thinking of ourselves as "city people" somewhere along the line. The apartment in the city took on a certain unlived-in quality, and large quantities of our belongings made their way up to the country a bit at a time, as if we were stealthily burglarizing ourselves.

Eventually—inevitably—I began to think of spending more time in the country myself, and decided to try my hand at commuting. As it happens, Pleasant Valley, at ninety miles from the city and about half an hour from the nearest railway station, is just a little beyond normal commuting range for this part of the country, which was exactly why there remained farms, woods, and empty land, and why we had chosen it in the first place.

Still, there *were* people who commuted; I knew that. The Hubners, from whom we had bought our house, had lived here for more than thirty years, during which time Mr. Hubner had traveled down to the city and back five days a week on the train from Poughkeepsie to his job at a large oil company's headquarters on Forty-second Street—at least a two-and-a-half-hour journey each way. Mr. Hubner, whom I had only met briefly, was not a great advertisement for daily commuting, all things considered. Tall, stooped, frail, and rail-thin, he walked with some difficulty, as if afflicted with permanent fatigue, and had the look of someone who might have had a stroke, on top of a lifetime of rising at five in the morning to make it to his desk by nine. Still, there were doubtless other factors involved than commuting, I told myself. Plenty of other people did it, and were perfectly healthy, I supposed—though I hadn't met any of them.

It was, of course, possible to commute by car—to somebody who lived in Los Angeles, say, the distances involved would doubtless seem modest—but at the time we had only one car, and Margaret would need that. Besides, a second car seemed like an expense and a complication I didn't need (little foreseeing that I would one day own three cars, a truck, two horse trailers, a motorcycle, three tractors, and two four-wheelers).

A further problem lay in the geography of New York City. As everybody knows, Manhattan is an island. Previous experience had taught me that you can make pretty good time in the morning down to the end of the Saw Mill Parkway, just beyond the city (if you are careful not to get caught up in the early-morning rush-hour traffic to White Plains). After that, you come to a grinding halt any later than about six-thirty in the morning, since all traffic coming from the north has to pass over one ancient, narrow bridge to reach the Henry Hudson Parkway on the west side of Manhattan, which means that you really need to be on the road, bright-eyed, bushy-tailed, and moving, by five in the morning at the latest.

The same was true coming home, in spades. It can take an hour or more through clogged streets just to make it from Rockefeller Center to the George Washington Bridge if you leave the office any later than four-thirty in the afternoon. Anyway, the whole point of commuting is to put the time involved to good use—reading manuscripts, catching up on my correspondence, perhaps even dashing off a few pages of writing—which I wasn't likely to do at the wheel of a car. The train seemed like a better—and more civilized—bet, though something in me rebelled at becoming a commuter, perhaps because of all those *New Yorker* cartoons and short stories about men in Brooks Brothers suits, raincoats, and hats, carrying a briefcase, with a folded copy of *The New York Times* under one arm, patiently waiting for the train at commuter stations in southern Connecticut or on Long Island. I didn't see myself as one of them, and as it happened, I wasn't about to become one.

I put some time into studying the possibilities. There were, it appeared, two train services to the city, using the same tracks, but distinctly different. Metro North, the New York commuter railway, left Poughkeepsie for the city at frequent intervals, but stopped at almost every station, however small, on the way. Amtrak, a more recent service, stopped at Rhinecliff, about half an hour north of our house, on the Hudson River. The Amtrak trains were coming from places like Montreal—they were faster, more comfortable, usually had a dining car and Pullman lounge cars with reserved seating, and stopped only once or twice on the way into the city. By leaving the house at six in the morning, I could be at Rhinecliff before seven, park my car, have breakfast on the train, read and work, and be at my desk in Rockefeller Center by nine. If I caught the 5:40 P.M. from Grand Central Station in New York, I was in Rhinecliff by seven-twenty, and home before eight—a long day, but not, I told myself, worse than a lot of people's. There was even an Amtrak office in the lobby of our building in Rockefeller Center, so I could buy a ticket and book a reserved seat during the course of the day. I felt good about the whole prospect.

The first couple of times, it seemed fine. The trains arrived on time at Rhinecliff and left New York on time, the reserved seats were comfortable, even luxurious, the dining car in the morning served decent coffee and an assortment of pastries; on the trip home at night it was pleasant to order a drink, a bag of peanuts, stretch out my legs, and get in some valuable reading time—this, I told myself, was the life.

After a few days of it, two things did catch my attention. One was purely personal—I have always liked trains, and found them a singularly relaxing way to travel, so much so that I found myself nodding off by the time we were in Westchester, no matter how urgent or interesting the work at hand was. Far from getting more work done, as I had hoped, I was getting in an extra four hours or so of sleep. The other was that as I began to recognize my fellow commuters—it was pretty much the same small group every day—they seemed to me to have a certain distinctive zombielike appearance, a grayness and a fatigue that were unmistakable. Though all of them talked with enthusiasm about "the country life," which they swore by, and to a man boasted that the happiest day of their life was when they moved out of the city once and for all, they had the kind of pallor and nervous habits that one usually associates with prisoners, or passengers just released from a hijacked airliner, and a pronounced tendency to stare into the middle distance blankly, or to fall asleep with their mouth open. Like old Mr. Hubner, they weren't good advertisements for spending five hours a day on a train.

Or more, for after the first flush of enthusiasm, when everything went smoothly, Amtrak began to show its other side. I would rush to Grand Central, lumbered down with briefcases and shopping bags full of manuscripts and food, only to find that the train's departure was delayed, because of mysterious "problems up the line" that always went unexplained. Or I would discover, upon reaching the Rhinecliff station, that the train was delayed because of some mechanical problem and was still in Albany.

As the honeymoon wore off and I became a regular commuter, mysterious problems, I discovered, seemed to plague Amtrak, like some ship with a curse. One night I heard an enormous crash and looked up in alarm to find my window covered in blood and glimpse what looked like body parts flying past. The train halted, while the conductor went forward to talk to the engineer. We had struck a deer on the tracks, he explained when he returned. We would be halted for at least an hour, to "investigate" matters. Investigate what? I wondered.

That alone was enough to make me feel a certain waning of my confidence in Amtrak. The next incident was stranger. Poughkeepsie is about ten minutes from Rhinecliff by train, so at the sight of the Poughkeepsie station going by—at the time Metro North and Amtrak enforced a kind of mutual noncompetition clause by not allowing Amtrak passengers to get on or off at the much larger and more convenient Poughkeepsie station—passengers getting off at Rhinecliff knew it was time to stand up and collect their belongings.

One evening, on a night of torrential rain, the train went through Poughkeepsie, and those of us who weren't going on to Hudson, Albany, or points north got up and moved forward to where the conductor was waiting to open the door and let us off, only to watch the Rhinecliff station platform slip past while the train hurtled on in the dark toward Albany, or even Canada. Since Amtrak stations have long since given up having porters, the platform had been deserted, so it was possible that nobody had even noticed the train had skipped the station.

There was a short moment of silence, followed by noisy protests from the passengers. The conductor rolled his eyes, and reached up to turn on the intercom. "Hey, Ern," he said, "passengers say that was Rhinecliff we just went through." The conductor was an elderly railwayman of the old breed, with wire-rimmed spectacles, a plump red Dickensian face, a pocket watch on a silver chain with a Masonic seal in his vest pocket, and the shiny visor of his uniform cap set dead straight. He looked slightly out of place in the sleek modern train, with its pastel plastic paneling, bright red velour upholstery, and microwaved hamburgers.

There was a brief pause, a crackle of static, and the engineer's voice came snapping back, indignantly. "The hell it was," he announced. "That was Poughkeepsie. Think I don't know Poughkeepsie when I see it?"

"That was Poughkeepsie, gentlemen," the conductor said. "Rhinecliff in about eight minutes, please."

Several of the passengers pointed out the absence of well-known landmarks between the two stations. One passenger threatened to pull the emergency cord. The conductor glanced out the window for the sight of lights, then hauled out his watch, looked at it for a while, straightened up, and shook his head. "Ern," he said, into his microphone, "thing is, I got a hunch these fellows could be right."

"I don't see how I could have missed a station," the engineer said. He sounded less sure of himself now.

"Amen to that, Ern—but that's about the size of it."

"Shit."

"You got that right, Ern."

The train drew to a halt. The conductor looked out of the window again and shook his head. It was pitch-dark, with not a light in sight. Rain poured down like a rehearsal for a biblical flood.

We were about half a mile north of Rhinecliff, I guessed, by dead reckoning. I suggested that the train back up until we were at the platform.

The conductor sighed. Patiently, he explained that for safety reasons the train couldn't back up. This apparently was engraved in stone, absolutely forbidden, even unthinkable. We would have to wait until they could send some guys out with flashlights and a stepladder to get us off the train and walk us back to the station down the side of the tracks. I glanced at my briefcases and shopping bags, and said that sounded to me like a crock of shit.

At that the conductor withdrew in a huff, and some minutes later a group of oilskin-clad men arrived with flashlights, got us off the train, and walked us back to Rhinecliff, just as he had promised, like refugees fleeing from a firefight. I arrived home soaked to the skin, with muddy shoes, my shopping bags having burst open, so I had to carry all my work in my arms like a baby, while damp pages of somebody's manuscript fluttered limply behind me to the ground.

"Where on earth have you been?" Margaret asked. "Dinner has been ready for *ages*."

I explained, but she was reluctant to believe me. Still, my faith in Amtrak was shaken.

It was shaken still more by the next incident. The one thing you could rely on was that if you fell asleep, the Amtrak conductors would wake you up before the train reached your station (sometimes with less than a minute to spare, but still). Perhaps because I had been snippy to the conductor the night the train missed Rhinecliff, I woke up abruptly a few trips later with the vague feeling that something was wrong. The train was slowing down to stop, so I gathered up my belongings. "We coming into Rhinecliff?" I asked the conductor as he walked by. He raised an eyebrow. "Nope," he said. "Hudson."

Hudson! Hudson was a good thirty or forty miles north of Rhinecliff. I knew it only as a name on the map, and had no desire to go there. "Why didn't you wake me up?" I said. "You knew I was getting off at Rhinecliff."

The conductor frowned. "It's the passenger's job to get off where he's supposed to. By rights, I ought to charge you extra fare."

By this time we were coming into Hudson. Further argument would merely ensure that I got carried all the way to Albany, so I stumbled off onto the platform. Hudson (which has since been gentrified and is now something of a center for antique shopping) was then, as seen from the railway station, an unprepossessing place. The railway station itself, for that matter, was shabby and worn, totally devoid of any sign of life except for a large lady behind the glass of the ticket counter. Were there, I asked, any taxis? She did not look up from the *National Enquirer*. "Look out the door," she said. I did—there was nothing. "There's a pay phone out there," she said, pointing a thick thumb.

I found the pay phone, looked up the number of a taxi company in Hudson, and called. When I explained that I wanted to go to the railway station in Rhinecliff, where my car was parked, there was a moment of silence. "That's a long trip," the voice said, as if I had suggested driving across the Gobi Desert. "It's going to cost you." How much? I asked. "Fifty dollars." It was highway robbery, literally, but I was in no mood to bargain.

Half an hour or so later, an ancient, beat-up old rust bucket of a car pulled up, driven by a scruffy-looking youth. "Fell asleep on the train, did yer?" he bellowed, then burst into a fit of laughter, giggles, snorting, and snuffling that carried him all the way through Hudson and onto Route 9 South. He did not appear to own a handkerchief, I noticed, from the backseat, the torn vinyl of which was artfully repaired with duct tape.

Once we were through Hudson, however, his hilarity gave way to a darker mood. He had heard of Rhinecliff, of course, but he had never actually been there, or apparently anywhere else beyond a ten-mile radius centered on Hudson. Judging from his fearful expression, we might have been plunging deep into Indian country, with who knew what dangers on all sides of us. His hands gripped the steering wheel as if he were hanging on for dear life, and as we passed through one sleepy rural crossroads after another, he would shake his head in wonder and say, "Things sure look different down here." When we finally got to Rhinebeck and drove through it, it was as if it was his first look at Paris. "God*damn!*" he said, looking at the few feeble lights. "The whole *town* is lit up!"

By the time I had paid him off, tipped him, and given him precise directions for getting home—he seemed afraid that if he got lost he might end up in New York City, where terrible things would happen to him—it was nearly nine o'clock. I reached home about nine-thirty, and realized, as I stumbled wearily out of my car toward the front door, that in less than eight hours I would have to be setting out for Rhinecliff all over again.

Then and there, my life as a commuter came to an end, and I never looked back on it with regret. On the contrary, I've benefited from the technological revolution that seems likely to make all commuting eventually unnecessary—why ship the body back and forth from the country to the city, when most of the work it is doing can be transmitted by fax or e-mail anyway? Most of the people I see jogging along my country road in the early morning will be at their desk at home by 9:30 A.M., running a business—some of them large, worldwide ones. Real farmers—for whom farming is the first and only business—are giving way to gentlemen farmers, who run a company via a computer while raising cattle as a hobby, and who have to think hard before they can remember the last time they scraped the manure off their boots, put on a suit and city shoes, and went down to the city. So I'm not alone. One of our neighbors down the road has a cellular phone clipped to his overalls when he's plowing his fields, and picks up his copy of *The Wall Street Journal* before stopping at the Dunkin' Donuts early in the morning. I was just ahead of the curve for once, that's all.

OF COURSE there are a lot of other ways in which it's possible to merge in with the crowd (relatively speaking, since our total population is still about eight thousand) without standing out. Early on, I realized that wearing riding clothes is a mistake, except when actually on a horse. Breeches, boots, spurs, all give off an unmistakable and unwelcome message: gentry. The ticket is to follow local fashion, which is for "athletic" clothes (often worn by some of the most spectacularly unathletic-looking people in the world), running shoes and baseball caps with an appropriate local message ("Jones Septic," "New York State Sheriffs Association," "Steinbau Construction"). In the winter, down-filled jackets of the kind that make one look like the Michelin Man are a pretty good bet, preferably in camouflage pattern, worn with a fake-fur-lined hat with earflaps and heavy overshoes; in the summer, extreme high fashion for men favors T-shirts with an appropriate local commercial message, cargo shorts with enough pockets to carry a complete set of tools, and heavy ankle-length boots with Neoprene nonslip treaded soles an inch and a half thick—like Li'l Abner's boots, if you can remember Li'l Abner, or imagine him in baggy shorts and a Dairy Farmers Squeeze Harder T-shirt, with a beer belly. Jackets, shirts with ties, and "city" shoes, are hardly seen anymore, even on professional men, except on formal occasions like funerals and court appearances, and are usually a sign that the wearer is so old that his next stop is likely to be a room at the Victory Lake Nursing Home, on Quaker Lane, next to the Pentecostal church campgrounds. Women wear pretty much the same thing as men, but usually not in a camouflage pattern.

It's as if formality of any kind went out of fashion overnight around 1970, never to return—about the same time, curiously enough, that beards and cowboy hats came in, and most of the male population began to look like country-and-western singers. Until then, nobody in the Northeast wore a beard except for vagrants and a few very old farmers of Dutch descent, and cowboy boots and hats were pretty much relegated to the Southwest, but now on a Friday night—"line-dancing night"—Mackey's Pub (the successor to Cady's) looks like Tucson or Houston as the line-dancing regulars come trooping in, an endless succession of ex-urban cowboys and cowgals, dolled up in leather fringes, turquoise jewelry, rodeo belt buckles, and (for the cowgals) the obligatory but not always flattering combination of short skirts and cowboy boots. Since Margaret and I have been Santa Fe residents in our time, we never had any difficulty fitting in with this dress code—we have closets full of the stuff—though it took us a while to catch on to the trend when it first began.

Vehicles have a lot to do with it too, of course, this being America. When we first bought the house, the vehicle of choice was still a big old American car. Cadillacs, we discovered, were rather frowned upon; one of our neighbors down the road referred to a Cadillac as "a Jew canoe" (an expression I hadn't heard before then), which struck home since our vehicle at the time was a vast silver Cadillac Seville. Without giving the matter much thought, we eventually traded down to a Buick, a car that escaped pretty much unnoticed in the supermarket parking lot, but also didn't attract much in the way of admiring (or even critical) comments.

Once Margaret had brought the horses home, however, it was necessary to buy a vehicle that could tow a horse trailer, so we bought a Chevy Blazer (and a small two-horse trailer), back in the days before it had been dubbed a "sport utility vehicle" and become a rural fashion statement. In four-wheel drive, the Blazer could go just about anywhere off-road, not that we really wanted to, but it also seemed to fit in with where we lived, where people still liked their vehicles big, V-8 powered, American-made, and capable of four-wheel drive in the winter. What with the trailer hitch and an NRA Life Member decal on the windshield, the Blazer fitted in pretty nicely most places in Dutchess County, and certainly showed that we were just plain folks in this respect, at any rate. Maybe *too* plain, I eventually discovered.

It took me a while to figure out that at least so far as men were concerned, this was the one area in which a certain amount of ostentation was acceptable, even encouraged. Pleasant Valley was clearly not a place in which ownership of, say, an eighteen-karat gold Rolex wristwatch, a $5,000 Savile Row suit, Gucci loafers, or a crocodile leather briefcase were appreciated, or would even be recognized, but even the shabbiest-looking farming type was likely to have something special in the way of a vehicle under canvas in the barn, and to have strong opinions on the subject of overhead camshafts, tuned headers, and Hurst shifters. The internal combustion engine in all its forms was worshiped here, as it was in most of America outside New York City and Washington, D.C., whether it was in the shape of a collection of antique tractors, ownership of a truck with tires big enough to cross the Gobi Desert in midwinter, or a perfectly restored Ford Model A brought out to chug down to Pleasant Valley in on a sunny Sunday morning. A local doctor, a mile down the road from us, had a vintage Jaguar stored in a barn, his son had a red Ferrari 308, our builder had a beautifully preserved Mercedes convertible, *his* son a bright yellow vintage Harley-Davidson. In the winter these treasures remained out of sight, but in the spring and summer they appeared from time to time, usually with an awesome burst of noise, color, and speed down our narrow road.

Here, at any rate, was an area that interested me—and one that offered almost as many chances for prolonged social conversation as Margaret's pigs. Not being an enthusiast for vintage muscle cars or customized pickup trucks, I eventually bought a Porsche 944 in bright red, a fairly serious commitment to the automobile culture. Total strangers came over to take a look at it, and men we knew made special trips to examine it in our driveway and throw a few pieces of loose change onto the floor mats, a local tradition intended to bring good luck on the ownership of a new vehicle. The general opinion was that it was a pretty nice car, but probably not going to be much good in the snow, which turned out to be spot on. Mainly, it established me as a serious player in the car ownership stakes, and people who still referred to our house as "the old Hewlett farm" and didn't know my name nevertheless recognized me as "the guy who owns the red Porsche."

Eventually the Porsche gave way to a much-used Ferrari 308 GTS *quattrovalvole,* in Italian racing red, a car guaranteed to turn heads anywhere and conferring upon me major status as a serious car enthusiast—fearless as well, since the Ferrari not only attracted state troopers from one end of the Taconic to the other but required constant maintenance and repair, and spent a good deal of its life on a flatbed being trucked to faraway Ferrari specialists when it wasn't parked on the grass by the side of the Taconic so a state trooper could admire it while he wrote out a speeding ticket.

From the very beginning Margaret had been skeptical of the Ferrari. The day it arrived, I had reserved a table for a celebratory dinner at the Old Drover's Inn in Dover Plains, about forty-five minutes away, and looked forward to driving over there in the Ferrari. Being squeezed into the narrow confines of the cockpit, with a bellowing eight-cylinder engine sending out waves of heat and noise right behind her ears, was not Margaret's idea of the best way to turn up for dinner elegantly coiffed and dressed, but it was unfortunate that the air-conditioning failed as soon as we were on the highway, as well as the electric motors that lowered the windows, thus leaving us in an increasingly hot, confined space, until the atmosphere was that of a steam bath, if you can imagine a steam bath with loud engine noises and the odor of damp leather upholstery.

I remained enthusiastic about the car—as did every teenage boy in Pleasant Valley—but it was an increasingly difficult love affair. Beautiful and high-strung the car might be, but at crucial moments it had a tendency to fail me, often in public. If you drove it to the movies, there was a good chance the headlights would fail to pop up when you were ready to go; if you drove it to dinner, it would overheat mysteriously along the way, sending the oil temperature gauge needle spinning into the red, or the oil pressure would drop alarmingly. Either way, the evening was ruined. It ran through expensive tires at a terrifying rate, the spark plugs oiled up if you had to drive it in slow traffic for any length of time, and it had a way of dripping vital fluids when parked overnight in my garage, but never when it was in the garage of the Ferrari mechanic's shop. It was necessary to carry a paper bag full of fuses on board, since they blew at frequent intervals, and were of a size and type unobtainable in any ordinary garage or filling station.

Much as I loved driving it—not to speak of the fact that it placed me at the summit of Pleasant Valley car ownership—I vowed one day that if it ever dumped its entire load of coolant, or hydraulic fluid, or brake fluid, or transmission oil onto the garage floor again, I would sell it. The next morning, one of the girls who was working in Margaret's barn saw me in the driveway as I was picking up the newspaper and gave me a cheerful smile. "Hi, Mr. Korda," she said. "Say, did you know that your garage floor is covered in some kind of yucky green stuff?"

That very afternoon the Ferrari was on its way on a flatbed to be sold, leaving me for the moment without a serious vehicle to my name. It was a sad parting, and it took me some time before I was able to think about a replacement.

When I did, it was a very different kind of vehicle indeed that caught my attention.

*M*OST OF MY ADULT (and pre-adult) life I've wanted to own a Harley. I've always liked motorcycles more than was considered good for me, and indeed acquired my first one as a gift from my aunt Alexa when I was eighteen—much against my father's wishes, and over his protests. Even my uncle Alex, Alexa's husband and the head of the Korda family, was opposed to the idea, but he was not about to argue with Alexa, who was beautiful, headstrong, and about forty years younger than himself, and anyway Alex liked from to time to annoy my father, just to show him who was boss in the family.

Thus, when I was in the Royal Air Force, I had a big Vincent Black Shadow, one of those exotic motorcycles for which England was famous before the war, and immediately after it, and used to scare myself and anybody else who was on the road in the middle of the night going back and forth from wherever I was being trained to London on the weekends. In those days, before the Japanese reinvented the industry, British motorcycles, like British sports cars, leaked oil all the time—gray flannels and suede shoes saturated with the fumes of Castrol and spattered with engine oil were part of the sporty image that all young Englishmen craved. The trick was to place a roasting pan under the engine at night. In the morning it would be full of oil, and all you had to do was pour it back into the oil tank before you set off. (A pocketful of spare fuses was also a good idea—Mr. Lucas, after whom Britain's largest manufacturer of automotive electric equipment and headlights was named, was not known as "The Prince of Darkness" for nothing.)

I gave up motorcycles eventually, but never altogether willingly, and shortly after we moved to the country, when I was asked what I wanted as a present for my twenty-fifth anniversary at Simon and Schuster, I asked for a motorcycle. This caused a good deal of trouble—Richard E. Snyder, the president of S&S and my old friend, was even less keen on motorcycles than my father had been, and did not want to be responsible for losing his own editor in chief. Eventually he gave in, and I received a dark blue Honda 600cc Nighthawk at a black-tie dinner in my honor at the Four Seasons, in New York.

Over the years, I grew to like the Honda—it was easy to maintain, fast enough, and good-looking—but it lacked a certain panache, a character—in brief, it wasn't a Harley. Certainly, teenage boys would admire it, but when I was out on the road and a group of motorcyclists thundered toward me in the other direction, they would ignore me completely if they were on Harleys.

Generally speaking, all motorcyclists wave to each other as they approach; it's a kind of "knights of the road" gesture, the camaraderie of people who share a love of the motorcycle, the feel of riding in the open air, not cooped up inside a car, the sense of being part of an endangered minority—for motorcyclists of all kinds regard car drivers as a potential menace to life and limb, with some reason, since in any accident involving a car and a motorcycle, the motorcyclist is the one who is unlikely to survive.

There is one exception to this fellowship, however. Harley riders—the serious ones, at any rate—don't wave back to riders who aren't on a Harley. They don't even *look* at riders who aren't on a Harley. If you don't ride American metal, you don't exist.

Some of this feeling was true around Pleasant Valley—a feeling that a guy riding a Japanese bike wasn't really a motorcyclist, maybe wasn't even a patriot. Harley riders had an image—they tended to be big, broad-shouldered, beer-bellied, aggressively bearded, wearing oil-stained blue jeans and scuffed leather jackets and tattoos before tattoos were fashionable—and the bike itself, heavy, painted in outrageous metallic colors, covered in gleaming chrome and fringed black leather, was the central artifact of that image. If I stopped at any of our local biker hangouts—Morse's Tavern, where there was always a row of Harleys glinting outside, or Wayne's Biker Barn, down by the prison in Stormville, where the Harleys were neatly lined up by the score on the weekend, or on Sunday morning for breakfast at Marcus Dairy, in Danbury, Connecticut, the holy shrine of bikerdom in the Northeast—some guy would always come over, look at my bike, and give a contemptuous sneer. "It ain't bad for a Jap bike," he would say, "but it sure ain't no Harley."

Of course it also didn't leak oil like a sieve or vibrate so badly that bits and pieces fell off; you didn't need to take half the bike apart to get at the battery, and it actually had a fuel gauge, so you didn't have to guess how much gas you had left; but none of these things was the point—a bike was either a Harley or it wasn't, and if it wasn't, the hell with it.

Eventually I gave in, got rid of my Honda, and took myself off to the nearest Harley-Davidson dealer, Jim Moroney's in Newburg, New York, and bought myself a Harley-Davidson "Fat Boy" (named after the atomic bomb that was used on Japan in 1945) in metallic silver, with enough chrome on it to blind an admirer in the sunlight. This was a bike that required you to put on a pair of sunglasses before looking at it. It was everything a Harley should be—big, heavy, loud (with an unmistakable, throaty low throb), about as macho an object as it is possible to imagine.

I got on, struggled to learn how to shift gears (Harley-Davidson does everything a little different), and set off down the road toward the Newburg bridge. With each passing mile I felt more secure on the big machine—not surprising, since Harleys are not only heavy, but like most of their owners have a very low center of gravity—and more of a Harley type. As I rode across the bridge I saw a motorcyclist coming toward me on the other side of the roadway—even from a distance, I could see it was another Harley. There was also no mistaking the rider. He wore a leather vest; his bare arms were thick, heavily muscled, hairy, and tattooed; he was thickly bearded and wore what appeared to be a German army helmet on his head and an Iron Cross on a chain around his neck. His gloves were fringed black leather. As he got close to me, I raised my arm in a tentative salute, expecting him to ignore me. But no, his eyes took me in—I was riding a Harley. As he passed by, he raised his arm to return my salute, and I heard him growl, "Fuckin' A, man! Nice bike!" then roar away. I rejoiced. I belonged!

THE HARLEY not only brought me salutes, at last, from other Harley riders, but gave me a certain position in the community. To own a Harley is to be greeted everywhere by friends (a lot of whom you'd rather not be greeted by, but that's another story), to *belong*. The most unlikely people turn out to have owned one at some point, or plan to buy one in the future. There was a group of Harley owners who gathered at Van's, our local gas station, on Saturdays and Sundays, substantial men of a certain age who liked to get dressed up head-to-foot in black leather and go riding on the weekends, and it included some of the people we were often trying to coax out of their home to repair this or that on a wet winter evening. For a fellow Harley rider, they were willing to come—it was understood, Harley riders stuck together: "Ride to live, live to ride," what more could you say? There were cops who rode in the Blue Knights, the police Harley club, and retirees who rode in the Silver Knights, on huge Harley "full dressers" the size of a Dutch barge, complete with an intercom for the rear seat passenger (usually "the missus") and a stereo tape deck, and a Harley club for former IBM engineers and executives—in fact, once you were out on the road on a Harley, you soon discovered that despite the Hell's Angels/ Savage Nomads reputation of Harley clubs, there was hardly any group or organization that *didn't* boast a Harley club, with its own colors. Malcolm Forbes even had one of his own, for wealthy businessmen, called—what else?—the Capitalist Tools Motorcycle Club, and when I acquired his colors (bright red, with flame-painted Harley on silver wings embroidered on the back) after his death, I wore them proudly. It didn't really matter that much to people what the colors signified (though real bikers, among whom Forbes had the status of a kind of distant god-figure, usually recognized them); the main thing was that I *belonged* to something, even if it was only a motorcycle club.

Between the Harley and the pigs, I figured that we had gone as far toward becoming "just plain folks" as we were ever likely to, but the truth was that we still had a way to go.

CHAPTER NINE

Good Fences Make Good Neighbors

WHEN THE BACONS had their first child, they quickly outgrew the wing of our house in which they had been living. I hated the thought of their moving away—it was an enormous comfort to know that people you liked and trusted were living in the house, and only a few yards away from the barn in case there was trouble with one of the horses.

Pleasant Valley was not exactly a high-crime area, but any big house by the road is a potential target for thieves, of course. I had learned this lesson when we acquired from New Mexico a magnificent weather vane to go on the studio barn, in the shape of a large, lovingly detailed, and impressively well-endowed copper longhorn bull. Big, heavy, cumbersome, it had taken a great deal of effort to get it up to its place on the roof, where it was very much admired by everyone—by too many people, as it turned out.

One night, shortly afterward, I heard what I took to be the sounds of an animal outside. It was two or three in the morning, and I felt no need to get up and go outside. I peered out the window and, seeing nothing, guessed it was probably a raccoon on the garage roof, rolled over, and went back to sleep.

In the morning, as I was on my way to the barn, I stopped for a moment—something seemed wrong to me, out of kilter somehow, as if something was missing, but I couldn't think what it might be. I went on to the barn and forgot all about it until, an hour or two later, somebody working around the house said to me, "Say, what happened to that bull you people had up there?"

I looked up, and to my astonishment, realized that it had indeed gone. What I had heard in the night was the sound of thieves putting up a ladder behind our garage and clambering onto a high, steeply pitched roof to steal our weather vane. How they got it down, I couldn't imagine, but get it down they did. The deputy sheriff, when he arrived, was philosophical about it—these things were worth a lot of money, and got stolen a lot, he said. Mine would probably be on somebody's barn in Columbia County before long, or maybe out of state, or, given the price of copper, broken up and sold as scrap. I should get an alarm system before something worse happened, was his advice (which I took). "If you're going to replace it," he said, in a jocular mood now, "go for a cow next time. It's the bulls that get stolen, every time."

Eventually I replaced the bull—making sure this time that it was welded so firmly onto its shaft that any potential thieves would need to lug a power tool up onto the roof to get it off. Still, I couldn't help thinking that strangers—criminals—had been crawling around on our garage roof in the middle of the night while we were sleeping in our beds, not fifty yards away. We took to locking our door at night, and I was grateful that when we were away Richard Bacon was there to look after things. The thing was, I decided, to find the Bacons a house as close to ours as possible.

Very fortunately, Tom Kirchhoff, who had sold us our house, called in on us one morning on his way to the office to say that our next-door neighbors to the south were thinking of selling theirs. It was set on five acres, and only a five-minute walk away, across our lawn and through some woods. Would we be interested in buying it?

Up until then our only communication with these neighbors had been the occasional gunshot, or the snarl of a chain saw, so we followed Tom over to the house with more than the usual curiosity. My first reaction was to wonder how anybody could let their home deteriorate to this point. "They actually *live* here?" I asked, aghast. Tom shrugged. "Well, I don't say it's not a fixer-upper," he said calmly.

We made our way through a kind of tacked-on shed, thickly carpeted with discarded children's clothes. There was a sour odor in the closets that made one hesitate to examine them closely, and many of the walls consisted of bare insulation without any plasterboard covering. Somebody had been repairing a motorcycle propped up on milk crates in one of the bedrooms. "Could do with a good cleaning too," Tom said, glancing at the piles of junk and garbage.

This was an understatement. Long, low, and built with many poorly thought-out additions, the house showed every sign of being an abandoned experiment in do-it-yourself building, and no signs of ever having been cleaned. The top of the kitchen stove was coated with a thick layer of burned grease, and the oven was worse. One bathroom, inconveniently placed, had sufficed for a large family with many children and pets, none of them fastidious, and the idea of installing a water filter had not, apparently, occurred to anyone; the plastic tub/shower, the sink, and the toilet were stained a deep red by rust and thick, encrusted mineral deposits—"Looks like their water is pretty hard," Tom said cheerfully, which was putting it mildly. He looked a little more worried when he discovered that at some point the owners had given up on maintaining the septic tank—the toilet simply drained out into the woods, at the far end of the lawn. "I'm not saying there isn't work to be done," he said.

Above him, a hole in the ceiling was covered with duct tape. We peered into the garage—the floor was covered in a layer of thick mud, and the cinderblock walls dripped steadily.

"Nice and big," Tom said. "You could keep a truck in here."

"Better yet, a boat," I suggested. "There's a foot or so of water, and it isn't even raining."

Tom chuckled. He took us outside, put on his serious professional realtor expression, and gave us "the bottom line." We should buy the house, if only for protection. It was a mess, sure, but nothing that couldn't be fixed. The owner wasn't asking much—his wife might not have housekeeping skills, nor he any particular aptitude for home repair, but he was realistic about the value of his house. For $25,000, the whole thing would probably be mine, and the land alone was worth that much, or very nearly so. Besides, if it went to somebody else, who knew who our new neighbors might be—we could get lucky, or we could end up with people who were a real pain. We shouldn't have any problem picking up the house cheap; the owner was so far behind on his taxes that he *had* to sell, it was as simple as that, and rumor was that he was facing a divorce as well. Most of the money would go for back taxes and to the bank, but at least the seller, a local bartender, would get all his obligations off his back in one go, unless the poor son-of-a-bitch was deep in credit card debt as well.

Tom sighed. Anyway, he said, after it was fixed up, it would solve the problem of where the Bacons were going to live. A good cleaning, some new plasterboard, new appliances, new bath fixtures, a decent septic, and a water purifier; why, we'd never even recognize the place in three months' time—probably wish we were living in it ourselves. "It's amazing what a difference a good coat of white paint makes," he said—something which I was soon to recognize as his mantra.

Looked at in that light, it seemed a reasonable investment, much as I didn't want to add another house to my list of responsibilities, and we went ahead. As usual, more turned out to be involved than Tom had guessed, but he was by and large right, and the Bacons soon had a perfectly presentable and comfortable place to live in.

The experience made me think, however. At that time, I had just written a couple of successful novels, one after the other, and felt in an expansive mood. The idea of adding to our land was an attractive one—after all, the more land you had, the farther away your neighbors were. Obviously, Dutchess County wasn't the West—you couldn't put thousands of acres between yourself and the smoke from the nearest chimney—but it wouldn't hurt to buy up a little more land, if the occasion arose. And—miracle of miracles—no sooner had this thought occurred to me than the occasions started to arise.

There's a kind of mental telepathy in country life, when it comes to this kind of thing, as if your neighbors can actually read your mind—though the truth of the matter is that once you've bought the property to your south, then your neighbors in the other three directions naturally begin to wonder if you might be in the market for *their* place as well. Besides, there are plenty of people in a small rural town whose idea of a morning well spent is nursing a carton of coffee and a doughnut down at the town hall, schmoozing with the lady who looks after deeds, real-estate transactions, and property taxes, and therefore knows exactly who is buying, who is selling, and who is way behind on their property and school taxes. It is an old truism that there are no secrets in a small town, but it isn't necessarily the romantic ones that people are curious about—it's the ones that have to do with property that really interest people, not who is sleeping with the clerk of court while her husband is away at a weeklong business motivational seminar.

All these people can sniff out a buyer by sheer instinct. Before the ink was dry on the contract for the house next door, they were turning up at our doorstep with properties. Just down the road from us was an apple orchard that had been in the hands of one family for generations, but which suddenly might be available at the right price. One of the guys who worked there even turned up in person, to suggest that if I bought it, we could go in as partners on the apple farming—he would supply the expertise, the contacts, and the labor; I, no surprise, would supply the capital. Apples, he swore, over a cup of coffee in our kitchen, were gold on a tree, if you knew what you were doing. You brought in busloads of Jamaicans and paid them peanuts to harvest your crop, and you sold it in advance at a good price to South America, where they would pay through the nose for a fruit that didn't grow there. Brazilians saw American TV, American movies—they wanted to eat apple pie, just like Americans. Did I have any idea what a ton of Empire State apples went for in Brazil?

I confessed that I didn't. Well, he didn't either, as it turned out, because the market was so volatile, but it was a fortune, any way you sliced the goddamn apple—you couldn't lose. The only problem, he said, leaning over close to me conspiratorially, was that I had to act fast. The owner was Jewish, he confided to me in a hoarse whisper, and he would probably try to sell it to some Jewish businessman, who would cut him, the manager, out of the deal. What could you do? he asked. These people stuck together; in a way you had to admire them for that. I whisked him out the door as fast as I could, and as a result, perhaps luckily, never got into the apple business, but there were plenty of other opportunities knocking at our front door, most of which involved the farm business.

In the end, my next step was a timid one. The trailer to the north of us had been a thorn in my side ever since we bought our house. It wasn't visible—trees mercifully screened it from view—but it housed a shifting population of posthippies and kids who looked like bad news, centered around the young woman who lived there. I disliked the sound of loud music that wafted over late at night, however faint it was by the time it reached our ears. (The pigs were nearer to the trailer than we were, and unlike us, appeared to quite enjoy the music.)

Fate in the form of a sad-looking, elderly gentleman turned up in our path as we went out riding one morning. His daughter was moving away from here, he explained. He was trying to sell off her trailer and the acre it was on, and since we lived next door, he wondered if we were interested.

I made the deal on the spot, then shocked everyone by having the trailer torn down and plowed over, as Genghis Khan used to demolish cities that stood in his way, thus gaining an acre and eliminating the threat on our northern flank. Down at town hall, Tom Kirchhoff told me, the rumor was that we had gone crazy—nobody in their right mind would buy a trailer merely to tear it down, especially since under the new zoning laws it might be impossible to put another one there.

Still, this further purchase, even though it was only an acre, was duly noted down at the town hall, so it was hardly surprising when a bulky, well-dressed gentleman, a lawyer from Westchester as he introduced himself, turned up shortly afterward with a more substantial proposition. He, as it turned out, was also our neighbor, in the sense that he owned a big chunk of land that abutted ours—over 135 acres. This was a bigger chunk than I really wanted to swallow, especially since we weren't able to agree on a price, but in the end I managed to buy thirty-five acres from him, including a dilapidated old cow barn, and secure a lease on the rest. Margaret retained a strong interest in acquiring more, and based on what has happened to land prices, she was probably right, but as I pointed out, if we kept buying up every piece of land that was offered to us in order to keep neighbors at a distance, we would eventually reach the Canadian border, if we weren't bankrupted by land and school taxes first. As it was, when the tax bills started to come in, the meaning of the term "land poor," which often occurs in novels about eighteenth-century Virginia and the nineteenth-century American West, became clear to me for the first time.

In the end, over the next twenty years or so, we would only add another forty-four acres to our spread, a parcel of woods directly across the road from our house that I bought just to make sure we wouldn't wake up one morning to hear a bulldozer idling just below our bedroom windows—there's nothing like the news that somebody is going to put up fifteen or twenty houses right in front of you to make you wish you'd bought the land yourself when you had the chance, or so I keep telling myself every time I look at it. None of it is the kind of countryside that necessarily impels passersby to reach for their cameras, but it's all ours, every acre of second- or third-growth woods.

Sometimes, when I look back at it, I wish we'd begun by buying a place on the other side of the Taconic Parkway (the "good" side), with rolling fields, and open vistas, and neighbors who care about the environment, not to speak of a zoning policy that frowns on trailers, trailer parks, and fast-food outlets, or perhaps where so many of our friends live, across the state line in Connecticut, where there's a real, if slightly self-conscious, effort to keep the countryside free from the blight of commercialization and sheer bad taste, and a notable absence of garbage on the roadside. On the other hand, Pleasant Valley is America, not some upper-income country gentry theme park, and it includes pizza parlors, two Chinese take-out restaurants, a gym (though you might not guess it, looking at the crowd in the A&P), and, these days, a Blockbuster Video store, not to speak of neighbors whose idea of a weekend well spent is dusting their apple crop with poison and who let their kids ride trail bikes through the mud at high speeds, occasionally on other people's land. Love it or leave it, it's not Ralph Lauren country.

Then again, I tell myself, if you're going to live in the real country, you're just going to have to accept the fact that your neighbors, no matter how far off you manage to have them, are probably going to have a whole different view of life from yours. Ours certainly do.

CHAPTER TEN

Bats in the Belfry

WE PROBABLY would never have bitten the bullet and plunged into a full-scale redecoration of our house if it hadn't been for the birds, or the bats.

Animals outside the house were one thing—occasionally a skunk would wander past, on its way from digging up our lawns for grubs in the middle of the night, and leave its signature odor, or a possum would find its way onto our porch, but generally speaking the deer, wild turkey, foxes, coyote, and raccoons who were our most frequent animal neighbors caused us no problems (the occasional moose and black bear were said to be out there too, but I never saw one). Animals *inside* the house were a whole other story.

Mice we learned to live with, so long as they stayed within the walls or merely pitter-pattered above the ceilings on tiny clawed feet late at night. I had presumed that with cats in the house we would never be troubled with mice, so it was disconcerting to discover that the cats had no interest in them at all, as if they had never seen a Tom and Jerry cartoon. On several occasions a courageous mouse—or perhaps simply one who knew his cats—was observed to walk right past a lightly dozing cat without producing any reaction at all. The cat opened one eye, looked right at the mouse, and went back to sleep again with a yawn. Not my job, no concern of mine, the body language read, unmistakably.

Of course, in some ways that was better than finding nasty little bits of bloody mouse remains on the carpets in the morning, but at the same time it was disappointing; "doing what comes naturally" when it came to mice didn't seem to be programmed into our cats. The mice weren't afraid of them, and treated them with contempt, when they took notice of them at all. *Outside* the house, the cats might stalk the occasional mouse, not to speak of songbirds and chipmunks, but *in* the house a truce that Henry Kissinger himself might have negotiated reigned, and neither side broke it.

True, Irving, Margaret's old orange-and-white cat, was a prodigiously whiskered and dignified elderly gentleman and retired world traveler. He had spent many a night in places like the Beverly Wilshire Hotel in Beverly Hills, where there were no doubt few opportunities to pursue mice, and was now in any case well past his mousing days. When he died, his replacement, Queenie, while of a livelier nature, had been born with one stunted front leg—it was really hardly more than a flipper, with no claws or pads on it, though she could bat you with it pretty hard if you annoyed her—and at some point in her life her other, good paw had been declawed.

Shortly after Irving's death, Margaret went off to the Animal Medical Center in New York City with a city neighbor, her friend Phyllis Getzler, and called me at the office to say that she had found the perfect cat. I said that sounded like good news, knowing how much she missed Irving.

There was just one small problem, Margaret said, after a slight hesitation.

What was that? I asked.

"She only has one front leg, and she has a big lump on her belly that may be a tumor."

I suggested that with dozens of strays to pick from Margaret might at least have found one that had four legs, but I could tell that it was a waste of breath. Queenie, with all her problems, came home (after a detour in which the bottom fell out of her cardboard carrying case and she vanished among the cars in our garage, while Margaret, Phyllis, and the guys in the garage hunted her down on all fours), and lived on to great old age, making an appearance in *People* magazine in her prime and winning many fans. Still, mousing wasn't her specialty either, given her handicap, nor that of Chutney, who turned up at the door one day and became her companion.

The mice were not much bothered by other forms of attack, either, it transpired. Supermarket mousetraps didn't tempt them a bit, they seemed too smart to get themselves caught in the old-fashioned spring-loaded mouse traps, even when baited with peanut butter—the local can't-fail recipe—and poison they simply ignored. Eventually Richard Bacon put in prodigious square footage of mouseproof sheet metal, which pretty much confined them to the basement, and installed so many high-tech electric devices emitting noise at a mouse-specific frequency in crucial areas that we fought them to a draw. So long as they stayed out of the drawers and cupboards, we were willing to put up with them in the basement and the crawl spaces—a kind of DMZ—following the sound adage, What the eye doesn't see, the heart doesn't grieve for, which is not bad advice for anybody living in an old house.

If the cats were no help with the mice, they were even less interested in larger and more active intruders. For a while, fairly large birds got into the house somehow, flying back and forth crazily and crashing against the windows as if in a scene from Alfred Hitchcock's *The Birds*, a film that has always scared me, with good reason, if you've ever been in the same room with a panicked bird. Here too the cats were mildly interested, but clearly did not feel that this was any concern of theirs. They watched our efforts at bird-catching with amused tolerance but did not join in, as Margaret, more courageous in the face of feathered attack than me, attempted to trap a determined bird inside a Bloomingdale's shopping bag and get it out of the house. Eventually we were able to plug the holes the birds had been coming in through, but that didn't stop squirrels and bats from coming down the chimneys. The squirrels could be trapped in a cardboard box and taken outside, though they weren't happy about it, but the bats were another story altogether. Once they had made their way out of the fireplace and shaken the soot off their wings, they tended to fly around the room at a high speed—at just about human eye level, alarmingly enough—weaving in and out of the branches of the chandelier and emitting ultra-high-frequency squeaks, like tiny heat-seeking missiles. Despite an armory of high-tech bat-catching devices that included flyswatters, paper bags, and an old tennis racket, the bats proved almost impossible to corral once they were in the house. Besides, they were even better at hiding themselves than the birds had been, once they stopped flying. Roxie, it turned out, was pretty good at slamming them with a rolled-up newspaper, and appeared to have no fear of them whatsoever.

I don't think of myself as squeamish or faint of heart, but the bats did it for me. At that point I called in "the Chimney Doctor," who put wire mesh over the chimney tops and managed to prevent their being used as entry points by even the most determined (or luckless) of wildlife. Up to this point, in fact, we had not made much use of our fireplaces, on the subject of which Tom Kirchhoff had been gently discouraging, but the chimney man discovered so many things wrong with our chimneys that we decided to have him clean and repair them so we could use them more often.

This, as it turned out, was something of a mistake, and gradually evolved into a bigger (and messier) job than we could possibly have imagined, making me feel that the phrase "Leave well enough alone" probably ought to have been carved into the wood above our front door, or possibly above each fireplace. Every repair to the chimneys opened up a whole new set of problems in the labyrinth of flues, brick chambers, and connecting chimneys that lay behind the walls of the house.

By the time the chimneys had been cleaned, "pointed," and repaired, we learned more about chimneys than I had ever wanted to know, the most important thing being that ours had been built by one of the less gifted bricklayers of the eighteenth century. With seven fireplaces in the house, the chimneys took paths that were strange and hard to follow, even for a specialist in eighteenth-century fireplaces, and short of finding a chimney man with a promising six-year-old chimney sweep, like those in Dickensian London, it seemed unlikely that some of the mysteries would ever be resolved. My personal solution—to the deep dismay of the chimney man—was to have the more problematic fireplaces sealed off altogether. This was a wise precaution. Sealing them all off would probably have been even wiser.

I'm as fond of a good fire as any man, myself—not perhaps as fond as was Richard Nixon, who startled visitors to the Oval Office by keeping a cheery log fire blazing in mid-August, with the air conditioner turned up so that the room temperature was like that in a freezer—but once we started to use a few of our fireplaces regularly, it swiftly became apparent to me why the big beams in our dining room were so dark. When one thinks of the eighteenth century, one thinks of a big fire blazing in the hearth, with dinner cooking over it—and our dining room certainly had the fireplace for it, having once been a tavern—but what one *doesn't* think of is the smoke.

The eighteenth century (and a good part of the nineteenth) was the age of smoke—smoke from the fireplace (and smoking grease from the food cooking on it) turning the room blue, and mingling with the smoke from candles and men's pipes. In those days, if you were warm indoors, you coughed, you choked, your eyes ran, and you counted yourself lucky. If our beams were admired for their rough-hewn look and deep, dark color, it was because they had been pickled in smoke for a century and a half, turning the wood a shade that no decorator could match.

I am myself an indifferent maker of fires, and sensible enough to know it, but Margaret, having spent her early years in rural England and in Kenya, neither of them places famous for central heating, prided herself on her skills. Indeed, she could always get a fire burning, and keep it going, and knew how to build it so it didn't smoke—or didn't smoke most of the time, for no matter how carefully we tended our fires, every once in a while, with the wind in the wrong direction, or perhaps based on some other unknown parameter, smoke would come pouring out into the room. The big fireplace in my office, which had once been used for cooking, was a particular offender, no matter how many times the chimney man came back to work on it. Margaret would build a fire lovingly so I could enjoy it while I was working. For an hour or two, that would be fine; then, insidiously, smoke would start to seep into the room, and before I knew it I would begin to doze off, half-asphyxiated, and wake with the kind of headache that people who have tried to commit suicide by sitting in a car in the garage with the engine running complain of, if they survive. Worse still, whole areas of the room turned black from the smoke, and there was a fine layer of dust and ashes spread over everything.

In some places this kind of thing isn't such a big deal. For years, when we owned a house in New Mexico, we kept a fire going every night, and from time to time the fire would back up, filling the room with smoke and staining the painted walls and the hearth of the kiva. The attitude toward such incidents was *"Nada!"*—the caretaker simply came in the next morning with a spray bottle of Resolve, a pan of white paint, and a roller, and repainted everything that looked smudged. Unfortunately, this procedure doesn't work in a room where there is wallpaper or paneling, or anything else that can't be touched up with a fresh coat of white paint, so every time one of the fires started smoking became an emergency, with Margaret and me rushing around opening windows (not helpful), fanning with newspapers (also not helpful), and attempting to push the fire farther back in the fireplace (bound to add a deluge of cinders to the smoke). To all this too, the cats were as indifferent and unhelpful as they had been about mice. They quite liked to doze in front of a good fire, but at the first sign of smoke, they made a dignified exit to another room.

Eventually, step-by-step, what between the intrusions by wildlife, the smoke from the fires, the occasional mishap by a guest (Thank you, Diana Erwitt, for dropping a sixty-four-ounce bottle of Diet Coke on the pale blue living room carpet!), and the fairly constant wear and tear of the cats, the house became, at last, noticeably shabbier than it had been when we first moved in.

In a way, our relationship to it had changed too, without our noticing it—this was where we lived now, not the apartment in the city; most of our belongings had made their way here; it was, in short, *home*, place of our voter registration and primary residence. Since this had not been our intention originally, we had furnished the house in fits and starts, comfortably, but without much thought for the big picture. When we needed furniture, we drove down to the Paramus Mall, bought whatever seemed to fit in the space we had in mind, and brought it home in the Blazer. For the rest, we had left things pretty much the way Betty Kirchhoff, Tom's wife, had painted or wallpapered them before we bought the house. Not that there was anything wrong with that—Betty got most of it right, and we're still living happily over twenty years later with some of her choices—but if we'd known we were going to be spending most of our time here, rather than the city, we might have done some things differently.

Besides, over time, inevitably, we had begun to say about many things that fatal phrase, "Wouldn't it be nice . . ." Wouldn't it be nice to have a wider front porch, with a drain in it, so water didn't pool up when it rained? Wouldn't it be nice to have a larger refrigerator, with more freezer space? Wouldn't it be nice to have the television set in the library placed so that we could sit together and watch it, instead of sitting on different sides of the room, with our necks twisted? Wouldn't it be nice if it wasn't freezing cold in the corners of certain rooms? Wouldn't it be nice not to have a carpeted kitchen floor? (This had been an untypically eccentric solution of Betty Kirchhoff's to the unevenness of the kitchen floor, which on the plus side didn't show dirt, since it was in several shades of brown, but on the minus side looked ugly and was impossible to keep clean.)

This is a dangerous passage in the course of owning an old house—the dreaded moment when the list of changes and improvements one has been making for years is suddenly too long to ignore. Rule number one is that every change, however small and insignificant it may appear, will bring about a whole host of unwelcome and unexpected problems and expenses. Thus, for example, moving a painting from where it's hanging to someplace else, which sounds like a piece of cake, will inevitably reveal a deep gouge in the wall that it was concealing (in this case, due to the fact that it took me three tries to get the picture hanger hammered in correctly in the first place), a darker rectangle in the wallpaper because the rest of it will have faded in the sun, and the need for putting up a picture light where the painting is going because it's too dark to see it there. Plastering, wallpaper repair, an electrician, and more plastering and wallpapering are called for, thus turning something that looks as if it could be done in ten minutes into a project of several weeks that is likely to cost several hundred dollars. Then multiply this by many times. Rule number two with an old house is that behind every change, however small, lies the threat of "structural problems." There is no point in moving the refrigerator to exactly the spot in the kitchen where you want it if it's going to fall through the floor there. Rule number three is that no matter how carefully you plan things, the electrical outlets will turn out to be on the wrong side of the room, or inaccessible, once you've moved things around the way you want them, thus giving everyone seated in the living room a good view of an endless tangle of extension cords and three-way plugs on the floor. Rule number four is that everything will cost many times as much as you thought it would, and at least twice as much as was estimated by whoever is going to do it.

The final rule is that no attempt to redecorate or reconstruct an old house ends when it is completed—it ends when money or interest runs out, and we were no exception. There is always something more left to be done, whole areas left unfinished, projects that once seemed critical (or at least desirable) at which the owners have finally thrown up their hands and said, "Oh, for God's sake, let's not bother with *that!*" Thus our guest bathrooms remain in the same relatively primitive state they were in when we bought the house, despite occasional plans to upgrade them over the years. Thus many attempts to spruce up the cellar have petered out without changing it much. Thus the shower in my bathroom still can't be used, because it would require major construction to prevent leaks. Eventually you learn to live with these things, even to take a certain perverse pride in them. No matter how ambitious and all-encompassing your plans for renovation are (particularly when these coincide with some moment when you're feeling flush, and don't mind signing checks), you inevitably reach a moment when all you want is to get the plumber, the plasterer, the electrician, and their helpers out of the house, and get on with life again. So the refrigerator door still opens the wrong way, so the hot water still goes from scalding to freezing in less than one second (usually just as a guest is washing her hair), so half the wall plugs still don't work and spring brings a small Niagara of water coursing through the cellar—so what? You learn to live with it, and post small warnings where they can't be missed for guests. ("Don't use for hair dryer!" "Don't touch!" "No screen on this window, so please don't open!")

Before we learned all this, we sought the help of a friend, Thom von Buelow, a decorator who had performed miracles for us in Santa Fe, and explained to him that the house needed a certain amount of sprucing up, a discreet upgrade that wouldn't cost us an arm and a leg but would get rid of the damage from smoke, pets, and guests (not to speak of our own moments of carelessness) and correct some of the things we hadn't wanted to bother with when we first moved in. Thom was sympathetic, creative, understanding. With him on board, we passed many happy hours looking at swatches and paint samples—the honeymoon period of home decorating, when anything seems possible and the only question is whether it really makes sense to send to Florence or Milan for that perfect piece of cut velvet for the sofa in a house with cats. Thom had the advantage of knowing us, and an acute sense of what our breaking point was (I'm not thinking about money, I'm thinking about patience). The only disadvantage was that Thom's own home, an hour away in Westchester, was a model of perfection, the kind of house that made you feel you were living in a medieval peasant's hovel when you went home. A visit to Thom and his friend Marvin Sloves was enough to plunge one into self-loathing about one's closets, one's kitchen, one's bathrooms, one's whole style of life, while a walk around the house to see the swan pool (with live swans), the swimming pool cut out of the living rock, the pergola you could dine under alfresco, the flower gardens, and the herb garden made Harold Roe's limitations only too obvious.

Fortunately for us, Thom's own patience was unlimited, and his professionalism so highly developed that he was able to work with even the most difficult of local craftsmen. Electricians whose usual response to any suggestion was that it couldn't be done that way, did whatever it was exactly the way Thom wanted it done; painters mixed their colors over and over again until it was just the shade that Thom wanted. He had the magic touch of making everybody feel that it was important to live up to his own high standards. Even Harold Roe deferred to Thom, particularly after Thom had a life-size bronze statue of a stag delivered that weighed about as much as a small car and had four or five of us, including Harold and myself, move it back and forth across the lawns and the gardens until it was sited exactly where he wanted it to be. Whether by not allowing Harold to move it with his backhoe or by being willing to spit on his hands and help carry the immense weight himself, Thom managed to impress his authority on

Harold to a degree we had never achieved. In all likelihood it was simply that Thom seemed to know what he was doing and exactly how he wanted it done.

With his help, we managed to get the living room, the library, and the kitchen redone and to brighten up the halls, at which point we stopped, exhausted, and decided to live with the rest—a decision that now, many years later, seems to be good for the rest of our lives. Indeed, I have taken to applying what I call my "Ten Year Rule" to all changes and improvements. I based this upon the well-known British rule of the 1920s and early 1930s: government defense budgets should be drawn up on the basis that the United Kingdom would not be involved in a major war for the next ten years. From year to year the Ten Year Rule was invoked to hold down defense spending; as is so typical of government planning, it was still in force when World War II made it irrelevant.

My own version is slightly different. When I am advised by anybody that something needs repairing, I ask how long it will last before it collapses. If the answer is ten years or more, I leave it alone. This is, perhaps, part of the wisdom of age. When Vince the tree man, a perfectionist, tells me that our big trees are in need of yet more expensive surgery, I ask him how long they will last if we do nothing. "*Last?*" he asks, warily.

"Before they fall down."

He nods, stares at them, shakes his head. "Hard to say." He knows it's a trick question, but can't figure out the right answer.

I give him a lead. "Do you think they'll survive the way they are for, oh, say, another ten years?"

He sighs. "I guess so, sure, but—"

I silence him. "Ten years is good enough for me. Let's leave them alone."

Obviously at the age of thirty or forty one might not want to adopt this rule, but past a certain age, it makes sense. If the roof is good for another ten years, leave it be. If there's still another ten years of life in the living room sofa, don't re-cover it—especially if the cats are going to be sharpening their claws on it because it's been re-covered in nice new fabric. Ten years seems to me like the right amount of time to pick, and so far it's worked.

I just wish I'd thought of it years ago.

CHAPTER ELEVEN

Where Every Prospect Pleases, and Only Man Is Vile

WHEN FRIENDS TELL US how much they envy our living in the country, "peace and quiet" are the words that come most often to their lips—well, those and "simplicity," of course.

Oh yes, they say with a sigh, you're so *lucky* to have peace and quiet and the simple life—*you're* not kept awake by traffic noise or psychotic neighbors in the apartment next door, *you're* not running around town trying to fit three cocktail parties into one evening, followed by a dinner at the very latest new three-stars-in-*The-New-York-Times* restaurant, where you can't get a reservation with less than a three-month wait, and even then only if you know somebody who has just been profiled in *Vanity Fair* or *W;* then tomorrow, the same thing all over again, until one's poor, weary feet are just too tired to slip into one's new Manolo Blahnik shoes for yet another evening out. . .

Of course city people—New Yorkers particularly—tend to assume that once you're north of Yonkers you're deep in backwoods country, full of people with goiters and genetic problems who leave rusted-out pickup trucks on their front lawns like a scene from *Deliverance*, but despite all that, with unlimited peace and quiet. Guests coming to visit us—those we have been unable to fend off—stand in the driveway before they've even hauled their Vuitton luggage out of the car and exclaim how *quiet* it is, nothing but the sound of the birds, the wind in the trees, and the faint sound of the pigs snuffling in the distance—did they but know. "*Boy*, are we going to sleep tonight!" they say.

To those of us who live in the country, this is hard to understand. Personally, I never sleep better than on those nights I spend fifty-three floors up in the city. No mysterious snuffling outside the window in the middle of the night from God knows what kind of wildlife on the prowl, no owls hooting, no coyotes howling, no furious predawn catfights, no lost eighteen-wheelers careening down Gretna Road in the fog at sixty miles an hour in search of Route 44 as if the devil himself were driving a Peterbilt semi, no sudden change in the weather to wake you up to the sound of limbs crashing from your favorite trees and rain coming down in torrents, or, even more certain to rouse you from a sound sleep, the diesel roar of the big snowplows out on the roads punctuating that heavy stillness that tells you the path to the front door is going to have to be dug out in the morning before you can even make your way through the snow to the barn to start the real work of the day. And that's not even counting somebody pounding on the door at four o'clock on a cold, foggy morning to say that there are horses loose on the road, and are they yours?

Peace and quiet? I ask myself, as Margaret and I, with coats thrown over nightclothes and feet stuck hastily into cold rubber boots, grab big police flashlights, halters, and apples (the apples to tempt the horses to stop running and come close, the halters to put over their heads so they can be led). A quick look in our fields assures us, greatly to our relief, that they aren't our horses, but still, nobody who loves horses wants to see one get hit by a car, which happens all the time when they get out at night, so we head down the road on foot, waving traffic to a halt and looking for horses, which for such large animals have a remarkable capacity to make themselves invisible when they want to. Eventually we round up four of a neighbor's animals and get them back where they belong, then it's home to bed for an hour or so before it's time to get up. The neighbor, it turns out, has been sleeping soundly, unaware that his horses were cantering up and down the road in the fog, having the time of their lives.

Well, of course one wants to help—one *has* to help. Only the other day, a Sunday morning, I came back from a ride and as I approached our back field had the impression that a strange animal was following me. A stray dog, perhaps? But no, it seemed larger than that. A deer? Right size, wrong color. I looked around, but saw nothing. My horse was making a fuss, however, so it was clear that *something* was nearby. He came to a sudden halt; there was a Shetland pony, clearly lost, standing in the middle of the trail. One of the people who works in our barn managed to get the pony into a paddock and closed the gate on it, but nobody I telephoned was missing a pony or knew anything about it. Then I looked out the window to see a pickup truck being driven down the road very slowly by an elderly man who appeared to be looking for something, like Buster Keaton in *A Funny Thing Happened on the Way to the Forum.* I ran out and waved him down. Was he, by any chance, looking for a Shetland pony? Relief lit up his face—yes, by God, he was! His granddaughters' pony, it turned out, had broken out of its field in the middle of the night and made its way four or five miles cross-country (and across several roads) to our place. Very shortly his son arrived with a trailer and two delighted small girls, and the pony was on his way home, none the worse for the adventure. The son, who turned out to be the local distributor for Ben & Jerry's ice cream, came by the next day to fill our freezer with Chunky Monkey, Cherry Garcia, and New York Super Fudge Chunk. This was, as we say up here, right neighborly—but the point is that despite all appearances to the contrary there is always something going on up here, and very seldom a moment when somebody isn't pounding on the door or window to alert you to a new crisis or problem. By comparison, Broadway and Seventy-ninth Street on a Saturday night is quiet and peaceful.

WHEN WE FIRST moved to the country, I too was struck by the moments of silence. Here, I decided, was the perfect place to work—no noise, no interruptions, no distractions. Alas, that illusion evaporated quickly. It's in the city that you can find peace and quiet. I can be home all day in the apartment without anybody at all coming to the door, and the concierge downstairs carefully screens visitors. Here in the country, on the contrary, we can leave our door unlocked without fear, but a certain spirit of neighborliness prevails, which means that people feel free—dreaded phrase—*to drop in.*

As it happens, my office is in the part of our house that was tacked on to expand it at the beginning of the nineteenth century. I have what must have then been the family's big downstairs room, which has a huge fireplace suitable for roasting an ox, a front and a back door, and big windows on both sides, looking out over the garden on one side and toward the driveway and the road on the other. This is idyllic from one point of view—I have plenty of daylight, and great views in either direction—but it has certain disadvantages. Chief among them, I'm completely visible as I work at my desk. Anybody parking in the driveway can see me sitting there and make a beeline for my front door; anybody coming through the garden toward the front door of the house walks past my windows and can see me at close range. Short of hiding under my desk, I might as well be sitting in a shop window, like a whore in Hamburg's infamous Reeperbahn, or the red light district of Amsterdam. Of course the sight of an elderly man working away at a word processor isn't likely to get anybody's blood pressure rising, but it's hard to pretend that you're not at home when somebody is looking straight at you through the window from a distance of about six feet.

Of course this is part of country living anywhere—Margaret's father and mother used to lie on the floor of their house in a small Gloucestershire village whenever the vicar came to call, and I myself have been known to crouch behind the sofa in my office when a neighbor of ours comes to visit on Halloween with her dogs dressed up in Halloween costumes for canine trick-or-treating—but the problem is that you need to see the enemy before he or she sees you. If you're concentrating (or dozing at your desk), the enemy may be at your window staring in at you before you've had time to get on all fours behind the couch.

People in the country aren't ashamed to press their faces against the window, either. The general feeling is that if they want to see you, you'll probably be just as pleased to see them, so why be shy? And *nobody* telephones before coming; so far as the country is concerned, when it comes to dropping by, Alexander Graham Bell might just as well not have invented the telephone. Phoning before coming seems too formal, too citylike, and of course also carries with it the chance that you'll say don't come. The neighborly way of doing things is to simply turn up. The notion that one or both of us might be doing something we don't want interrupted has never occurred to anyone here, hard as Margaret has explained that I'm a writer, and might be doing *something*—thinking, at least, hopefully—even when it looks as if I'm doing nothing. The possibility that we might be taking a nap, or having a wild afternoon of sex, or don't want to see anybody for one reason or another, simply doesn't occur to anybody. What are neighbors for, if not to interrupt, after all?

This seems far-fetched to our friends from the city, who, as luck would have it, are usually here on the one untypical day when it's quiet as a tomb, so I thought it might be helpful to sketch out the chronology of a typical peaceful day in the country.

The phone rings at six in the morning. It's the man who delivers Margaret's hay and straw, calling to say that it looks to him like rain, so he's not coming today. No point in getting all that good hay and straw wet, is there? It is a bright, sunny day, so far as I can tell from bed, though who knows, of course, what it's like in Vermont. Since everything has been arranged for the delivery of several hundred tons of hay and straw, Margaret gets on the telephone to unarrange it all and fix a new date with the hay man. We get up, feed the cats, and have breakfast. It is still sunny.

The barn help arrives at seven-thirty. At seven forty-five, a knock on the door. One of the horses has thrown a shoe during the night. Margaret gets on the phone to send out an SOS to the blacksmith, whose wife will try to reach him in his truck. Margaret gets dressed and goes out to the barn; I get dressed, go down to the gym—Valley Fitness on Route 44—and am seated at my desk by nine, with my work neatly piled before me. The phone rings. It is the hay man again, saying the weather looks better and he's coming after all. I go out to the barn to pass the message on. Consternation. All the arrangements have to be made again now. I should have told him not to come.

Back to the house. The blacksmith's wife calls. He will try to get there today. I go out to the barn with this message, then sit down at my desk again. Ten o'clock—a tap at my window. I look up to see two small children gravely holding up cartons, their mother smiling encouragingly from the driveway. I get my wallet, meet them at the door, and buy several boxes of Girl Scout cookies. The mint-chocolate ones aren't bad.

A knock at the door at ten-thirty. It's the plumber. We don't have an appointment with him, and of course he didn't call, but he was passing by and thought he'd drop in and check out our water softeners, in case they needed more salt. I open the cellar door for him. "Must be nice to be retired," he says. "Stay home all day."

I refrain from comment and go back to my desk, just in time to see two Jehovah's Witnesses get out of a car with their pamphlets. They have seen me too, so there's no way to hide. I go to the door and explain that we're not interested, we're Anglicans. "Even Anglicans need to know the truth," the older one says. He has a tight collar and a neck like a turkey's. "Anglicans *know* the truth," I snap, and send them on their way. The Jehovah's Witnesses will be back—they own a huge model farm about twenty miles away, with a hotel and a conference center, so they don't give up easily.

Ten forty-five—one of our tree man's workers turns up, in a mammoth truck. He can see me at my desk, so there's no hiding from him. I go out to head him off at the pass. He was just passing by and thought he'd drop in and do some work on our fruit trees, which need pruning this time of year. It's all right with me, provided he doesn't disturb Margaret's horses in their fields. He should talk to Margaret before he does anything. He promises to, and I let him go.

Eleven o'clock—the mail person drives up in her red-white-and-blue van, honking furiously. I go out to collect the mail from her—she needs my signature for something. "It must be nice to be at home," she says wistfully. "No bother, no hassles, right?" Right, I say, and go back to my desk. When I look up, there's a man standing in the driveway, smiling tentatively. I try to ignore him, but that does no good—when I look up, he's still there.

With a sigh I get up, go out, and walk over to him. He has a sheaf of papers in his hand and hands me one. I look at it quickly. There's a smudged photograph of a lost dog. I commiserate briefly with him. "Don't much care whether the son-of-a-bitch comes home or not," he says, "but the kids do—you know how it is." I promise to keep an eye peeled for Snapper—funny name for a dog, I think, and hope it isn't because he behaves like a snapping turtle, of which we have plenty in the local ponds—then go back to my desk and try to summon up my concentration again. I remember reading that Samuel Taylor Coleridge had been writing his poem "Kubla Khan" in a drug-induced frenzy of creativity when he was interrupted by a knock on the door from a gentleman from Porlock, the local village, and was never able to resume the poem or rediscover the ending for it that had been in his mind. My heart goes out to Coleridge, not normally one of my favorite English poets.

Eleven-thirty—an enormous truck backs into our driveway, barely missing the gateposts, and moves off toward the barn. I crane my neck to see what it is and recognize the propane gas emblem. The propane deliveryman nearly always checks the tank for the tack room heater by the barn but goes off without checking the big tank for our generator for some reason—perhaps because it's harder to get to. There is nothing for it but to get up and intercept Vern (his name is embroidered on his jacket and painted on the side of the door of his truck), who says Yup, sure he will make sure to check both tanks, no problem. "Must be pretty nice to work at home," he adds, giving me a mildly resentful stare, as if I were Charles Darnay's uncle, the awful marquis, in *A Tale of Two Cities.*

I get back to my desk just in time to see his truck rumble off down the driveway without stopping at the generator tank. With a sigh, I add the propane company's name to the list of people I have to call: the plumber, who went off to get more potassium salt and has failed to return from his mission; the man who comes to service the generator, who came yesterday without calling to warn us, left to get a replacement part, then vanished, leaving the door to the generator house wide open; the people who took the tractor away to service it and have failed to bring it back (and who aren't answering their phone); the landscaper, who has approximately three times as many clients as he can handle and parcels his work out to reckless teenagers while he goes through what appears to be a protracted spiritual or religious crisis (he will eventually quit because I took the name of the Lord in vain while talking to him); the lady who does our garden, who has put a handsome flower bed a hundred yards from the house, requiring us to drag the garden hose over to water it. . . .

The propane company's answering machine is on—not a good sign. In any case, the local propane company was taken over by a bigger one, then that was taken over by an even bigger one, and now *that* has been swallowed up by a national chain, so when you do get somebody on the telephone, they are more likely to be in Tennessee, sitting in front of a computer screen, than in Pleasant Valley, right opposite the flower barn, where they used to be, and where you could drop in on your way to pick up *The New York Times* and ask why the hell they missed the big tank again.

The same thing happened with the garbage companies around here. In years gone by they were small and local, and when we had a problem I simply drove off to see the man in charge at his office, an air-conditioned trailer by the dump with a row of Jaguars, Mercedes, and BMWs parked outside and a receptionist who looked like a model from the pages of *Heel and Garter*, in a micro-mini and a blond beehive. Now, however, the garbage haulers are all part of one big national company, and the name on our bill seems to change every month.

Twelve noon—Margaret comes in from the barn, hopping mad because I told the tree man to prune the fruit trees, and he has scared the horses and set them running. That's all we need—another lost shoe or, God forbid, a lame horse, she says vehemently. I point out that I told him to be careful and to talk to her first, but of course he didn't. We decide to break early for a bite of lunch. It's been a busy morning in the barn, what with the blacksmith, the hay man, and the vet, who dropped by to look at one of the horses.

Twelve-thirty—an old rule of country living states, "Never sit down to have lunch, because the moment you do, somebody will appear at the door." The truth of this is borne out as we sit down at the kitchen table. Just as we are raising sandwiches to our mouths, a knock at the door. The guy from the tractor dealership is standing there, wearing a cap that reads "Been There, Wrecked That!" holding his bill and eager to talk about what they've done and why it took an extra day to do it. I point out that it's lunchtime, but that's a bad move—for a moment it looks as if he might take it as an invitation, but no, he gives it some thought and says, "Yup, it sure is. I figured I'd find you home, see?" He takes me through every item on the bill—the tractor appears to have had the equivalent of a triple bypass—if it's all the same to me, could he have the check now? Since he is obviously prepared to stand there all day if necessary, I go back to my desk, write out a check, and put it in his hand. "Must be pretty nice having lunch at home," he says. "Got to try it myself one of these days."

Margaret goes off to put the tractor away—it's her baby, and she takes a proprietorial view of it; in fact it may be the only tractor in Dutchess County that gets washed every time it's used—while I finish my sandwich with only one more interruption, this time by the Federal Express driver, who has a package he won't leave without my signature, even though the label reads "No signature required."

Then it's back to my desk, when one of our neighbors comes roaring up the driveway in a new sports car that he wants to show me. This is, by the way, as much of a tradition as the modern world still affords, now that barn raisings and harvest are no longer celebrated. It is customary to drive a new car to the homes of all your friends and neighbors so that the man of the house can walk around it and kick the tires admiringly. At the very least you have to sit in the car, ask to have the hood opened so you can look at the engine (no great knowledge is required—an appropriate comment is, "Say, will you look at *that!*"), and drop some loose change on the floor as a good-luck token. Since our neighbor has taken over my place as the local Ferrari owner, he will need all the loose change he can collect, I think to myself—wait until he sees what his first service costs!

Three o'clock—a neighbor drops by to say hello and tell me all about his recent surgery. Hard to say I haven't time to hear about it, so I listen, face fixed in an expression of friendly concern, mind fixed on my desk and longing to get back to it. Still, this is neighborliness, if that's what you want; after all, it's presumably one of the reasons why we moved to the country in the first place. If you can't tell your neighbors what happened to you and how you're feeling, then what are neighbors for? They have to listen to you and express sympathy, and you have to do the same for them. You might just as well live in the city, otherwise, where nobody listens or cares.

Three-thirty—a surprise. The cable television guy who was supposed to be here last week to fix our picture—we get God knows how many channels, but they all look as if colored cornflakes are flailing around behind the screen—turns up at last. He just happened to be passing by, saw our name on his list, so he dropped in. I take him to the television room and explain what's gone wrong and that I haven't been able to clear the problem up myself. I know I'm going to feel pretty foolish when he touches a button and everything turns clear and sharp instantly, but no, no matter what he touches, there's no improvement. He looks at the picture, shakes his head, pokes around, pulling the cables out of their sockets then sticking them back in again. If anything, the picture is worse. He rubs his chin thoughtfully and says, "It beats me too." He might try putting in a new converter box, but he doesn't have one with him. He promises to bring one tomorrow, swears that he'll call before coming, and goes. He will not be heard from again without numerous calls to his head office, each of which produces a computerized voice-mail menu that, even if you follow the directions faithfully, will eventually land you in limbo, listening to seventies soft-rock music while waiting for a customer representative to pick up—estimated waiting time twelve minutes, but don't bet on it.

That's it until four-fifteen, at which point it's teatime (we're English). Margaret and I take a cup of tea standing in the kitchen. I eat a shortbread-with-stem-ginger biscuit from the English grocery in Clinton Corners. There are moments when being English makes sense, and tea is one of them. The barn help have gone home, and for the moment peace and quiet reign, just as in the imagination of our city friends. There are deer and wild turkey feeding on the lawn (one of the cats is looking at them, trying to decide whether they just might be too big to be easy prey), birds at the bird feeder, a family of crows squabbling in the background.

Back to my desk just in time to see the plumber return, just six hours after he departed, to refill the water softeners. As I lock up the cellar, he stretches. "End of a long day's work for *me*," he says, with the slight edge of a worker bee talking to a drone who has been home all day.

It's plain sailing from here on in, with a good chance of no more interruptions until it's time to close shop. That's not to say that you can rely on that. One memorable late afternoon a hot-air balloon came down on our land; on another an airplane with an eighty-year-old pilot crash-landed a little up the road from us (he had run out of gas), bringing every emergency vehicle in the county in for the rescue; on other afternoons we have dealt with everything from trespassers firing gunshots in the woods opposite our house to one of our horses being severely wounded by an arrow from an unobservant (and trespassing) bow hunter. Still, by and large, as the sun begins to go down, the pace slows, there are fewer interruptions, there's at least some hope of getting a bath and a drink in peace. That's if the plumber didn't accidentally turn off the hot-water heater while he was working on the water purifiers, of course, in which case we'll have to put in an emergency call for him, and he'll arrive during dinner.

He's certain to say that it sure does smell good before he goes.

CHAPTER TWELVE

One Left-handed Clevis, Please

PROBABLY THE WORST THING that's happened to country life in America is not, as our local farmers like to insist, the federal government's irrational ban on the use of DDT on apples—"Been spraying apples all my life *and* eating 'em, and it never did *me* no harm," as one of our neighbors said firmly—but the more insidious takeover of the local hardware store by big national chains.

It used to be that the real center of country life was not the Masonic temple, nor even the feed store, but almost invariably the local hardware store, with its wooden floor scarred by generations of work boots, its endless dusty bins full of mysterious bits and pieces of plumbing, and its seemingly random array of merchandise, apparently beyond the powers of any one man to know, or to find any one item in.

The old-style hardware store owners and their clerks (all of whom had the look of having been apprenticed at the age of fifteen and kept out of sight until they were as worn, bent-over, bald, and sharp-tongued as the owner himself before they were fitted out with a shop apron and turned loose on the customer) managed somehow to know their stock by heart aeons before the computer age. You could push your way through the creaky door of Crispell in Hyde Park, or H. G. Page & Sons in Poughkeepsie, or Williams Lumber in Salt Point, or Rhinebeck Hardware, or Roger & Sons in Hudson, confident that if you asked for a galvanized stove bolt, one of the clerks would nod without looking up and say, "Two rows down, big bin on the left by the floor," and there they'd be in every possible size and thread known to man, all neatly labeled.

Stand in a hardware store, and if you weren't careful your mind would reel at the sheer quantity and diversity of the stock: chains and ropes of every size and thickness, farm gates, tools, plumbing parts from floor to ceiling, electrical goods and fittings, ladders, paint, kitchenware, parts for milking machines, old-fashioned items like manure baskets and mousetraps and milk cans cheek by jowl with more modern items like Weedwackers and electronic garage door openers, enough power tools to blow the mind (as well as countless fuses), long rows of things more unfamiliar than anything an archaeologist could find in an Egyptian tomb, some of which looked as if they'd been put on display before World War I, and probably were.

When we first moved up to Pleasant Valley, the local hardware stores were much the same as they'd been since the turn of the century, and the best places to go for advice on almost anything you needed to know about home or garden. They were pretty much 100 percent masculine institutions—there was usually a selection of local heavyweights, big, bulky men in overalls or outsize blue jeans, crowded around the counter chewing the fat with the clerks: dairy farmers, contractors, and the like, plus people like Buddy Brandow, a highly regarded master carpenter and local hardware store sage (his wife was reputed—correctly—to be the best baker in town, and they had a singularly beautiful daughter), or Tom Kirchhoff, or Harold Roe, or Turk

Daley, or anybody else who could spin a trip to the hardware store for an eye bolt or a hacksaw blade into an hour or so of chat and gossip.

If the clerks didn't have the answer to your problem, somebody else in the store was sure to—one way or the other you could be certain of getting all the advice you wanted (and more) about heat-taping your pipes for the winter or caulking the tiles in the bathroom or getting an air conditioner to stop leaking moisture onto the floor simply by going down to the hardware store and asking, though you might find it hard to escape, or to reconcile the many different and conflicting replies; the hardware store was a church in which everybody followed his own particular brand of religion, and no two men were ever likely to agree to the best solution for your problem. The final word on matters like this was reserved for the owner or the oldest clerk, to whom everyone deferred. At most, an argumentative and born contrarian like Harold Roe might shake his head in disagreement, and add, with respect but a certain stubborn defiance: "Well, maybe you're right, but I'd still do it my way if it was me."

At H. G. Page's, we actually found plumbing fittings that matched those of the late 1930s and early 1940s that the Hubners had installed in our house, cartons of them stacked away in one of the back rooms. "Don't get much call for these no more," the clerk said, unwrapping the items we wanted from pages of newspaper from the 1940s, but one of the rules of the hardware business is, or used to be, Never throw anything away—no matter how old-fashioned or useless an item may appear to be, somebody is sure to come in looking for it one day. A visit to the hardware store was like a visit to the Smithsonian Institution, "the nation's attic," and many of the items in stock looked as if they belonged there.

My feelings about hardware stores—the real, old-fashioned kind, not the new ones that are controlled by national chains—have always been deeply ambivalent. In my heart of hearts I know that I am no "danged do-it-yourselfer," as Harold Roe liked to call those who bite off more than they can chew in the area of home repair and upkeep, instead of calling on an expert (him). It's not that I'm necessarily all thumbs; I just don't have a gift for using tools, and am therefore more likely than not to make a mess of even a simple task. Nowadays I've managed to live with that—at sixty-seven I've learned to say no to any task more demanding than, say, hanging a small picture or changing a lightbulb—but when we first moved up to the country, I still regarded this kind of thing as a challenge to my masculinity, feeling that a man ought, by God, to *know* how to install a new timer or figure out what's wrong with the tack room gas heater. I was always ready to drop whatever I was doing, grab a Phillips-head screwdriver, and come to the rescue, or to get down on my hands and knees to put together one of those things that comes labeled Some Assembly Required. One of my first purchases after we bought the house was a big red toolbox, which I filled with all the things I thought I might need, under the skeptical eye of the hardware store clerk. I saw myself, tools in hand, as a weekend Mr. Fixit, even though as a child I was a dismal failure as a model builder and accomplished nothing in shop class except to give myself a jagged L-shaped scar on my left index finger, which I can still see clearly today every time I make the mistake of starting some task that involves tools.

Bitter experience soon put an end to this illusion, but not before I had developed a kind of fascination with hardware stores. Never mind what I was sent there to buy, I always managed to come home with some tool or device that seemed absolutely necessary, with the result that our drawers are full of objects the use of which I've long since forgotten, most of them still in their original wrapping. There is nothing quite like a good hardware store to bring out this kind of Walter Mitty feeling in even the most clumsy of do-it-yourselfers—the sense, standing there before all those power tools and pliers and saws, that we are all, after all, descendants of *Homo faber*, the maker and user of tools, and that we therefore ought to be able to fix the screen door ourselves, rather than pay somebody to do it for us.

Very fortunately Richard Bacon, like most men born and bred in the country, could fix almost anything, including projects that I'd started and abandoned when it was clear that I didn't know what I was doing. Still, however shamefaced I felt at having to ask Richard to finish up what I had begun, it only took one trip to the hardware store to convince me once again that *this* time I'd get it right. Looking through the house, I can still see evidence of my handiwork—gouges in the wide-plank floors, places where a picture or a mirror has been hung too high or too low to cover the dreadful mess I made in the wall trying to put in a picture hanger, a row (thank goodness, almost invisible) of small plastic and Velcro clips along the baseboard at one side of the dining room, where I attempted infelicitously to conceal an extension cord, innumerable lumps and bumps on the woodwork where I drilled screw holes, only to change my mind....

If I spread my custom out among several of the nearby hardware stores, it was partly because Pleasant Valley's was the smallest of them, and therefore the least exciting, and also because somebody once sent me down there, as a joke, to pick up a left-handed clevis (for those who aren't into hardware, it doesn't exist), thus causing a good deal of merriment in the hardware store at my expense and forcing me to take my business to Salt Point, or Rhinebeck, or Poughkeepsie for a while, where none of the clerks had heard the story. The clerks were by and large an ill-tempered and impatient lot to begin with, rather like the masters at an English boarding school for boys.

At about the time we redecorated the house—an experience so deeply traumatic that we tend to date other events by it—I began to notice a change taking place at the hardware stores around us. It was small, at first, but it gathered speed alarmingly—the "housewares" made their way from the dim back of the shop to the front, the walls were painted in bright colors, tiles covered the old wooden floors, whole sections of the store were given over to "decorating" wares, the area around the cash register became crowded with things like trivets, dishcloths, and scented candles, while the merchandise that had been the staple of the hardware store since the nineteenth century retreated step-by-step to the darker corners or, where available, the basement. This process was accelerated as the big national chains took over the stores, imposing their own brands and their own idea of merchandising on what had once been a family-owned business. They also brought with them their own catalog and a microfiche reader (soon to be replaced by the computer), so that the clerks no longer had to know the stock by the heart—it was the customer's job now to know what he wanted and to find it, and with this reversal of roles the clerks themselves changed, the old guys who knew exactly what size box spanner you needed and where to find it giving way inexorably to pimply youths who knew nothing (and cared less), and eventually to young women.

Of course there are few exceptions left—Page's in Poughkeepsie is still a kind of shrine to the building trades, the holy of holies for plumbers and electricians in search of something, and Williams in Salt Point still has a certain old-fashioned, frowsy charm too, together with a paint mixer that seems to date from the dawn of the industrial age—but the old-fashioned hardware store is now largely a thing of the past, and all thumbs though I may be, I miss it. There was a certain integrity to the old hardware store that most businesses lack: a willingness, even an eagerness, to embrace the whole crazy diversity of human need and invention; a stubborn determination to keep right on stocking items that sell for only a few cents apiece and put them in tiny paper bags, and to hang on to things that might sit on the shelves gathering dust for twenty years; as well as an acceptance that even when there's a new way of doing something, plenty of people will still want to keep right on doing it the old way, and that they should be catered to and not simply told, "They don't make them that way no more, they're all plastic these days."

*I*T'S NOT ONLY the old-fashioned hardware store that has gone the way of the old-fashioned grocery store; the old-fashioned family-owned drugstore has gone too (Pleasant Valley's gave up the ghost about ten years ago and moved out of the center of town, to be replaced by a national chain with young women in white coats behind the prescription counter instead of the local pharmacist who knew everybody's medical history and business, and dispensed advice along with every sale), and was soon followed by the old-fashioned butcher's shop (with a real butcher) on the main street, now replaced by Poppa's Pizzeria. We still have a feed store—two in fact, one in the center of town, the other on the outskirts—and they seem likely to survive, only because there is no new or efficient way to sell horse feed, let alone pig pellets, hamster food, cracked corn and poultry feed, and the like. One of them has branched out into domestic pet supplies, the other has added a tack shop of sorts, but the substance of the business wouldn't seem very different to a farmer from the turn of the century.

Now that Pleasant Valley's hardware store has become part of a national chain—and taken on with it a certain non–Pleasant Valley suburban ambience, in which lawn care and housewares outrank farm equipment and tools—the nearest thing we have to an old-fashioned, traditional, small-town business is the Pleasant Valley Department Store, which somehow manages to retain its own identity though the big shopping malls in Poughkeepsie and Wappingers Falls, with The Gap, and Victoria's Secret, and Old Navy, are less than half an hour away.

Maybe the Pleasant Valley Department Store has survived because it doesn't even attempt to compete with the big guys—it offers, as it always has, a firm sense of rock-bottom rural values and does not challenge its customers with displays of clothing in sizes smaller than they could squeeze into, or sexier than they would dream of wearing. Fashion hasn't raised its ugly head here, not so as you'd notice anyway, as you squeeze your way past tables piled high with nondesigner blue jeans, bulky sweaters, watch caps and face masks in every possible color, and rack after rack of oilskins and assorted foul-weather gear.

Here, at least, is a place where it's not hard to find large and even extra-large sizes, and where the stock, packed into a crowded Victorian storefront, includes (but is by no means limited to) work clothing, children's clothing, work boots, sneakers, winter gear for people who work outdoors (or hunt) in below-zero weather, fishing tackle, bait, ammunition, knives, goods for sewing and knitting, lanyards for the coaches of local school sports teams, work gloves for every possible profession and climate condition, hand warmers and foot warmers of every description, a full range of clothing in hunter orange and in camouflage patterns suitable for each season, not to speak of the kind of things that you can hardly find anywhere else these days, like big red-and-black-checked flannel shirts, deer hunting caps with earflaps that tie down, bright red suspenders, and overalls with a pocket or sewn-on tab for every tool known to man.

This is Polarfleece city. Underwear leans toward the warm and the outsize, and doesn't get any sexier than Fruit Of The Loom, but if your main concern is keeping warm and dry, this is the place to go. They've been selling big 100 percent cotton bandanna handkerchiefs since long before they started to become fashionable—in fact I'm not sure that anybody involved in the store knows they've become fashionable, or would care.

There's a certain comfort in the survival of places like this, a sense of tradition and a respect for local custom that is—or at least ought to be—part of small-town life. The arrival of Pizza Hut, McDonald's, Dunkin' Donuts, the A&P, CVS Pharmacy, and Blockbuster in a small town is convenient, and probably inevitable, but they don't celebrate diversity; on the contrary, they signify uniformity, the imposition on small-town life of an artificial and carefully articulated commercial reality that is just as much at home in Bangkok or Moscow or on any highway in America as in Pleasant Valley. Enter McDonald's or Pizza Hut, and you could be anywhere in the world—anywhere in America, at least—but enter the Pleasant Valley Department Store, and you could only be here, where older residents are still in touch, spiritually if not physically, with the rural past, even as it recedes and erodes around them, and where grandparents still bring their kids in for a new pair of sneakers or a school sweatshirt and, in the case of grandfathers, sometimes hang on to buy the kid that all-important first pocketknife.

There's no pressure to buy here, no effort to sell, no talent for display or merchandising, not even, so far as one can see, any attempt to replace the old-fashioned cash register with its tinny ring with some newfangled silent computer, but the proprietor, who seems at once aged and ageless, has all the time in the world to spend on his side of the counter describing the merits of each penknife in the display case, and demonstrating how sharp their blades are. Judging from the boxes they come in, some of them have been there since the 1940s, but penknives don't become obsolete, so that's okay. Neither he nor his customers (nor the members of his family who work here) seem in a hurry.

With the sad disappearance of the real hardware store, the department store is the last vestige—together with the feed stores, themselves something of an anachronism—of an older, quieter kind of small-town life, one over which the outside world has little influence, and where a trip to Poughkeepsie to shop is a major event and undertaking, reserved for such formal—and potentially life-changing—purchases as a suit, or a wedding ring, or a suite of bedroom furniture. Everything else you need is here, if you aren't too fussy.

That world has vanished, swept away by four- or six-lane highways and shopping malls, and soon no doubt to be further reduced by Internet shopping and the like; but we are fortunate to retain some last traces of independent small-town life, and even if the hardware store has gone the way of the buggy whip, I still take the time to buy my socks down at the Pleasant Valley Department Store, where, if nothing else, they know me as the fellow who bought the old Hubner place.

CHAPTER THIRTEEN

Nature Green of Tooth and Claw

LIVING IN THE COUNTRY, it's easy to persuade yourself that Mother Nature is in charge and knows what she's doing. At some point in the early spring the forsythia will begin to show signs of life, at some point in the late fall the leaves will turn red and start to drop, the whole landscape around you is constantly regenerating, and there's nothing you have to do about it except sit back, pour yourself a glass of wine, and enjoy the spectacle. Farmers know better than this, of course, since they spend their lives struggling against Mother Nature and her capricious and destructive ways.

When we first moved up to the country, I took the broad cosmic view that, in the words of Dr. Pangloss's famous remark to Candide, "Everything is for the best in the best of all possible worlds." Mother Nature would provide us with an ever-changing wide-screen, Technicolor, Todd-AO spectacle, and all she needed was an occasional lick of help from Harold Roe and his mower.

What I had failed to understand is that Mother Nature really isn't a domestic goddess at all—her intention, if she has one, appears to be to sweep away all traces of human habitation and construction and return the land to what it was before the Native Americans walked across what is now the Bering Sea from Asia and began to mess with the North American continent. If there's one thing Mother Nature doesn't care about, for example, it's lawns.

Which is a pity. Even here, far to the north of suburbia, the lawn is seen as a sign of civilization, a barrier against chaos and anarchy, much as Hadrian's Wall must have seemed to the Romans in Britain. On our side of it, neatness, safety, civilization, paved streets, togas, and steam baths; on the other, barbarians who paint themselves blue and worship oak trees by sprinkling human blood on them. Those who lived behind the Great Wall of China must have felt the same, as well as, more recently, settlers on the American frontiers who built log forts and palisades to discourage the marauding Indians.

The lawn separates what's ours from what's somebody else's, of course, but it also separates what's ours from what's Mother Nature's. *Here,* a nice flat green space, with flower beds, perhaps a pool, teak lawn furniture; *there,* within sight, a tangle of trees, vines, undergrowth—prickers that tear the skin, poison ivy and poison oak and poison sumac, countless things with thorns—not to speak of God knows what kind of wildlife, from biting bugs of every variety to snakes and snapping turtles. Admittedly, Dutchess County isn't Rwanda or Borneo—it's very hard to come to any real harm in the woods, except at the hands of trigger-happy hunters, but at the right time of year you can certainly come home with enough insect bites, rashes, and poison ivy blisters to keep your dermatologist busy for weeks.

The people who settled this part of the world in the seventeenth and early eighteenth centuries didn't know anything about lawns, of course—they built stone walls instead. If there's one thing that was and remains in good supply around here, it's stones—you can clear a field of stones with prodigious labor (I know, since we did it), but at the first frost a whole new crop of stones comes up to replace them, and plowing simply brings even more to the surface. The settlers had to fell the trees, pull the stumps out with teams of oxen, then remove countless tons of stones before they could plant a field. What they did with the stones was to build walls—nothing elaborate, just a visible, solid barrier between "civilization" (a plowed field) and "wilderness." As the farmers gave up or moved west, much of the land they cleared with such effort has been reclaimed by second- or third-growth woods, but anywhere you look you can see miles of stone walls, fallen in, broken down, or scattered now, but still testifying to that remarkable determination to tame as much as one could of Mother Nature's wilderness, and to set up a firm barrier against her encroachment. Nowadays it's become the thing to build "decorative" stone walls—Mexican immigrants are the only people up here now who seem to know how—but the stone walls of the early settlers weren't intended to be decorative. They defined your property, of course, and prevented your livestock from wandering, but they also marked the line at which your small patch of civilization ended; and when push came to shove, you could always take cover behind them and open fire if the Indians or the redcoats were coming.

Since everything else up here grows in profusion—just when you thought you'd whacked back enough, it's time to start whacking back some more—it naturally seemed to me that the lawns would do the same. After all, every spring—even as I write this, the tree man and his crew are out there, pruning away like crazy and feeding it all through their industrial-size Woodchipper into a huge dump truck—the trees have to be pruned, and although Margaret complains every year that they're stripping everything bare, by next spring there'll be even more to prune. Nature loves excess, it seems—look away for just the blink of an eye, and the birch trees around the house have grown back enough twigs to tear the cedar shingles off the roof and fill the gutters with debris, while the apple trees have put out enough suckers to reach the telephone and power lines—but she doesn't necessarily lavish her cares upon things she regards as artificial and manmade. She loves poison ivy, for instance—can't apparently get enough of it—but couldn't care less about our flower garden.

My own relationship with lawns is based on a deep misunderstanding. As an Englishman, my idea of a lawn was formed by the one outside the big old house where we lived near Denham, at the beginning of the war, or the one around the old "manor house" at my uncle Alex's Shepperton Film Studios, or the ones at Magdalen College, Oxford—huge expanses of grass as flat and green as a billiard table, lovingly maintained by devoted groundsmen and gardeners. There used to be an old joke about an American tourist who visits an Oxford college and is awestruck by the beautiful lawn. How do you get it to look like that? he asks the elderly groundsman; What's the big secret? No big secret, sir, the groundsman says. Just reseed it as necessary, make sure it gets plenty of water, cut it regularly, and roll it daily—then keep on doing all that for five hundred years.

Of course in England (and Ireland) hardly a day passes by without a few hours of gentle rain, and the winters, while wet and miserable, are not particularly cold, which makes it the ideal climate for lawns. Dutchess County, on the other hand, has severe winters, with lots of snow and ice, and summers when the temperature rises into the nineties and droughts are not uncommon. When there's a drought, the last thing you want to do is water your lawn—living on well water, you soon learn that there are more important things than a green lawn, bathing and flushing the toilet being among them.

Then too, there is the question of size. The Hubners, when they owned our house, kept sheep, and though the sheep eventually went when the Hubners got too old to look after them, the lawns on which they had lived and grazed remained. The house was surrounded—very prettily under the right circumstances—with perhaps five acres of rolling lawn, in front of the house quite flat but elsewhere sharply sloping, with fairly steep contours. There seemed no way to make all this look like the great lawns of Oxford, even had Harold been the man to do it.

For one thing we seemed to be dealing with a different kind of grass, spikier and apt to turn brown at a moment's notice, except for a strip in front, deeply shaded by big trees, where the old roadway had been incorporated into the Hubners' property to straighten out Gretna Road. Here the grass was patchy, partly because there was only a very thin layer of soil over the crumbling blacktop of the old roadway, partly because it was so shady.

Since I could see this strip easily from my window while I was working, I wanted Harold to fix it, but he was deeply resistant. He saw his job as mowing lawns, not making them grow better, though when questioned on the subject he grudgingly suggested that putting down grass seed for shaded areas and a good lawn fertilizer might help. His own preferred solution, almost needless to say, was to bulldoze the entire stretch, remove the layer of old blacktop, put in fresh soil, and roll it flat. "Cheaper in the long run," he maintained, but a bulldozer was exactly what I was trying to avoid.

Eventually, with Harold looking on my efforts skeptically, I purchased a hand spreader for lawn fertilizer and the right kind of grass seed, and spent many restful afternoons going up and down the area spreading seed like Millet's sower (to be seen on the spine and the title page of every Simon and Schuster book), then pushing the fertilizer spreader back and forth.

For quite some time the only result that I could see was a vast increase in the number of birds around the house, many of which swooped down and ate my grass seed the moment it hit the ground. Then, after several rainstorms, the grass started to come up in big clumps and hummocks, the bright kelly green of the "Kiss Me I'm Irish" ribbons and plastic derbies at the Saint Patrick's Day parade, with large areas that not only remained grassless but seemed to have sprouted a kind of sickly bright green moss. There was a certain depressingly funereal look to the whole area, like that of a cemetery in a movie of a Stephen King novel, and though Harold did his best to kill it all off by running his tractor back and forth over it with the blade set so low that it scalped the grass rather than just cutting it, within a day or two it grew back, thicker than ever. "You put too much fertilizer on it," he told me, and he may have been right—overenthusiasm has always been my biggest fault when it comes to gardening—though it's also possible that the man at the Agway sold me the wrong kind of fertilizer.

In any event, one whole area of our landscape looked as if it had been painted in by the scenic designers of MGM for *Finian's Rainbow* in the days when Technicolor was still more of an art than a science, and remained that way until a fortunate collapse of our septic system made it necessary for Harold and Turk to dig the whole area up with a bulldozer and a backhoe and put in an enormous cement septic tank. Even then, after topsoil, reseeding, and rolling, it still looked a different shade of green from the rest of our lawns, and certainly lacked a cricket-pitch smoothness.

Then there was the "soft spot" in our lawn, a trough of ground that turned into a bog after even the lightest of rains and remained pretty squelchy underfoot even in a drought. Here too, Harold's preferred solution was to backhoe a drain, then fill the whole area with topsoil and start again. To demonstrate his point, he would run his tractor over the area, despite our pleas to leave it alone and just let the grass grow high there, thus producing huge, deep tire ruts, as if a passing tank had crossed our lawn by mistake.

I found the trick was to look in that direction as little as possible. Harold, on the other hand, couldn't take his eyes off it. Its chief attraction for him was that it ended in a shallow, rocky stream, heavily overgrown with reeds, which attracted the occasional pair of ducks or geese. Harold had in mind a vast earthmoving plan worthy of Stalin or Mao Tse-tung at their most ambitious: not only to dig up the soft spot in the lawn and put in a drain that emptied into the stream, but to whack back the reeds and convert the stream into a pool; or, alternatively (and more ambitiously), to put in a long culvert and fill in the stream, thus enlarging the lawn and giving him a bigger area to mow on that side of the house. I preferred to leave it to the ducks as it was. That we were deeply resistant to this plan, even at its more modest level, made Harold only that much more determined to show us how wrong we were by bogging his tractor down in the lawn every time it rained.

Still, by simply turning a deaf ear to Harold on this subject, we managed to keep it on the back burner for years—he had plenty of other ambitious plans involving earthmoving machinery, culverts, and drains, though this was his favorite. The uneven texture and color of the lawn, however, remained both an annoyance and a mystery, even to Harold himself. He did not necessarily share our taste for the smooth, green lawns of our dreams, but he had a certain pride in the way the place looked. If guests were coming up, he would arrive unbidden, to "gussy up" (a favorite phrase of his) what could be gussied up, though his ideas about what constituted gussying up did not always correspond with ours. As for the lawn, he took grass samples to the Cornell Agricultural Extension and came back with a complicated regimen of fertilization of his own devising, which seemed to make no difference at all.

Eventually, even Harold agreed that expert advice was called for, and a "lawn doctor" was called in to analyze our problem—a specialist, as it were, to Harold as the general practitioner. The lawn doctor, a heavyset, red-faced, bespectacled man in a grass-green T-shirt (what else?) and khaki trousers, like a larger version of a painted garden gnome, tested the alkalinity of the soil, took samples of our earthworms, and consulted gravely with Harold. When I managed to break into the conversation, he kept me at a distance with scientific jargon: pH levels, soil bacteria, acid rain. He was, I realized, a figure straight out of Molière's *Le Médecin malgré lui*, determined to use the language of science to keep the layman at bay. My job was to sign the checks, not to ask questions.

I had expected that Harold's nose would be put out of joint, and that he would be argumentative, to say the least—accepting advice was not one of Harold's strong points—but perhaps because we had left the choice of expert to him, they showed toward each other the ponderous courtesy of seventeenth-century doctors discussing a baffling case, and eventually new mixtures of exotic fertilizers were applied, we invested in garden sprinklers and hundreds of yards of hoses, and Harold sprayed, dusted, limed, and rolled the lawn with a heavy roller studded with spikes he had built himself, reminiscent of a medieval instrument of war, to encourage aeration of the soil. "The expert said your worms wasn't doing the job," Harold explained. "This will."

Oddly enough, whatever we did, our grass never came up as green, dense, or long-lasting as the grass the Highway Department sowed on either side of the roads, and which stayed miraculously green even through the snow—but then the Highway Department wasn't putting their money on earthworms to do the job; they sprayed their newly seeded grass with liquefied cow manure that brought tears to your eyes from a hundred yards away.

In some places, where we despaired of getting the grass the way we wanted it, we gave in and actually put down squares of sod, which arrived looking like neat, bright green squares of cake, and—to our surprise—thrived remarkably. The only trouble with the sod was that it required a great deal of watering at the beginning, made the rest of the lawn look even worse, and by comparison was somewhat artificial-looking in color, like AstroTurf.

The sod never did quite blend in, but since it was near the house, and thus the first thing you saw when you got out of your car in the driveway, it gave a false impression of smooth opulence. Quite a few people commented on how great the place was looking. In fact, it was. So it didn't look like Hampton Court, or the grass courts at Wimbledon; still, after much work and money, it was a lot better than it had been, and every morning I got up and took my glass of grapefruit juice outside to enjoy the sight of it—all these acres of bright and dark green, unquestionably *ours.*

After incredible amounts of work, worry, and money, our lawns were looking good enough to be a pleasure to admire from the windows. When I came up from the city, I got out of the car and was bowled over by the sheer, smooth greenness stretching before me. Admittedly, the lawns of our friends in Westchester looked better—but after all, this was old farmland, and up to a few years ago had been trimmed by sheep rather than mowers. For up here, in farm country, they were pretty fine lawns, if I did say so myself.

It was therefore with some dismay that I rose one morning to find that our lawns had been trashed, as if somebody had attacked them savagely with a pitchfork during the night, uprooting whole chunks of it and exposing bare earth in places. When called over to examine the destruction, Harold nodded sagely. "Moles," he said.

Moles! How *many* moles? I asked. It looked to me as if it would take a whole army of moles to do this much damage.

Harold stuck his hands in his overall pockets glumly. Moles were hard workers, was the thing. It didn't take that many of them to do a lot of damage. He could put poison down, of course, underground—that ought to take care of them.

But I knew that was a nonstarter. Margaret would certainly not want to use poison, first of all because of the risk to the cats, who might either eat it or eat a mole that had been poisoned, and secondly because she was firmly opposed to all forms of biological warfare directed against small furry creatures, whatever their species. She had been against using poison to bring down our mouse population in the cellar, and she didn't want it used on the rats in the barn, either, so she certainly wouldn't want it used on the moles.

Harold nodded—a stubborn man himself, he had a good deal of respect for Margaret's stubborn streak, even when he disagreed with her. There *was* another way, he said, which Richard Bacon had suggested to him—you drove plastic stakes into the ground that gave out a sound the moles didn't like. Richard, it turned out, had found these in a high-tech garden catalog, and they naturally appealed to him as an expert on electronics of all kinds. The devices, he explained, were battery-powered and sent out a high-frequency signal that drove the moles away. What about the cats? I asked. But that had been thought of—the frequency of the device was aimed precisely at moles: it was guaranteed not to bother domestic animals of any kind (except, presumably, for the few people eccentric enough to keep moles as pets). Even Harold, whose faith in any kind of machinery that wasn't diesel-driven was limited, seemed convinced, and before long the antimole devices were in the ground, humming away, no doubt, at a pitch unbearably painful to small underground burrowers. Before putting them in, Harold had gone to great lengths to get the lawns back in shape, replacing the divots, reseeding the patches that had been dug up, gussying everything up as best he could. Deep underground, one hoped, the moles were in full retreat. The lawns grew back, as pretty as a picture, the moles having presumably made their way down Gretna Road to attack old Mr. Tokar's lawn, or the Vandenkamps'.

Then one morning I woke up to find that it had happened all over again, even worse; in a few places even the antimole devices had been uprooted. This seemed to me like the work of something larger than moles, and my first thought again was of vandals—angry teenagers on a rampage, perhaps. Summoned to view the battle scene, Harold's expression was glum. We could forget about teenagers, he said. It could be that his first guess had been mistaken—*he* wasn't the kind of man who would never admit he'd been wrong, no sirree—this was clearly the work of *skunks,* not moles, and in retrospect he thought skunks may have been to blame for the previous attack on our lawn too, though it was hard to be sure.

Up until now, I had always had a certain friendly feeling toward skunks, of which there were plenty around the house. Admittedly, it was no fun when one of them sprayed, but that apart, they were fairly quiet and attractive nocturnal creatures. Occasionally one of them would turn up on the porch at night, drawn to the food we put down for the raccoon family. Since we didn't own a dog, the skunks weren't threatened by anything on our property—the cats sometimes followed one of them around, not with any evil intent (a skunk is more than capable of taking care of a cat), but more out of sheer curiosity. Indeed, one of our neighbors kept a pet skunk (its scent glands had been removed, of course), and it was reported to be highly affectionate.

The problem, Harold explained, was grubs. At certain times of year grubs multiplied underground, and the skunks were crazy about them. They were such a great delicacy that whole families of skunks would gather at night to dig up a lawn with their powerful little claws, and go on doing it until the grubs' cycle was over. The only way to stop it was to kill the grubs.

Fortunately, Margaret's aversion to the use of poison did not extend to larvae and grubs. An expert was called in who put down whatever the situation called for, the grubs died off, or perhaps simply went into the next cycle of their existence as full-fledged bugs, and the skunks left our lawns alone for the time being. The moles, if they had ever been responsible at all, vanished.

The lawns renewed themselves, though not quite as opulently as before, with many rough spots and bare patches where the skunks had outdone themselves grubbing.

Somehow, in the end, the skunks won. Though their depredations became rarer over the years, they still managed to uproot a patch here, a patch there, enough to keep us on our toes, and when we did finally manage to get a piece of lawn back to a certain level of perfection (by Dutchess County standards of perfection, if not those of Westchester or England), some subterranean problem nearly always led to digging it up and starting from scratch again, with a whole bunch of raw, rocky earth.

In the end we learned to live with compromise, on this as on so many other issues. We joked about putting down AstroTurf, but the truth is we simply accepted the adage that green enough is good enough, and tried to look at the place from a certain distance.

As a matter of fact, when some enterprising fellow and his wife turned up at the door with a folder full of eight-by-ten color photographs of our property taken from the air, the first thing I noticed was how green it all looked—as smooth and green as a bowling lawn from one thousand feet up, all the bumps, soft spots, and patchy areas totally invisible.

I bought three full sets of pictures, I was so impressed.

CHAPTER FOURTEEN

Manure

LOOKING AT PATCHY GRASS is one thing, but looking at a pile of manure is another. Hardly anybody *likes* manure—Larry McMurtry once quoted a cowboy's proud boast: "Twenty-five years a cowboy, and never stepped in horse shit yet!"—but there it is: manure is a fact of life, and on a horse farm it's even *the* fact of life.

Of course it wouldn't be a farm without a manure pile. Horses produce a lot of it, winter and summer, day and night, and one of the first big questions when it comes to keeping them on your own property is where you're going to put the manure pile. And of course, what you're going to do when it gets too big.

Placing the manure pile isn't too hard. It has to be fairly near the barn, since the help isn't going to want to push a loaded wheelbarrow any farther than necessary, particularly in midwinter or a rainy day;

and the general opinion is that it probably shouldn't be visible from any of the windows of the house, or from the porches. A secluded spot, maybe a couple of hundred yards from the barn, one that doesn't leach into a stream or risk contaminating the well, is just the ticket. Then all you have to do is dig a hole about the size of a swimming pool, line it, brace the sides with stout logs, and wait for it to fill up with horse shit.

It's what you do when it fills up that constitutes the harder part of the problem.

Naturally, the more horses you have, the faster it fills. We began as a comparatively modest three-horse, one-groom family barn operation, with Margaret's old Thoroughbred Tabasco, her new young quarter horse Missouri, and my quarter-horse mare True Grit (Malplaquet had been retired to a farm on a lesbian commune in the Adirondacks).

Missouri, a handsome dapple gray, though now snow-white, is still alive and ridden every day as I write this over twenty years later, and went on to take Margaret to a stunningly successful record as a United States Combined Training Association competitor. True Grit (known around the farm as Grits) did not endear herself as Missouri had. In the first place, it was Grits who broke Margaret's leg by kicking out at her while we were riding together on the Rockefeller estate at Pocantico, which was why Margaret was on crutches when she first showed me the house; and in the second place, Grits, though a very good-looking bay, disliked other horses, children, most people, and all dogs. She was like the linear descendant of Woodrow Call's mare The Hell Bitch in Larry McMurtry's *Lonesome Dove*, for those who know the novel (or the miniseries) by heart.

The hope had been that when she was up in the country, with plenty of space and nice big fields, Grits's character would improve, but this turned out to be a delusion. She snapped, ground her teeth, and kicked out at anything and anyone that caught her eye. In Central Park she had developed a strong dislike for the joggers and runners who were beginning to take over the bridlepaths and who actually resented the presence of horses. Those who ran close to her very often regretted it, particularly if they came up from behind. Once she had her teeth into a runner's shoulder, she could lift him right off the ground without breaking stride.

Dogs didn't scare her a bit. She was not a western horse for nothing—far from being afraid of dogs, she would fix one that annoyed her with a beady stare, wait until it was close enough, push it under her with a forefoot, then trample it. Many dog owners thought it was good fun to let their dogs off the leash to run after a horse, barking like crazy, but Grits usually managed to teach the dog (and its owner) a lesson about showing respect for horses, and who belonged on the bridlepath. Most horses are terrified when a dog chases them, but Grits always kept her cool, pinned her ears back flat against her head, and waited for just the right moment, when the dog was exactly in range, before landing a kick that sent the dog flying like a football. Dog owners screamed and shouted abuse (or burst into tears), but as I pointed out, their dogs *were* supposed to be on a leash at all times, and the bridlepath *was* for horses. . . . On the other hand, the mounted cops in the park tended to take Grits's point of view, and thought she would have made a pretty good police horse.

Grits's view of the world did not improve once she was in Pleasant Valley and away from the stress of urban life. Even Roxie Bacon, who had a magic touch with horses, worked around Grits with a certain caution. In the end, Grits was moved to a farm across the road from us, and to replace her, I bought a big quarter horse named Hustle from Katherine Boyer, a chestnut with a white blaze, a far better horse than I needed and altogether one of the most lovable horses you could ever hope to meet. If ever a horse had a winning, noble character it was Hustle, though there was something of the holy fool about him too, as if he were the equine counterpart to Dostoyevsky's Prince Myshkin.

Hustle was amiable, reliable, a strong jumper, and apparently determined never to let his rider down. He never kicked, never bit, and never failed to get you over a fence—however badly you placed him, however off balance you were in the saddle, however frightened you were as the fence loomed up before you, Hustle simply gathered himself up, took a good look at the fence, and compensated for your errors. Even if you came down in the saddle like a sack of potatoes as he landed, or pulled on the reins just when you should have left him alone, he didn't hold a grudge. He was the gentlest of horses, far more talented than his rider, in my case, and to this day is still remembered with affection by anyone who knew him. "Oh, you used to own Hustle," they'll say to me; "He was *some* horse."

People who don't know horses don't realize how greatly their characters and personalities differ. Like people, some of them are irritable, some of them are courageous, some of them are lazy, some of them temperamental and high-strung; unlike people, none of them is simply no damn good—horses only turn mean or vicious when they've been made that way by people. It's the whip, the curse, the heavy hand on the reins, and the use of cruelty as a means of control that makes for problem horses—though once a horse *is* spoiled by somebody else's carelessness or cruelty, it's very hard to retrain, whatever the "horse whisperers" may say.

In any event, once we had our horses installed in a barn with six stalls, the first thing that caught Margaret's eye was the empty stalls. Empty stalls exist to be filled. If you want to keep to four horses, say, build a four-horse stable; if you build a six-horse stable, you'll soon own six horses. Nature—and a horsewoman—abhors a vacuum. Over the years our horse population varied, usually four, rising to a maximum of five (our practical maximum, as we use one of the stalls to keep hay and straw in) as Margaret sought that rarest of animals, the perfect event horse, sound, competitive, and reliable, with a winning spirit. Eventing is a tough sport, combining as it does three phases; the horse has to perform flawlessly in the dressage ring, go hell-for-leather over stiff cross-country obstacles against the clock, then put in a perfect round of stadium show jumping. Some of them made the grade, some didn't. A very sweet Appaloosa gelding named Cheyenne turned out to suffer from narcolepsy, and actually fell asleep, or went into a coma, as he went over a jump, landing with a crash on the side. He always staggered to his feet looking embarrassed and perplexed—as if asking himself, "How on earth did *that* happen?"—but it tended to keep him from winning blue ribbons at events, and there was also a certain risk to the rider of a broken neck, so he went, to be replaced by a Dutch warmblood (Dutch warmbloods were very much in fashion among event competitors at the time) with some other problem. What they all had in common was they produced horse shit.

SOMEHOW it had never occurred to me to ask what we were going to do with manure once the manure pit was full. On a lot of horse farms, of course, they don't bother. When the pit is full, they dig a new pit next to it, and so on, but ours wasn't that kind of horse farm. Then too, it's not just horse shit, though there's a lot of that. It's also the bedding from the stalls—in our case, Margaret and Roxie being traditionalists, straw rather than wood shavings (you can't even give manure with wood shavings away to gardeners, who only want the kind with straw). Wet straw mixed with manure takes up a lot of space, and every night produces wheelbarrows full of it, steaming away on a cold day.

I had vaguely imagined that mushroom farmers would be beating a path to our door for our manure pile, but it turned out that the mushroom growers were mostly in Pennsylvania, and had plenty of local manure to draw on, so that was out, and although Asians from Poughkeepsie occasionally showed up out of the blue asking if we could let them have some of our manure for their vegetable gardens, they only took away a couple of tubs of it at most, whereas we had tons of the stuff. No matter how much they took away to put on their bok choy, it wasn't going to help us much.

In the end Harold solved the problem by bringing over his manure spreader and spreading the manure over our back fields, where it looked unsightly but eventually disappeared. That is the time-honored farmer's method—returning to the land what you've taken from it—

and there is a lot to be said for it, if you are a farmer. Farmers *like* the sight of a field covered in manure, and even enjoy the smell—it's money they're smelling, not manure, as they think of the crop coming up—whereas we tended to view our land as a kind of park to ride over and didn't much like to see tons of manure spread all over it, much of it in big, uneven clumps, since spreading manure evenly did not turn out to be Harold's greatest talent. Yes, eventually it would go, and eventually the grass would come back fuller and thicker (making more mowing for Harold, and thus providing, on an hourly basis, a classic win-win situation), but in the meantime it looked like hell. Besides, the manure spreader was a big piece of equipment, and towed behind Harold's Kubota tractor, it tended to catch on small trees and brushes and yank them right out of the soil—useful "whacking back" from Harold's point of view, but not from Margaret's.

In the long run, a solution was found on the nearby farm of Paul Wigsten, a transplanted New Yorker with Pleasant Valley roots who had taken over his grandparents' farm on Wigsten Road and was going into the business of raising gourmet organic vegetables. Wigsten was willing to take any amount of manure—he must have put tons of the stuff on his asparagus beds alone—and this took some of the pressure off. Even so, the manure pile had a kind of life of its own, requiring a small army of heavy machinery to keep it under control. At regular intervals the manure pit overflowed, and Margaret had to send out anguished SOS calls to everyone involved to get rid of it.

Indeed, it was the manure pit that made me hesitate to take on any more animals. Both Margaret and I had always admired Highland cattle; there were several herds within a few miles of us, and there was a part of me, certainly, that yearned to sit on the porch with a drink in my hand, looking at my own Highland cattle in the fields.

For those who don't know what they look like, Highland cattle have long, curving horns and a thick, shaggy, honey-colored coat that hangs all the way down to the ground in the winter, making them look like yaks, or old Victorian tasseled sofas on the move, and are only about half the size of normal cattle. In short, they're a very appealing breed, with soulful eyes, big wet noses, and the look of a child's drawing.

The problem is that they produce about the same quantity of cow pats as normal-size cattle—and you need to spend a fortune in fencing, since Highland cattle, just like their larger relatives (and unlike horses), enjoy spending their leisure time leaning against fences until they've knocked them over, so they can go wandering over the countryside finding more fences to destroy. Between the fencing and the cow manure, Highland cattle are a challenging proposition—far more so than the currently popular "exotic" livestock, like llamas, alpacas, and designer goats—but not less tempting to a certain kind of personality for that. Then too, while it may be very nice to look at them from the porch in the spring, or the summer, or the early fall, it has to be a whole different story dealing with them in the winter—say, on a morning when it's ten below zero, there's a whiteout blizzard raging, the help hasn't shown up for work, and they need to be fed and watered. . . . To this day, every time we pass by the nearest farm with Highland cattle on the way to Rhinebeck or Red Hook to go to the movies, I catch a gleam of desire in Margaret's eye and have to remind her of how hard it is to get rid of our manure pile as it is.

There's a certain symbiosis to country life—eventually most things, however improbable, get recycled in one form or another. When we built an indoor riding ring and were looking for the right kind of material to put down as footing, we started with one made of finely chopped old tires, which turned out to be pricey, dusty, and not a success, and eventually opted for shavings from a local broom factory, which seemed, upon use, to break up into just the surface Margaret was looking for. The old-timers may not have known the word "recycling," but they understood the concept, and had always practiced it.

Indeed, we recycled ourselves, in our own modest way. The pigs' droppings, for instance, when gathered by the Bacons for their vegetable garden, produced so many melons that we couldn't eat them all and had to give them away to everybody who stopped at the house, along with immense quantities of tomatoes and zucchini, none of which anybody in the country wants, since they already have too many of their own.

In the end Margaret grew rather proud of the manure pile, and would actually show it to visitors touring the property. The kaiser, she never failed to point out, had caused the royal apartments at Potsdam to be built above the stables; he believed the odor of horse manure to be healthy, and credited it for the fact that he never caught a cold. Most of our guests did not seem convinced by this, and many looked as if they wished they were back in the city, or had chosen to spend the weekend at some more conventional country house—one with a pool, say, or a tennis court, instead of a manure pile.

On all sides of us, our friends boasted just such amenities. To the north, near Hudson, the Buchmans not only had a pool and a tennis court but a pool house with a wet bar, a kitchen, and a steam room; to the south, in Cross River, Dick Snyder, then emerging as the boss of S&S, had not only the pool and tennis court but a system of specially made waterfalls and rock pools for his collection of fabulously expensive rare Japanese goldfish; only forty minutes away from us our friends Marvin Sloves and Thom von Buelow had a pergola under which they served elegant candlelit dinners. We had a manure pile, and while it can't be said that people came from far and wide to see it, it least it confirmed that we were real country people, not citified weekenders.

After all, a manure pile is the basic element of country living. You only have to walk past it and take a good, deep breath to know that you can't get more country than that!

CHAPTER FIFTEEN

The Wrong Deer

The Wrong deer

OF COURSE THE HARDEST PART about running a farm—or keeping a country house—is, inevitably, help. For years we were lucky—we had Dot Burnett, Harold's sister-in-law, in the house, and Roxie Bacon in the barn, and whenever we went out to dinner in the country people tended to sigh in envy, then say, "You're so lucky to have Dot!" or "You're so lucky to have Roxie!" and we knew it was true, especially when we heard other people's horror stories. We *were* lucky.

As the number of horses rose and Margaret began to evolve from being a pleasure rider who occasionally competed in a few local shows and events into a committed (and successful) event competitor, Roxie began to need a helper.

This was a difficult problem—it involved not only finding the right person but dealing with Roxie's belief that she could do it all herself, despite being a full-time wife and mother, now, of three small children. The truth was that she did not much welcome the presence of strangers in the barn, which, together with the paneled tack room that Richard had built, was kept spotlessly clean, with everything exactly where Roxie wanted it. The phrase "a place for everything and everything in its place" might have been coined to describe Roxie's barn, and one could have eaten off the floor of the aisle, had one chosen to, so it was not easy to find her an assistant.

Horses thrive on a routine, and dislike it very much when their routine is upset by even the most minor change. Roxie's routine was ironclad, which suited the horses as well as her—since the barn was not more than fifty yards from the house, it was possible to look out a window and tell the time of day by what Roxie was doing in the barn, so regular and precise was her schedule. You didn't need a watch or a clock.

This, like the manure pile, tended to set our house apart from those of our friends, many of whom came to the country for the weekends precisely to escape from the demands of routine and schedules. They got up late, pottered around antiquing in the local stores, had long lunches, did a little gardening, or took a late afternoon snooze, whereas our lives in the country were more or less determined by the rigid schedule of the barn. *We* got up early to get the riding over early in the day, and much of the rest of Margaret's day after riding was still determined by the horses. In the summer she would lead them down to the back fields to graze, riding one of them bareback with a rope halter (often wearing only her bikini), while the rest followed along like well-behaved children; then, after tea, she would bring them back, to be groomed and fed before Roxie went home. Barn check was a fixed ritual, performed by Roxie every evening except on her day off, when Margaret would do it, going out to the fields to check on the horses for the night in the summer, or picking out the stalls in the winter, while the horses peacefully chewed their hay and made soft, blowing noises of contentment.

In addition to this daily routine, there were the regular visits of the feed man, the hay and straw man, the vet, and the blacksmith. The blacksmith was a major figure in our lives, of course. Hard as it is to find and keep a good vet, getting a good blacksmith to shoe your horses rivals getting an appointment with a fashionable Fifth Avenue cosmetic surgeon, or even surpasses it, in difficulty. A blacksmith is no blue-collar worker in iron and aluminum—the good ones are artists at what they do, like chefs, and can make the difference between a lame horse and a sound one. The really good ones are constantly on the move from one client to another in their specially equipped truck, and even fly down to Florida, or North Carolina, or Kentucky to shoe clients' horses there. And it isn't enough to have a blacksmith who turns up regularly on schedule to shoe the horses every four or five weeks—he has to be able to come in a hurry when there's an emergency, if a horse throws a shoe, for example, or has a hoof problem. We were fortunate that we eventually ended up in the hands of a real artist, Tom Pavelek, and his visit too became a fixed part of our routine—one saw the truck arrive, then heard the ancient, familiar noise of the forge and the hammering of hot metal against the anvil, sounds that might have been heard unaltered in any Roman encampment.

There was a certain idyllic quality to it all, not to be found at the homes of people who didn't live on a farm, a sense that one lived to some degree to the rhythm of the seasons and the animals, a degree of peace that you can't find in a pool or on a tennis court. Somehow, country living tends to put other things in perspective—whatever your own personal problems may be, the geese will arrive and depart at the same time every year, the Vandenkamps' cattle will come in from the fields on schedule (*they* don't need a watch to tell them what time it is), each of our horses would have its head sticking out over the top of its stall door expectantly at exactly seven-thirty in the morning, when Roxie arrives, come good weather or the storm of the century, to get the morning feed ready. Life goes on, in its own placid way and at its own pace, and you might as well slow down to match your own to that of the seasons and the animals, which perhaps explains why, by and large in the country, the phrase "eleven in the morning," when it refers to an appointment, can mean any time between, say, nine o'clock and lunchtime. Who's counting? The concept of *mañana* is by no means limited to Mexico—it thrives in most of upstate New York, though not, it almost goes without saying, in our barn.

Barn help is by nature temporary. Young women do it for a while, then move on, usually just after they've settled into the job and you've grown used to them. We've had young women in our barn whose résumés have contained everything including topless dancing, teaching, and cooking, but barn work is backbreaking labor; it may seem to have its attractions on a warm, sunny spring morning, but it's a whole different story when it's twenty below and snowing, and you have to break the ice in the horses' buckets before they can drink.

Despite the hard work—caring for horses hasn't changed much, if at all, in several thousand years, and still involves the shovel, the pitchfork, and the wheelbarrow, not to speak of hauling fifty-pound bales of hay and endless buckets of water—it's mostly young women who want to work with horses these days; very few men want to do it anymore other than Mexican immigrants, many of whom don't speak English or know anything about horses or have a green card, and therefore offer the prospective employer three different ways of getting into trouble.

During Roxie's first pregnancy we brought Margaret's goddaughter Tamzin over from England, and later her sister, but that was hardly a long-term solution, and over the years we went through a good many people. A certain urgency made itself felt when the Bacons told us they were looking for a house of their own—with three children, they needed a larger place than our little house down the road, and perhaps more important, they wanted to put down roots and own their own house rather than living, however financially advantageous it was, as our tenants. When they found a place they liked, across the river, it meant that Roxie would no longer be a two-minute walk from our barn in case of an emergency, which meant we needed to find a reliable, experienced adult, somebody to be relied on if things went wrong.

Eventually Margaret settled on Lee Matheson, a sturdy blond woman, to move into the tenant house and be Roxie's understudy. She was pleasant, hardworking, responsible, grown-up, and, Margaret assured me, good with animals. I nodded vaguely. The barn was Margaret's area, and I appeared there only to get on my horse in the morning, or in moments of great crisis. If Margaret and Roxie were agreed on Lee Matheson, I had no doubt they were right. I did notice, whenever her name was mentioned, that the fact that she was good with animals came up again and again, like a mantra. Even people who were outside the horse world, so to speak, would say, "I hear you guys hired Lee Matheson—she sure is good with animals."

I didn't give this much thought. In the country most people are "good with animals," or at any rate pretty used to them. Our vet's wife, for example, Dale Mountan, creator of the Jack Russell calendar, owned between six and twelve Jack Russells—her truck, usually a big utility vehicle, actually seemed to shake, rattle, and roll when she parked it, from the sheer energy and frenzied barking of all the dogs it contained—while the Lynns, a couple who bought a nearby horse farm, kept about a dozen cats in their house, all strays, most of them with some life-threatening disease or injury, and in need of constant nursing; they bought kitty litter by the truckload. Just below our neighbors the Vandencamps, a couple lived with donkeys and a flock of guinea hens—perhaps the noisiest imaginable combination—while over in Millbrook there was a man who had whole herds of alpacas and llamas. Down the road from us was a young couple whose menagerie included a children's pony, a Great Dane, several small, yappy terriers, innumerable cats and kittens (there was nearly always a Free Kittens sign taped to their mailbox), not to speak of chickens, domestic geese, and ducks—and that was only what you could see from the road! Even farther down the road was a large pond with a resident population of very large and aggressive domestic geese, who had learned to surround every car that stops at the T junction in front of their pond, where a conveniently placed stop sign gave them a perfect spot for ambushing motorists. Presumably somebody must have rolled down the window and fed them at some point—in any case, they acted like highway robbers, waddling out quite swiftly for such large and ungainly birds, firmly blocking drivers from turning right or left, or even backing up. At their best, geese are ill-tempered birds, but these geese had a nasty streak, and a mean look in their black, beady eyes. Failure to feed them made them hiss and peck away at the paint of your car, and honking at them merely provoked them to greater fury. Next to the geese was the farm of a local printer who raised draft horses, huge gentle animals with hooves the size of dinner plates, which he sometimes trotted down the road, pulling a carriage. There was no shortage of people on all side of us with every kind of animal.

Gradually, however, it dawned on me that Lee was something special, in a class by herself. Of course she had horses, dogs, cats, all the usual things—not to speak of a grown-up daughter, Jessie, and a much younger boyfriend who looked like an outlaw biker but was in fact rather shy and sweet—but she was also a certified New York State wildlife rehabilitator, which meant that she could keep at home all those animals that you're not supposed to—that would otherwise be illegal to have, in fact. When people found a fawn whose mother had been shot, or baby raccoons who had lost their mother, or a baby crow that had fallen out of its nest, or anything else in the way of lost, orphaned, or wounded wildlife, they called Lee. The only things she wasn't supposed to deal with were raptors—hawks and eagles—which had to be handed over to a raptor rehabilitator, who would do what he could to save them, then turn them out in the wild when they were strong enough, or old enough, to survive on their own.

Of course Lee was supposed to turn her charges back out into the wild too—that's the whole point of rehabilitation, and the reason why the state doesn't allow well-meaning citizens to turn wild animals into pets. In the meantime, however, her house—our house, actually, into which she and her boyfriend Randy soon moved—became home to a growing menagerie of animals about which I received reports from time to time from Margaret. When I finally went over with her to pay a visit, I was astonished—there was a baby deer, a tortoise, two baby raccoons, innumerable birds, a skunk, all of them friendly and well behaved, and living in reasonable harmony with the domestic animals. The baby raccoons were alarmingly friendly, and enjoyed climbing on Margaret's shoulder and playing with her hair.

My own taste for hands-on experiences with wild animals—or domestic ones, for that matter—is rather less enthusiastic than Margaret's. I am happy to watch, but all things considered I can live without having two baby raccoons playing with my hair, or playing hide-and-seek in my pockets. Still, even I had to admit that there was something charming about the whole scene, though I had no particular desire to replicate it in my own home.

Every once in a while, however, I would receive a bulletin from the rehabilitation front. It was always heartening to hear of the rescue of some small damaged creature, though few of these stories, I began to discover, had happy endings. Animals returned to the wild were often killed by predators or turned on by their own species, and not all of them thrived successfully in captivity, however loved and cosseted. The raccoons, once they were past the Stieffel-stuffed-toy cuddly-cute stage and big enough to live outside, were placed in a fenced-in field with their own little house, but a bigger predator, a coyote perhaps, or more likely an adult male raccoon (male raccoons, however cute they look, have strong territorial instincts and, like lions and most other predators, a deep dislike of other males' offspring), managed to get in, killing one and savaging the other, which was very depressing to everybody.

When Lee managed to rescue another fawn that had been left motherless by a hunter or a careless driver, she decided to keep it in one of the stalls in our barn. Margaret didn't mind. The horses accepted the tiny newcomer easily enough—they liked deer a lot more than they liked pigs—and for a while the barn had something of the appearance of the Peaceable Kingdom, though admittedly there was no lion lying down with the lamb. The fawn quickly won everyone's affection and seemed to fit in very nicely—a baby deer, perhaps because of *Bambi*, can tug at the heartstrings of even those who aren't sentimental about animals, not that there was anybody in that category in Margaret's barn. I could foresee—having read *Bambi*—many tears ahead of us, particularly when the fawn was old enough to be returned to the wild, but in the meantime it seemed a sensible and happy temporary arrangement.

One evening, as we were dressing to go to dinner in Rhinebeck, a cry came from the barn, where Lee was checking on the horses. Margaret went down to see what the problem was, and came back with bad news—Lee's deer had escaped. I sighed and hurried to finish dressing. Dinner, I could foresee, would have to wait until we had found the deer and returned it to the barn—no simple task, since daylight was fading fast. Guests would be waiting for us in Rhinebeck, but I could see from the expression on Margaret's face that we weren't going anywhere until the deer was safely back in its stall—live with a real animal lover, and you get to know pretty quickly when the situation is nonnegotiable. I had once, at Margaret's urging, picked up a stray kitten while I was riding, and it bit through my glove so deeply that I had to go to the emergency room at the hospital in Tarrytown (where Margaret herself would be taken, after Grits broke her leg) for a tetanus shot. I had once braked to avoid a raccoon in the middle of Route 9 one rainy, foggy night because Margaret would have been upset had we hit it, with the result that I went into a skid and put the car straight into a steel barrier, while the raccoon walked away calmly, unscathed. We weren't going to have dinner until the deer was found; I knew that.

I hurried to provide us all with flashlights, and we rushed off to the barn to form a search party. There was no sign of Lee's deer in any of the paddocks behind the barn, so we gradually moved down to the last fence line, then beyond into thin woods that led steeply downhill to a small stream (which Harold had been eager to dam, but settled for building a bridge so we didn't have to splash through when we went out riding). The air was full of insects, which I swatted at ineffectually while searching through the undergrowth for the deer, trying as hard as I could to avoid poison ivy, to which I am fiercely allergic. I glanced at my watch—it seemed to me likely that we would be very late for dinner. I hoped the people we were meeting would have the good sense to order. From above me, I could hear the others forming a line like old-fashioned beaters at a pheasant shoot and making soothing noises, their flashlights winking through the woods.

It was quite dark now. Every once in a while I would set off something, a rabbit, perhaps, or some nocturnal animal, but there was no sign of the deer. How far, I wondered, would a fawn that was used to humans wander? Surely its instinct would be to return to the barn, not to move farther away from it? Then, all of a sudden, my flashlight beam reflected off two shining eyes, not more than three or four feet away, in a bush.

I looked closer, and saw the deer standing there, trembling slightly. The poor thing looked terrified, presumably because it had wandered away from its temporary home and was now lost in the woods. I memorized the spot—I did not think the deer would move—and went back up toward the fence line until I could make out the dark shapes of a couple of people. I whispered to warn them that the missing deer was very close to us. Margaret went off down the hill with somebody else, and I was happy to leave the deer to them—short of throwing my jacket over it, I didn't have a clue how to get my hands on it, and the last thing I wanted to do was to hurt it.

Eventually, the deer was surrounded, calmed as much as possible, and carried carefully back up to the barn. I went on ahead, and, to my surprise, found Lee waiting outside the sliding doors at the back of the barn. It occurred to me to wonder why she wasn't out there in the dark, looking for her deer, but before I could ask, she gave me a big smile, full of relief. "It's okay," she said. "She's back in her stall, poor thing. She must have been terrified once she was out of it, because I found her hiding right on the other side of the barn. I was just going out to tell everybody to stop searching and come on in."

I looked into the stall, and there stood the fawn, peacefully eating. It looked just like the one that had escaped, all right. It also looked pretty much the same as the one we had found in the woods, and which was just being carried into the barn by Roxie and Margaret.

We had the wrong deer.

The newcomer, of course, had to be carried back out to where we had found it, and left there. It didn't seem upset or frightened now, though no doubt it was puzzled. I worried that its mother might refuse to have anything to do with it—animals very often reject young that have been handled by human beings—but the next day we saw a deer with a fawn very near to our fence line, and since it seemed improbable that we had more than one on our property, we decided that mother and child had been reunited after the kidnapping.

To this day I remain skeptical of amateur attempts to alter the course of nature—not that I'm not sympathetic whenever Margaret is tempted to rescue something. It's just that it's very hard to know if you're doing the right thing when you interfere with Mother Nature, or to guess what the consequences will be.

We put out cracked corn in the winter to feed the wild turkeys and the deer, and it's hard to imagine that's likely to upset the balance of nature, but we don't put out food for the coyote, of which we have quite a few. Is it because they're meat eaters, scavengers, or perhaps more sensibly because we don't want to encourage them to hang about the house, where they are only too likely to go for one of the cats? For whatever reasons, we pick and choose which species we're going to help, and which we're not.

All the same, when Lee and her family finally moved away to a home of their own, I missed the news bulletins from the animal rehabilitation front—even when it *did* involve rescuing the wrong deer.

CHAPTER SIXTEEN

The White Stuff

UNTIL WE MOVED UPSTATE, I'd never given much thought to snow.

I don't mean that I was unfamiliar with snow. I went to school in Switzerland, so I had plenty of experience with the stuff in large quantities, but in Gstaad, high in the Berner Oberland, snow was thought of mostly in terms of skiing, and the more of it, the better.

The Swiss don't fight snow, the way Americans do; they simply learn to live with it. Take roads, for instance, or driveways: instead of plowing the snow away until they reach the road surface, then putting down salt, the Swiss simply drive on the snow. With every snowfall the road level rises, and of course it is necessary to drive slowly, carefully, with both hands on the steering wheel and chains on all four wheels, but then the Swiss aren't exactly daredevil drivers even when there isn't any snow, so life goes on—it just takes longer to get where you are going.

Of course it sometimes snows in New York City too, and very occasionally a blizzard will paralyze the city for days, stranding buses and burying parked cars, but it doesn't happen often—indeed, New Yorkers tend to date other events by these rare big snowstorms—and unless you own a car that is parked in the street, or don't own a good pair of waterproof boots, a snowstorm is a minor inconvenience at worst. Besides, however much it snows in New York City, it isn't the responsibility of the average citizen to do anything about it—that's the job of the mayor, and the Department of Sanitation, certainly not *my* worry.

The first clue I had that things were different in Pleasant Valley was when we bought the house. I noticed that each section of the cedar shingles of the roof was crisscrossed in a big "V" pattern by what looked very much like long extension cords that plugged into outlets set just above the gutters. What was all that? I asked Tom Kirchhoff, pointing at it. Tom shook his head. I would be better off having all that junk removed, Tom said—his guys could do it. Old Mr. Hubner had put up electric heating wires to melt the snow and ice off the roof, but in Tom's experience they didn't do the job, and besides they were dangerous; there was always the possibility of fire or a short circuit—in short, it was one of those solutions beloved of your typical do-it-yourselfer like Hubner that caused more trouble than the problem itself. You got rid of the snow and ice but risked burning down your house.

Was snow and ice on a roof a big problem up here? I asked. Tom stared into space—I had not signed the contract yet, and he didn't want to scare me off—still, he owed me a reasonable answer to the question. Well, he said, there was no denying you got your share of the white stuff up here, but you just had to use your common sense, that was all. Worst comes to worst, you could always get up on the roof and brush the snow off, if it was a really big snowfall, sure, but I'd probably never need to.

I looked up at the roof and tried to imagine standing on it with a broom trying to brush snow off. I put the picture out of my mind. On the way home, I noticed that where the Poughkeepsie city limits began—unlike rural Pleasant Valley, Poughkeepsie had a city water system—some of the fire hydrants had long red rods sticking up from them like radio antennae, maybe about six feet high, with a tiny metal flag at the top. I had seen these before, and wondered vaguely what they were, but it now suddenly dawned on me that they were for snow, so that the firefighters could find the hydrants even if there was six feet of snow on the ground. The thought came to me that a bad winter's day in Dutchess County might involve something more serious than a greater difficulty than usual in finding a taxi, or having to slip a pair of galoshes over one's Gucci loafers to go to lunch.

This prediction would soon be justified by events. In the meantime, a further warning note was given by Richard Bacon, when we first met him. Had we made arrangements for snowplowing? he wanted to know. The thought hadn't even occurred to me, I was ashamed to admit, and was happy to agree that Richard should buy a used snowplow and have it fitted to his old Scout. He too was dubious about the wires on the roof, and took them down for us as well as finding, in one of the disused chicken houses, the dozens of storm windows that we were going to need, and that I hadn't though to ask Tom Kirchhoff about—who has storm windows in a New York City apartment? (It almost goes without saying that although most of the storm windows had little numbered lead disks that were supposed to match similar disks set into the window frames, since no two windows in the house were the same size or shape; most of the corresponding disks on the window frames had been removed at some point, so putting up the storm windows was like a gigantic jigsaw puzzle that had to be put together while standing on a ladder.)

Still, the full meaning of the word "snow" didn't strike me until we woke up one Sunday in November—way ahead of every prediction—to an ominous dead silence broken only by the noise of the big snowplows and sanders out working on the roads. I turned on the radio. The Taconic Parkway was closed, there was a litany of closings (including Sunday schools), and more snow was reported to be on the way. Then the radio went out, along with everything else electric—a car, as we later discovered, had skidded into a telephone pole on our road, breaking the power cable (in Pleasant Valley, real men don't believe in snow tires, despite ample evidence every winter to the contrary).

So we settled in for a cozy snowbound Sunday, which at first seemed idyllic but rapidly, as we got tired of doing without light, heat, the stove, or being able to flush the toilets or have a bath, began to lose its charm.

At some point in the day it dawned on me that this snow was *my* responsibility, not the mayor of New York's, which is not to say that I could stop it or make it go away any more than His Honor could, but in the future it would be up to me, say, to get a path dug from our front door to the driveway, or make sure we owned a battery-powered radio, or keep up a stream of calls to Central Hudson to find out when we could expect the electricity to come back on, not that anybody at Central Hudson was picking up the phone, needless to say. . . . So long as Richard Bacon was around, I could be sure that the basics would be taken care of, but still, there it was: deep down where it counted, it was my snow, and my problem.

With Richard's help, I drew up a list of things that we might need to keep on hand—fortunately, I had already put steel-studded snow tires on the car (illegal in our state, but very effective)—and was soon to discover that no matter how well-thought-out your shopping list is, it doesn't matter, since everybody waits until the first snowstorm of the year before buying what they need, so anything you might want to buy is out of stock. All the same, it was an impressive list: snow shovels, a snowblower, bags of salt, snow and ice scrapers for the cars, as well as tow cables and jumper cables, heat tape for the pipes most likely to freeze, hot air blowers and heat lamps for larger areas like the crawl spaces under the kitchen, a battery-powered portable radio, flashlights, lanterns, enough spare batteries in every conceivable size for a polar expedition, spiked contraptions—rather like medieval torture devices—that could be buckled onto one's boots to prevent slipping on ice, chemical foot and hand warmers, a scavenger pump in case of a sudden thaw, purse-size spray cans of whatever it took to unfreeze frozen car locks, and big bags of sand and extra kitty litter to put in the trunk of the car in case we got stuck (according to local lore, these were also useful in increasing traction on the rear wheels, which is why any serious accident in the winter up here leaves long trails of kitty litter on the road).

The list left me in no doubt that winter north of New York City is a serious business, and I was mildly grateful that the first early snowstorm had given me a much-needed heads-up to start preparing for the next five or six months—for just as there were early snowstorms, like this one, there were late snowstorms to worry about too, with stories of huge snowdrifts and blocked roads on Easter Sunday.

Harold Roe, an inveterate reader of *The Farmer's Almanac*, perhaps the most pessimistic publication in the world, was a fountain of knowledge on the subject of past and future winters. At the drop of a hat he would stop what he was doing to regale us with horror stories of winters past: when the Hudson froze over so solid you could drive a truck across it; when roofs collapsed under the weight of snow, suffocating people in their beds; when snowdrifts blocked the roads for days on end and National Guard helicopters dropped bales of hay for cattle. He also had plenty of gloomy predictions of worse to come, if *The Farmer's Almanac* was to be believed. "There it is, right there in black and white!" Harold would shout triumphantly, producing from his pocket a well-thumbed copy full of bad news for everyone except the local snowmobiler community and hibernating bears. It would be the coldest winter on record since 1940, or 1840, it wasn't clear which; Christmas would bring arctic conditions and huge snowfalls; we would still be shoveling snow and chipping away at ice in March, possibly even at Easter, Harold predicted with glee. "Better bring out that long underwear," he recommended—his own, he gave us to understand, was already on, November 15 being his date for making that change. Better safe than sorry, was his motto.

But the truth was, the first winter wasn't so bad. It was cold all right, there was a good deal of snow, the electricity failed more often than I would have thought possible in a civilized country, and we discovered that certain rooms—and certain areas in other rooms—simply couldn't be heated, wouldn't warm up even if you cranked the thermostat up to ninety, and that here and there where some plumbing genius had placed the pipes too close to an uninsulated wall they were guaranteed to freeze the moment the thermometer dropped. The local Caldor had a sale on cheap electric space heaters, and we bought half a dozen of them, put them as close to the cold spots as we could, plugged them in, and let 'em rip, despite many childhood warnings on the dangers of unattended electric fires, and they helped a lot, to the extent that you didn't need to wear gloves and an overcoat in the kitchen anymore. At least it was a sharp, clean cold that, when it was windy, cut like a knife, unlike the milder but damp and bone-chilling winter cold of postwar England, when people had huddled in front of a single, dark red bar of the electric fire for warmth and struggled home through greasy, soot-flecked fog.

Still, winter is winter, and while Harold Roe's worst prognostications didn't all come true, we learned to have a certain respect for the approach of white stuff in any large quantity. We got used to the endless problems of frozen pipes and frozen gutters, and to mornings when the purse-size de-icer spray came in right handy, but it was the days when there was no going down to the Taconic to the city, or coming up it, and the mornings when we did in fact have to get up on the roofs and push the snow off that gave us a healthy respect for snow. True, there was a certain coziness to being up in the country when snow fell, but there was a sense of isolation as well, a feeling that it would be a risky business just to drive down to the Grand Union supermarket in Pleasant Valley, less than a mile away, let alone to New York City; that we were, in fact, marooned.

We never took up snowmobiling, to Harold's disappointment—two minutes on a snowmobile was enough for me—but we learned the pleasure of riding across an untouched field of snow on a horse the morning after a snowfall, or of trotting down the road in the early morning, before the snowplows had cleared it. The horses seemed to enjoy snow too—they huffed and puffed and snorted, breathing out great puffs of steam from their nostrils, apparently delighted at the way their hooves sent the powdery fresh snow flying. Out there, in the silent country, there was a sharp, sudden pleasure at the sight of a red fox moving across the snow in the early morning, or, close to the house, that of a male cardinal feeding off birdseed on the snow beneath the kitchen window—a splash of vivid bright red against pure white. City dwellers for many years, we had forgotten what snow looked like when it *didn't* turn black, sooty, and grimy overnight; our fields were spotlessly white, and stayed that way, except where a predator had caught some hapless creature and left a few drops of blood and a flurry of tiny footprints at the crime scene.

Sometimes it almost seemed enjoyable, the snow, especially when you could shake it off, get inside, and warm up in front of a fire with a cup of tea in your hands, but it was impossible to ignore its immense potential for screwing things up. It wasn't just a question of stopping the commuter trains, or blocking off the Taconic so you couldn't get down to the city for an important appointment—these were minor things, after all. It was the sheer difficulty of dealing with livestock when the snow drifted up to the top of their fence line, or turned to ice, so they ran a constant risk of slipping and breaking a leg, that made one long for spring and understand why dairy farmers yearned to sell out to real-estate developers and move south to Florida, and why so many of their children ran away from home by the age of sixteen, usually to go south or to California, where you didn't need to own snow tires or snow shovels or have to get up at three in the morning to milk the cows on a day when the windchill factor made it feel like fifty below. . . .

The pigs, to our surprise, didn't seem to mind snow much—they huddled together for warmth and grew thick, bristly coats that made them look even more prehistoric. On the other hand, it was hard to keep them watered when their water bucket kept freezing over, and they were too far away from the barn for us to run an outdoor extension cable to them so they could have a heater in their water, which meant a lot of buckets to be carried in the freezing cold.

Eventually, all this kind of thing would get sorted out, by trial, error, and common sense—the horses got run-in sheds so they could shelter from the snow or the rain and electrically heated water feeders in their fields, the pigs got a ready-made shed, we learned that the first thing we had to do after a storm was to run the snowblower down to each field to make a path, then from the barn down to the manure pile, so you could get a wheelbarrow down there and back. Still, there was always a sense, when the snow started, that you never knew how much you were going to get, and that no matter how well prepared you thought you were, you might not be well prepared enough.

Plenty of people weren't, even old-timers and fourth- or fifth-generation locals who might have been thought to know better. Harold, never far removed from his trusty police band radio, brought us all the local bad news on those days when he wasn't off with his elderly pals cutting up a storm on snowmobiles—so-and-so's house caught fire, he would tell us gleefully, because they was using a space heater, and the fire department couldn't get there because the drifts was too high; so-and-so had a heart attack feeding his cows and by the time they discovered him his body was frozen solid, except where the coyotes had chewed on him; old Mrs. So-and-so couldn't get through the snow to get her medication renewed, and went off her head, right there in her own house; the so-and-sos slipped right off the road into a ditch on their way to potluck supper at the Masonic temple, despite Harold having told them a thousand times to put a couple of sacks of sand in the trunk to weigh the back down. . . .

To listen to Harold was to get the idea that Dutchess County was a winter war zone, and while of course that was true enough, connoisseurs of winter misery were quick to point out that *real* winter didn't begin until you were north of Albany—Fort Drum, up near the Canadian border, was so cold that the United States Army used it for arctic warfare training, and Buffalo, out to the west, had a well-deserved reputation as the snowfall champion of the eastern United States. From the point of view of New Yorkers who lived in Schenectady, Syracuse, Troy, or the Adirondacks, Poughkeepsie might as well have been Palm Beach. "Shoot!" people in Binghamton were inclined to say, when they heard where you were from—"Down there in the south, you think a *foot* of snow is a lot!" All the same, there was no denying it: New York State had plenty of winter, enough for everyone, and while it certainly got worse the farther north you went, Dutchess County residents didn't need to hang their heads in shame when it came to cold weather, or when comparing notes about it with somebody who lived, say, in Utica. There were days, indeed, when it seemed that the entire population of the county—perhaps due to the local prejudice against snow tires—was sliding off the roads at the same time.

Our own road seemed to turn into a skating rink at the first sign of snow, and also had an unfortunate tendency to attract dense banks of fog, so we could usually tell how serious a storm was in its early stages by the number of people who hit our privacy fencing. If more than three people turned up at the front door during the course of an evening with a dazed look on their face to ask if we'd mind their making a call to the sheriffs or for a tow truck, you could count on six inches to a foot of snow by dawn, as well as several hundred dollars' worth of fence repair. Even though we knew the road intimately, there were nights when it was as featureless as the arctic wastes and you had to creep along in first gear, with the passenger leaning out of the window, trying to keep the edge of the road in view and figure out where it ended and the fields began, this being caused in part by a strong local reluctance to waste good money putting cat's eyes or reflective lines on county roads. Let the state waste money on that kind of thing! was the local view when it came to marking roads, so much so that it sometimes seemed possible that highway superintendents owned tow-truck companies and operated like the wreckers on the Cornish coast, who used to lure ships onto the rocks with false lights, then pillage the wrecks. On the other hand, it may also have been a combination of stubborn conservatism and stupidity, neither of which was in particularly short supply.

The amazing thing was that the house stood up to it. Gales that brought down trees from one end of the county to the other did not lift a single cedar shake from the roof; rainstorms biblical in proportion were nevertheless absorbed by gutters built back when the United States was young; snow that made the owners of brand-new lockup storage units tremble for fear of their roofs collapsing didn't give us any problems at all—unless you consider standing on a slippery, steeply slanted, icy roof in a twenty-mile-per-hour gale with a broom in your hands a problem. On bad days, when snow was banked outside up to the level of the doorknob, the house survived unscathed. Admittedly, gusts of snow came pouring in from badly sealed doors and gaps in the window frames; admittedly, since the Founding Fathers had never heard of insulation, certain parts of the house, including one or two of the bathrooms, could have been used for meat storage; admittedly, given all the electric heaters, hot-air fans, and heating tape we were running, our electric bill in the winter resembled that of a small arctic nation—Finland perhaps, or Iceland—but all things considered, the people who had built the house had looked Old Man Winter in the eye and knew how to deal with him, though my guess was that people in the late eighteenth and early nineteenth centuries probably spent a lot of time indoors bundled up in bed, which might explain the high birth rate.

From time to time snow got the best of us. I remember being stuck halfway up the Taconic, unable to drive farther north, nor for the moment to go back south to the city either; I remember creeping home from dinner across the river one night with Margaret, in a blizzard that almost buried my car—even with snow tires, the Porsche wasn't the ideal snow vehicle—creeping at four or five miles an hour up hills that in normal circumstances we would hardly even have noticed; I remember an early snowstorm, before the trees had lost their leaves, when we stood outside in tears listening to cracks like cannon shots as all around us big trees, unable to bear the weight of the snow, collapsed and fell, and the awful helplessness of knowing that there was nothing we could do about it. . . .

Yet snow, we came to understand, was a shared experience, and each heavy snowfall somehow made us more firmly a part of the community. Snowstorms, like the Blitz in London, tend to bring out the best in people and bind them together. You get to know the drill. When you hear the news on the radio the night before, you get out the flashlights and make sure your boots and heavy mittens are where you can find them. In the early morning you open the door—if you can *get* it open, of course—and look out to see how much snow there is. Sometimes you get off lightly—a sigh of relief and another cup of coffee. Other times, there it is, by God, *tons* of the stuff. You struggle into warm clothes, a wool cap, goggles, mittens, boots, then stomp through the snow to the shed where the snowblower is kept. There's always a moment of hesitation as you pull on the starter; then the engine coughs and roars into life, and you're on your way—though after a few minutes of pushing the machine back and forth on its little rubber caterpillar treads even the toughest hands tend to freeze solid, like claws. About the time you get finished is when your snowplow guy turns up and undoes a good deal of what you've done, ignoring your hand signals completely. You also try to overlook the fact that the snowplow picks up all the gravel from the driveway and redistributes it onto the lawns, from which it will have to be swept, come spring. Eventually, once you hear the big sanders go by, you make your way cautiously (*you* may have snow tires, but an awful lot of other people don't) down to Pleasant Valley to shop for whatever little is left at the Grand Union (even the prediction of a small snowstorm turns people into maddened hoarders who can strip whole sections of a supermarket bare while you're still sitting at home with a drink in hand, listening to the evening news). Then somebody you know only slightly, by face perhaps rather than name, comes up to you in the pet food aisle (where everything our cats like has already been bought, leaving only things they wouldn't eat if they were starving) and says, "How are you folks making out up there at the old Hubner place? Is everything okay?" in a voice that tells you that he actually *means* it, that he really cares, that if you *did* have a problem he would do his best to help, that we are all in this together, and you feel as if you belong in a way you hardly ever feel when there isn't a crisis or a problem, and the roads are clear, and the supermarket hasn't been emptied as if by a marauding army. . . .

Really, it's almost worth it, I tell myself—it's *almost* possible to pity those who live farther south, below the snowbelt. So I persuade myself every year; and one of these days—who knows?—I may succeed.

CHAPTER SEVENTEEN

Viva Zapata!

SOMEHOW FOXHUNTING, right from the beginning, failed to hook us. Maybe we just weren't cut out to think of ourselves as "gentry"—Pleasant Valley, unlike nearby Millbrook, was rather more full of potential *tricoteuses* than of aristocrats. Or perhaps it was reverse snobbery—the local foxhunters simply didn't seem to Margaret the kind of gentry she had grown up surrounded by, or considered herself to be. Certainly they were not the kind of hard-riding, fast-living people I associated with foxhunting, and their relationship with their nonfoxhunting neighbors was less squirearchical than testy and self-defensive. They were, in fact, a beleaguered minority, and like most beleaguered minorities they alternated between arrogance and a desperate desire to please, the latter taking the form of unlikely attempts to show the community that foxhunting was democratic, environmentally sound, a great American sport, and good fun for the fox, none of which, as it happens, I believe.

Perhaps inevitably, therefore, Margaret was drawn into competition instead, beginning with the odd local "hunter pace" and moving on to small local horse shows. It had escaped my attention somehow that she was fiercely competitive, perhaps because, unlike my ex-wife, she wasn't interested in competing with *me*, but the very first time she arrived home in triumph with a blue ribbon, I could see that this was going to be more than a passing phase—despite years of world travel, modeling, and giving dinner parties, she had apparently always been a competitive athlete waiting for the opportunity to get out there and win, and determined to make up for all those wasted years of entertaining, high living, and posing for the camera.

After a couple of times as a spectator, I resumed an old interest in photography, not so much out of any passionate need to take photographs as because I discovered that unless you have something in your hands at a horse show, you will quickly be handed a horse to hold, or worse still, a brush or a bucket. For a brief period we toyed with the notion that I might compete too. My big chestnut quarter horse, Hustle, was a gifted jumper—a good deal more gifted than I—but I didn't get much pleasure from riding in horse shows, and always found I got enough competition in the normal course of a working week without having to drum up more opportunities to compete on the weekend. Eventually I had to replace poor Hustle, who developed cancer, with a lively little dapple-gray quarter horse called Handsome Devil (perhaps not a good sign, now that I look back on it), whom we renamed Zapata.

For a small horse, Zapata had a remarkably thick, muscular neck, like that of a stallion, which, had I thought about it, I might have recognized as a sign of trouble. A "backyard horse" who had lived with one family and been ridden by the daughter most of his life, he was used to getting his own way, and the general opinion was that he had been "cut," i.e.

gelded, a little later than he should have been, which tends to leave horses with a few of the stubborn and rambunctious habits of stallions.

Indeed, Zapata turned out to have a mind of his own, to put it mildly. He had the build—and the temperament—of a small tank. Unlike Grits, with her marish ways, Zapata wasn't particularly nasty—kicking or biting wasn't necessarily his thing—but he didn't respond well to taking orders from his rider, and he took a certain devilish pleasure in doing the unexpected and sending his rider flying. Horses are said to have "a good mouth" when they respond sensitively to the bit, and "a bad mouth," or even "no mouth," when they do not. Zapata was definitely in the latter category—you could pull the reins until you thought your arms were going to pop out of their sockets without slowing him down or stopping him, if he didn't want to slow down or stop. Conversely, if he didn't want to move forward, no amount of squeezing him with your legs, or even kicking him, would move him one step forward.

He was a pretty good jumper, but you could never be sure whether he was going to jump a fence or change his mind at the last second and come to a screeching halt, sending you flying over his neck like a launched missile; and certain things, like ditches, he simply would not jump, even with Roxie on his back, or better yet, on foot behind him with a whip. Even two people behind him, with whips and a length of rope to put behind his hind end to *pull* him over the ditch, were not guaranteed to do it—"He no do ditches," we took to saying, though every once in a while Zapata would confound us by jumping a ditch with no fuss at all, as if just to show he could.

Zapata was full of tricks, some amiable, some not. Short and compact, he could drop a shoulder so quickly that you came off before you even had time to notice you were airborne. He was small enough that you didn't feel that it was a long way down to the ground, but when you went sailing past his head unexpectedly, it did seem like a long way down. He did this to me early in our relationship, with consequences for my right rotator cuff that keep orthopedists and physical therapists interested and prosperous to this day. He wasn't one of those horses that ran for the barn the moment he had ditched his rider. Usually he stopped, took a good look at you, as if to say, "Gotcha!" then went some way off to graze peacefully, having put the whole incident out of his mind.

He was therefore perhaps not the ideal horse for me to compete on, but Roxie was determined that I would do so, and since keeping Roxie happy was important to us, I reluctantly agreed to give it a try. My reluctance, as it turned out, was nothing compared to that of Zapata's. Some horses like the excitement of competition, but he hated every minute of it. Unlike horses that are problem loaders, he wasn't all that hard to get into a trailer, which tended to give those around him the false impression that he would be cooperative once he arrived at the other end. A close look at his eyes, however, would reveal a steely determination to screw things up at the first opportunity.

We picked a fairly easy place to begin—the local Pleasant Valley Horse Show, which was, and is, about as easy as it gets. I wasn't the only adult competing, but there were certainly a lot more children than adults, and more ponies than full-size horses—a small, dusty ring, haphazard parking (parking control was in the hands of one of the local mentally handicapped, whose job this had been by tradition for many years), dogs yapping everywhere, babies crying, the smell of hot dogs and Italian sausage from the food stand in the air. There's some level of small town below which you don't get an annual horse show, but for that the town has to be very small, or totally lacking in civic pride and feeling, neither of which was true of Pleasant Valley.

My task was simple: to take Zapata around the ring at a walk, a trot, and a canter. "You can't go wrong," Margaret said as I mounted, and even I, scarcely an optimist when it came to this kind of thing, couldn't see how I could. Zapata, squeaky-clean, shiny, and groomed to within an inch of his life, seemed steady enough, though a little glum, his head cocked slightly to one side as he examined the ring with a certain skepticism, as if saying, "You think *I'm* going to do that? You've got to be kidding!" Roxie, biting her lower lip with anxiety, held him tightly enough to convince him that there was no point to backing up, so he simply stood there glumly, snorting ever so slightly to show his displeasure and swishing his long tail loudly—a sure sign of discontent.

"Just get him on the correct lead at the canter," Margaret said to me as my name was called, but as it happened, that good advice was wasted. The judge, an ample lady of a certain age, was seated on a wooden folding chair in the middle of the ring as she called me in. I rode in, halted, bowed, then walked Zapata toward the outside of the ring, at which point he took the bit between his teeth and broke into a gallop, headed straight for the judge, while I tried desperately to stop him. We missed the judge by a few inches, and Zapata would probably have run her down on his second try had she not abandoned her chair and her clipboard and made a dash for safety. For a large lady, she could move pretty quickly when she had to, I thought.

I took Zapata back to my handlers, who looked grim as I dismounted. "You shouldn't have let him get away with that," Margaret said. Roxie looked close to tears as she led Zapata back to the trailer. "I bet he'd be a lot better at an event," she said, as if she was trying to cheer me—or herself—up.

There are three phases in eventing—dressage, stadium jumping, and cross-country—and it almost goes without saying that nobody, not even Roxie, thought that Zapata and I could be trusted to perform the first two. The general feeling was that Zapata might do better in the open country, however, over fences, than in the more formal atmosphere of the show ring, provided there were no ditches on the course, so we were entered in a cross-country event up at Old Chatham, New York, about an hour or so north of Pleasant Valley. The fences were not terribly challenging, it seemed to me as I walked the course, and very much like the ones at home—there seemed no reason why Zapata shouldn't get around them perfectly well.

The first fence was built in a kind of trough, a narrow natural valley with thick woods on the right and a steep hill on the left, at the top of which was the refreshment stand. This too was an advantage, as Roxie and Margaret explained it, since it would make it more difficult for Zapata to run out on the first jump—the natural lie of the landscape would funnel him toward the fence, and after we were over the first one safely, why not the rest? I cannot say that I could actually imagine myself holding up my blue ribbon as I did a victory gallop, but I felt a certain modest confidence, having practiced hard over fences at home for several weeks, though some of that evaporated as Zapata was cajoled and threatened into the start box, which he disliked very much indeed. I heard Margaret and Roxie cheering as I came out of the box, and from a distance, a loudspeaker announcing that Michael Korda on Zapata was on course. It seemed to me that we were going a lot faster than necessary, but on the other hand, at least we were going in the right direction, so I let Zapata have his head.

There was perhaps a hundred yards or so between the start box and the first fence, just enough to give the illusion that things might go better than I expected—certainly there was no reason for Zapata to have a problem with the first fence, which was a lot easier than many of the fences we had practiced over at home, and not in any way threatening or unusual. Nevertheless he put on the brakes at the last second, nearly sending me flying over his head.

Practically speaking, one refusal pretty much guaranteed that I wasn't going to be in the ribbons, but the main thing was to keep going, so I swung him back, aimed him at the fence, and gave him a couple of taps with my stick just so he understood that I meant business. He took off like a rocket straight for the fence; then, at the very last fraction of a second, just as he should have been going over it, he dropped his shoulder (a favorite trick of his), veered sharply to the left, avoiding the fence completely, and took off at a gallop up the hill, snorting, bucking, and kicking as he went.

Like a missile that has gone off course, he was aiming directly for the food stand, where a good-size crowd was gathered. At first, as we came up the hill toward them, people laughed and even applauded, but then, as it became apparent that I couldn't slow Zapata down and that his intention appeared to be to go right through the crowd, sending small children, babies, dogs, and old people flying, people began pushing, shoving, and running to get out of his way.

I was too busy trying to stay on him to notice much—by this time I had lost a stirrup, and my seat was precarious—but I saw a blur of alarmed faces, mothers grabbing tiny tots and running, people dropping their containers of coffee and their Danish pastry as they took off in every direction. The proprietor of the food stand had his hands over his eyes as we approached him at high speed.

Then, apparently satisfied with the amount of chaos he had caused, or perhaps calmed by the smell of Danish pastry, Zapata abruptly halted, gave a couple of loud snorts of satisfaction, put down his head, and began to eat grass calmly.

Roxie, when she came up, was in tears. I dismounted and handed her the reins. "I don't ever want to do this again," I said—I didn't add that Zapata would surely have agreed—and I never did. Thus my collection of ribbons, hanging from a wire next to the fireplace in my office, consists of a handful of oddly colored trophies—no blues, no reds—most of them for things like hunter paces, where you can win a ribbon for showing up alive and breathing, on a live horse, whereas Margaret's fill room after room in the house, from floor to ceiling, and the tack room, an endless array of ribbons, most of them blue and red, plus row after row of plaques and silver trophies in every possible size and shape. Perhaps it's just as well. There's only room in a family for one champion, and I'm always happy to tag along as "the husband" when Margaret is accepting trophies or attending USCTA dinners.

As for Zapata, he was retired to a farm in nearby Red Hook, where, surprisingly enough, he is used to give riding lessons to children. Perhaps he likes children better than he likes adults, or perhaps it's just that he isn't being asked to compete, but I've not had any complaints or heard about any kids being injured, so it's a happy ending for him.

I'm glad. He had a lot of character, for a horse. I'm not too sure that he may not have actually had a sense of humor, which is rare enough in people, let alone in horses.

CHAPTER EIGHTEEN

The Acropolis

The indoor ring

WHEN MARGARET FIRST STARTED EVENTING, she competed fairly close to home. The events were small, local, never overnighters. Then, as she got better at it and developed not only a real taste for it but a certain reputation for winning, she began to travel greater distances, to bigger and more serious events, in New Jersey, Vermont, Pennsylvania, Maryland.

Little by little her establishment was increasing in size and complexity. Perhaps the most serious step we took—certainly the one that impressed locals the most—was the construction of an indoor riding arena. This is, for those who don't know, a big building, intended to provide an indoor area of at least twenty meters by seventy meters, without any columns, for exercising and training horses. The Lakehurst blimp hangar is certainly bigger, as are the hangars at major airports in which jets are serviced, but for Pleasant Valley our arena represented about as big a building as anybody had ever put up on their own land for a noncommercial purpose.

Tom Kirchhoff, to whom we had entrusted the project, was cheerful but cautious. The Kiehl brothers in Red Hook, who specialized in steel agricultural buildings, could put the thing up in no time, he said optimistically, but a lot would depend on the ground. It was the preparation—putting in the foundation, giving the whole thing a solid base—that would take time and, possibly, cost extra money. After all, you didn't know what you were going to find until you started digging, that was always the problem. Tom gave me a man-to-man smile—we were standing on the remains of a trailer on cinder blocks on one acre, which we had bought mostly to get rid of the kids who lived there, and which would now serve as a part of the site for the indoor arena. "You must be in some kind of trouble with Margaret, to put this up," he said. No, I told him. I had offered her a choice between a diamond bracelet and the riding arena as an anniversary present, and she had chosen the arena. Tom nodded wisely. "Well, I'll tell you this," he said. "By the time it's done, you're going to wish she'd picked the bracelet."

As Tom described it, the building, big as it would be, was simplicity itself to erect. You sunk your prefabricated structural steel cantilevered supports into concrete foundations, bolted on your overhead beams, fastened on roof and side panels, and put in sliding doors at both ends, and there you were: a riding arena. Of course before any of this could happen, there was a lot of work to be done. Your concrete foundations had to be set in good, solid, dry ground—not rock, of course, because rock would need to be blasted and jackhammered, and that would raise the cost of preparing the site to who knew how much—and of course when all *that* was done, and the structure was up, you needed to put down your base of gravel, sand, and whatever we were going to use as a footing on absolutely flat, level, dry ground if the ring was going to be any use at all. There was more to putting up a building like this than most people thought, Tom warned.

The truth of this was brought home to me almost immediately, when the excavators struck not only rock—no great surprise in Dutchess County—but, more alarmingly, an underground spring.

Probably nothing would ever get built in the country if it weren't for the sense of self-importance that undertaking a large construction job lends to the person who is paying for it. At the Grand Union supermarket, at Cady's Bar, at Van's gas station, where the local senior-citizen Sunday Harley riders gathered to chew the fat and exchange motorcycle tuning tips, at the feed store and the car wash, I was temporarily elevated to the status of pharaoh, Sun King, John D. Rockefeller Jr. Who can fail to be impressed by a man who is pouring his own money into the local economy, keeping dozens of honest, local, God-fearing, Republican-voting working men gainfully employed, and improving his own property (thereby increasing his own share of local school and property taxes)? I was as welcome everywhere as the hero of *The Music Man* in River City, even to those people, of whom there were many, who didn't have a clue what we were building, or those who did have a clue and thought it was a pretty silly way to waste good money. I basked in a warm glow of appreciation.

On the other hand, this being a small town, there were also no secrets. Everywhere I went, even to the local health food store for a new supply of Mom's Meatless Meat Balls (a specialty that exists nowhere outside Pleasant Valley, so far as I know), people shook their heads and commiserated. "I hear you struck rock," they would say sadly, to which I would reply, "*And* an underground spring!" at which they would sigh and say, in the case of women, "Oh, my!" and in the case of most men, "Son-of-a-bitch!" It's not just that news is instant in a small town—was always instant, long before CNN—it's that people here are of farming stock, and even if they've gone into insurance, or health food, or opened up a nail-and-hair place, indoor work, they have sons, brothers, relatives of every kind, who still work with bulldozers or backhoes and know their way around a construction site. Rock and underground springs, they understand. Rock and underground springs mean time and money. Rock and underground springs mean going over budget.

That was soon confirmed. "We're going over budget," Tom said, as we looked down at a series of large holes that seemed as if they had been dug by artillery shells. What he was thinking, he explained, was that maybe it didn't make much sense to keep on digging as if we hoped to go all the way to China. Sure, we could keep on blasting rock, but we were just likely to get down to more rock, plus water, which was worse. Instead of digging down, maybe we should be *building* a foundation—raising the building up, so to speak. He showed me what he had in mind on the back of an envelope. He would build a low cinder-block wall about 200 feet by 75 feet, fill that in with sand and gravel, just like filling a swimming pool, then tamp it down solidly and build the arena on top of it. On the outside of the wall, he would put down more fill and grade it gently to hold the wall in place, so the arena would appear to be built on top of a low hill. With a little bit of grass seed and a few trees, the whole thing would look perfectly natural. It would even give the building a certain presence—like the Acropolis, he suggested.

That seemed to me unlikely—all drawings of the arena made it look pretty utilitarian, though we had sprung for the optional transparent panels around the top third of the walls and for the adjustable overhead ventilators on the roof—but it was a nice thought, even though half the diners in our part of the world were now called the Acropolis, as immigrant Greeks began to take them over, much to the alarm of local residents, who couldn't figure out what moussaka and spanakopita might be, or what they were doing on a diner menu.

In any event, since the choice seemed to be between picking a different site—with a chance that we might run into the same problems there—and doing what Tom suggested, I agreed. How much more would it cost? Tom shrugged. It was hard to say. He would try to keep it to the minimum, but we would need an awful lot of bank-run gravel.

Up until now bank-run gravel had not played much of a role in my life, but once the cinderblock wall was up, which took hardly any time at all, the huge trucks from our local sand-and-gravel company began to arrive and unload in a seemingly endless convoy. Up the road they would come, truck after truck, with a heavy diesel roar, then they would unload, hurtle past my windows in the opposite direction, back to the gravel pit, and return, heavily loaded again, eight hours a day. I had thought a few truckloads would do it, maybe a dozen at most, but it gradually dawned on me that we were talking about *hundreds* of truckloads, earthmoving on a scale that would have pleased any pharaoh, though of course we were using diesel trucks for the job instead of slaves.

Eventually, after several days of trucks tipping their loads into the walled-in area that would become the foundation for our arena, Tom told me we were done. I breathed a sigh of relief. "Yup," he said, "we've got all the bank-run gravel we need. Now we start bringing in number 2 item." "Number 2 item," it appeared, was finer, and of course more expensive. Since it crushed down, we would need a lot of it.

The endless parade of trucks resumed, until it seemed that I must have bought the entire gravel supply of Dutchess County, but eventually the area inside the walls was filled to the very top, at which point the trucks began to reappear with topsoil, to form a low rampart around the outside of the wall, which would be bulldozed down into a gentle slope, of natural appearance.

By the time all that was done—and paid for—the rest was positively anticlimactic. The steel structure rose, as promised, swiftly; the roof went on without any problems; electricity was brought in; sand and sieved dirt were trucked in to form the floor of the ring (and would eventually have to bulldozed out and replaced with more exotic, and expensive, footing that wouldn't freeze or clump up, like rubber chips or broom shavings); hundreds of feet of plywood "kickboard" was installed around the inside of the ring (so the horses, if they kicked out, wouldn't hurt themselves against the steel supports); and the arena was ready for use. It did run over budget (what big construction project does not?), but as promised, it looked as if it belonged where it was, on top of a gently sloping hill, even if the hill was artificial, and by the time trees and grass had been planted, it seemed as if it had always been there.

All that remained to be done was to get a meticulous German craftsman to come in and install his own "Rainmaker" system—a series of fine overhead copper pipes, suspended from the beams by thin wires, with a pump and individual control valves that allowed you to mist each section of the ring to keep down the dust, even in the winter, since the Rainmaker's fine spray didn't freeze up, the way a steady drip would have done—and Margaret was in business.

Not literally, of course, since we were spending money rather than making it, but I took a perverse pride in the arena, looming just over the tree line on the far horizon, as seen from the house. It might not be the Acropolis, but it was the largest building I had ever caused to be put up, and remains so to this day. Apart from maintenance, and the occasional severe winter when Detlef Juerss and his men have to get up intrepidly on the roof with snowblowers to take the weight of the snow off it, it has only produced minor problems—mostly because it provides a perfect nesting place for pigeons. At one point we tried putting up inflatable dummies of birds of prey, but they didn't frighten the pigeons a bit. We discovered a company that produces long strips with wire nails, like the kind that you see Indian fakirs lying down on in cartoons, but we would have needed miles of the stuff, and it wasn't cheap. In the end Mother Nature solved the problem in her own way—every once in a while a peregrine falcon that was smarter or bolder than the rest would swoop in and kill a few pigeons, and for some time the rest of them would move out and go elsewhere, like people moving out of a neighborhood in which there has been a series of brutal murders or muggings.

Even the old-timers who still referred to our property as "the old Hewlett farm," or if they were somewhat younger, "the old Hubner place," now paused and scrutinized us with new interest, asking, "Say, ain't you the folks who put that big arena up by the road, on the old Hewlett farm?" and nodded sagely when we admitted we were, as if to say, no doubt, "Well, ain't it the truth? Some people got more money than sense!"

That said, the arena at least gave me a yardstick by which to measure other projects. For example, Margaret's plan to build run-in sheds for each of her horses so they could shelter from the wind and the rain when they were out in their field seemed, by comparison, small potatoes. Even her decision to build a big barn to store her truck and her two trailers, a fairly formidable undertaking on the face of things, seemed relatively minor compared to the arena. I eventually did draw the line at reconstructing the old red barn on our property and turning it into a house, after discovering that we would have to get the permission of the Department of Environment and Conservation to redirect a small stream that was part of a protected wetlands complex. Instinct told me that anything involving bulldozers *and* environmental lawyers would consume more time and money than I wanted to think about.

As for Margaret's arena, every time I see it, I think to myself, "My God, we actually *built* this!"

Pretty much the way the ancient Greeks probably felt about the Acropolis, come to that.

CHAPTER NINETEEN

"Do You Know Egg?"

TRAVELING WITH MARGARET to events, or driving to see her compete, gave me a certain feeling for diners. Food doesn't play much of a role in the eventing world, except for feeding the horses, of course. There's always a food stand at a horse event, usually serving the kind of food that cardiologists warn us against, but then people who are doing hard physical work and who tend to think that five in the morning is late to get up aren't likely to eat granola, or low-fat anything, when they take a break. Egg, sausage, and cheese on a roll is more likely, and every variation of hamburger. In the evening, eventing people are usually too tired to go looking for great or interesting restaurants—and anyway, they have to get back to the stables for the barn check before going to bed themselves—even if there were any great or interesting restaurants to be found, which is seldom the case, so it's usually a choice between eating at the motel, if it serves food, or at a diner.

Throughout most of the United States a diner is a pretty safe bet, and indeed in many places it has achieved a kind of cultural status, about as close as our society comes to a secular equivalent to medieval churches and cathedrals, particularly as diners in the more prosperous parts of the country get fancier and fancier. Still, there's something about a fancy diner, with acres of tinted, beveled mirrors, fake patent leather upholstery in designer pastel colors, art deco chrome accents, and—God help us!—in some cases, a theme, that seems contrary to the whole idea of good, cheap, simple food served twenty-four hours a day.

In our part of the world the old-fashioned diner was in the process of extinction when we first moved up to the country, a victim not so much of any change in taste on the part of the customers, who knew what diner food was and liked it that way, as of change in the diners themselves, and how they were run. It was Pleasant Valley's misfortune not to have a proper diner—another consequence of being too close to Poughkeepsie, where there were plenty of diners, since it was a prosperous market town, as well as being the home of Vassar College. That is not to say that Poughkeepsie was Paris on the Hudson, but if you wanted a diner meal in the middle of the night you could find it there, and it was only a fifteen-minute drive from Pleasant Valley to downtown Poughkeepsie.

When Poughkeepsie collapsed shortly after World War II—a victim of people and businesses moving out of the city to the new suburbs, of the federal government's decision to rip the heart out of the old downtown area to put through not one but *two* four-lane highways, and of the new shopping malls that were going up everywhere on farmland all around the city to support the developing suburban sprawl—the diners collapsed with it. Poughkeepsie became the kind of city that you were warned not to visit at night (or advised to go armed when visiting), and people started eating at franchised restaurants, dimly lit "steak and brew" places, fast-food places, Chinese restaurants, instead of the old reliable diner with its feisty, knowing waitresses in pink uniforms, its revolving glass refrigerator case for pies, and its cups of coffee endlessly refilled without your having to ask for more.

Pleasant Valley didn't have a diner, but there were plenty around us, if you didn't mind driving—and after all, the whole reason for diners is to provide food for people on the road; the car and the diner go together, almost as symbiotic as the car and the gas station. Fifteen minutes away, in Millbrook, there was a diner; half an hour away in Red Hook there was another; and in rural Millerton, a little farther, still another, all of them the good old-fashioned kind built like railway dining cars, long and aluminum-clad, with the usual long Formica counter and vinyl-covered booths inside. There was nothing fancy about the food; it was basically your standard diner fare, all the usual sandwiches, meat loaf, homemade pies—and of course eggs.

Eggs were at the very epicenter of diner culture. When I was a child, my father had a friend, a fellow Hungarian named Laci Bus-Fekete, a Hollywood screenwriter, who was enormously fat—far too fat to be comfortable on a plane, or even in a train compartment. The Bus-Feketes, when they traveled from coast to coast, always went by car, in a big old Cadillac with strong springs for Laci's weight and plenty of room for his bulk in the front seat. Both Bus-Feketes were gourmets, and when I grew up I wondered what they found to eat as they crossed the United States. Finally I worked up the courage to ask. "It's very simple," Laci said. "We stop at a diner three times a day, and eat eggs—scrambled, or fried, or poached. If there's one thing you can rely on, it's the eggs in a diner, anywhere in America."

The central importance of eggs in diner cuisine was brought home to me also, some years later, by my friend Carlos Castaneda, whose books I edited and published. At one point in his apprenticeship as a sorcerer with Don Juan, his Yaqui Indian mentor, he annoyed Don Juan, who decided he needed a lesson in humility and ordered him to take a job as a short-order cook in a diner for six months. Carlos was to get his hands dirty, to work long, exhausting, sweaty hours instead of going to an air-conditioned classroom to teach, or sitting at his desk writing. Carlos, short, swarthy, stocky, looked like a Mexican, and in southern California most of this kind of work is done by Mexicans, so it was unlikely to occur to any prospective employer that he was a UCLA professor and best-selling author. At the first place he went to, the owner of the diner looked him over, and after a pregnant pause stared directly into his eyes. "I've got just one question," he said, leaning forward intently. *"Do you know egg?"*

"Do you know egg?" After the six months were over, Carlos used to tell this story and roar with laughter until tears ran down his cheeks. Knowing egg was what it was all about when it came to working in a diner, and a man who knew his egg could find work anywhere. That was the whole thing, Carlos would explain; you had to know how to handle all the egg orders exactly, even when they were coming faster than bullets from a machine gun, when the truckers stopped for breakfast. Everyone was hungry, in a hurry, and when it came to eggs, everyone wanted theirs done *exactly* the way they liked them. A man who ordered two eggs over easy wanted them over easy; nothing else would satisfy him. A man who wanted two four-minute poached eggs wasn't going to be happy with eggs that were half a minute more or less than that. At five in the morning—really, from five to eight in the morning—you might get hundreds of orders for eggs, and you had to produce them fast and get them just right, or you weren't doing the job. There, on the stove before you, you would be scrambling eggs, poaching them, frying them, dozens of eggs all cooking at the same time, and you not only had to keep all the orders clear in your mind, you had to have a sense of the egg, to know your egg. You had to have *Fingerspitzengefühl:* your instincts had to tell you when it was exactly the right moment to put the two pieces of toast on the hot plate and flip the eggs off the grill and onto them so they would arrive at the table just as ordered, not too runny, not too hard, just right.

Carlos hadn't started off knowing egg—he had faked his knowledge to get the job—but he learned fast. He would hold up his hands—solid, thick hands, with short, blunt-tipped workingman's fingers—and show me the burn scars. "Egg," he would say. At breakfast time, when you were working like a crazy person, you got splattered with hot grease, or you forgot to wrap a towel around the handle of a skillet when you were turning over a Western omelet. Every day you took your share of burns, cuts, and scalds, but you moved the eggs.

Don Juan had been right—the work taught Carlos humility, renewed his quest for exactitude, brought home again the vital importance of getting things right. Besides, he would add with a grin, if the bottom ever fell out of the writing business, or even the guru business, which he had never wanted to be in anyway, he could always fall back on egg—a man who knew egg could always find work somewhere, no questions asked.

The first sign of the collapse of the old-fashioned diner business in our part of the Northeast was that they no longer knew egg. Scrambled eggs arrived either burned or too runny; fried eggs were never done exactly the way you had ordered them; omelets were limp and greasy; poached eggs—forget about it! Your poached egg requires real skill—it shouldn't be served up wet, so the piece of toast underneath it is soggy—and egg skill was lacking, a dying art in our part of the country, where without knowing it we badly needed Carlos Castaneda.

It wasn't just egg, either. The tuna salad sandwich, another diner staple, was all wrong. Tuna salad needs to be white, with tiny crisp chunks of celery, and without any fishy taste or odor. Generations of American kids who wouldn't eat fish to save their lives have been happy to eat tuna salad sandwiches at diners because they didn't taste like fish at all. All of a sudden, they began to taste and smell fishy, perhaps because they were made with darker, cheaper canned tuna instead of albacore solid white meat tuna. The consistency was wrong too, either too sloppy (too much mayonnaise) or too chunky (not chopped fine enough, nor blended long or vigorously enough).

The worst was pie. Pie was right there with egg, at the very heart of diner culture, and people would drive miles for a diner that served great pie. But then, gradually, great pie vanished, for the simple reason that diners were no longer baking their own, but buying pie instead from big commercial bakers, who delivered tasteless apple pie with a crust like rubber and lemon meringue pies that were six inches tall, even without the layer of whipped cream out of a spray can, and had no taste at all. The pies were all huge, unnaturally colored, far too sweet, and totally artificial.

It was one of those curious phenomena of American business life. Diners in the Northeast had been small, family-owned businesses, but running a diner meant long hours of hard work, and not too many people wanted to do it anymore—certainly their children didn't. So the diners were taken over by Greek immigrants, who saw a good opportunity, like the Koreans who took over big-city grocery stores or the Indians who bought small motels all over America. The newcomers didn't mind working hard for long hours, but on the other hand, they themselves weren't people who ate eggs and bacon for breakfast, or a tuna sandwich for lunch, or a piece of homemade pie with a cup of coffee in the middle of the afternoon. In short, they were making their living producing food they didn't know or like themselves.

At the same time, since nobody wants to work in the kitchen of a diner (despite Carlos Castaneda's example), these jobs became a mainstay of employment for legal and, in many cases, illegal Mexican immigrants, and they too didn't have a sense of what a tuna salad sandwich ought to taste like, or even a BLT—in fact, in many diners there was no longer anybody in the kitchen or in management who had any idea what the food ought to taste like, except perhaps for the waitresses. Eventually the customers themselves ceased to remember what the food was supposed to taste like, or no longer cared, and that was it, so far as diners were concerned.

With a few exceptions. There's a diner up near Cobbleskill, where Margaret occasionally competes, where the customers—solid upstate New York citizens, all of whom have the look of serious eaters, most of the men in bib-front overalls and John Deere tractor caps, their ladies apparently untroubled by any desire to diet themselves down to Julia

Roberts's weight—sit down to dine at five o'clock for the special meat loaf dinner, with gravy, mashed potatoes, two vegetables, homemade coleslaw, and a roll and butter, and where they still actually bake their own pies and the fried onion rings aren't greasy and rubbery. There's not a lot of conversation—just steady, purposeful chewing, with an occasional pause for a sip of coffee. Most people end their meal with a sigh, and say, those that can still speak, "My land, I don't believe I could eat another mouthful!" but then order a piece of pie à la mode anyway. It's sort of a ritual with us to stop there on the way home from walking the course for a cup of coffee and piece of pie.

I don't think I'm going to give the directions, since I've no desire to see it turned into a tourist trap, but on the other hand, Cobbleskill is a pretty small place, so it would be hard to miss.

Since Pleasant Valley never had a full-fledged diner to begin with, we lost nothing close to home. The Great Little Restaurant on Main Street—where I had experienced my septic tank epiphany—was really a restaurant as opposed to a diner; that is, it didn't have chrome-plated selection units for the jukebox at each place and you had to ask for ketchup, as opposed to having a bottle at each place along the counter, and at each table. Besides, while it opened "early in the A.M.," it wasn't open late at night, or twenty-four hours a day, like the Acropolis in Poughkeepsie. The Village Restaurant, while often referred to as "the diner," wasn't, alas, a diner at all but a "family restaurant" again, open at or before dawn, but closed by 9:00 P.M.—as if to make sure that you couldn't get a BLT and a beer after the movies—and didn't have the unmistakable truck-stop chic of a real diner. When Pleasant Valley residents wanted to experience real diner meals, or felt a yen for a tuna melt at 2:00 A.M., they had to drive ten or twenty miles or more, not as far as Cobbleskill, to be sure, but maybe up to the Taconic Diner, right on the Taconic Parkway near Old Chatham, which was pretty much your traditional diner experience, with waitresses whose love lives kept them in endless, intimate conversation with each other and the customers, and great tuna salad sandwiches that didn't taste a bit fishy.

There were places closer to home where, for example, you could get Harold Roe's favorite dish—fried bologna on white toast with mayonnaise, and a side order of potato salad—but with the collapse of the traditional diner, it was tough to find a quick, decent meal.

Change, however, was in the air, had we but known it.

CHAPTER TWENTY

A Nice Cup of Tea

DINERS APART, we lived for quite a while in the country before the food problem ever came up in any serious way. We brought most of what we needed up from the city, and that was that. When we went out to dinner, it was generally without gourmet expectations, except for a grand occasion or special guests like the Goldmans, when we would drive to Rhinebeck, twenty miles away, for a perfectly decent meal.

Margaret, as it happens, is a gifted cook, but as the horses began to take over her life, there simply weren't enough hours during the day to do the kind of cooking she liked, nor was it easy to find the ingredients she wanted in Pleasant Valley. We maintained a kind of ambitious supply train from the city to the country, which at times seemed as circuitous and difficult as the Berlin airlift, and requiring much the same kind of organizational genius. I would have to shop for what Margaret needed at Zabar's or Fairway, on Broadway, or at her favorite butcher, Harry Oppenheimer, on the Upper West Side, then pack everything into coolers with refrigerator gel packs, transport them to the office on Friday morning, unpack and store everything in the refrigerator there, and hump them down to the garage in Rockefeller Center at the end of the day, together with wine from Sherry-Lehman, fresh bread and croissants, and whatever else was on the shopping list. Some days it felt as if I needed a column of coolies to drag it all down to the garage.

Hoping to take up some of the slack in the kitchen, I enrolled myself in the adult education course at the Culinary Institute of America in Hyde Park and embarked on a full course in Chinese cooking. The Culinary Institute is a full-fledged cooking university, sited in a former seminary, and perhaps one of the largest and most respected institutions of its kind in the world. At first, it was daunting to undertake the ABCs of Chinese cooking in kitchens designed for a full complement of professional restaurant chefs, but the atmosphere was, I soon discovered, the reverse of intimidating. Our teacher plied us with Chinese rice wine and tiny Chinese snacks until the atmosphere was positively convivial as she taught us to cook a variety of basic Chinese dishes. My fellow students—it was a small class of about twenty—were divided into two distinctly different groups: those like myself, determined to learn to cook *something*, and an older, more convivial group of retirees who were happy enough to spend a few hours tasting what the rest of us had cooked and comparing notes. I became quite proud of my newfound ability, except when it came to dishes containing tofu, for which, it appeared, I did not have a magic touch. The most difficult part about putting what I had learned to use at home, however, was finding ingredients like Chinese cabbage, bok choy, and fresh ginger. There was, it appeared, a Chinese grocery store hidden away in a strip mall in the suburbs of Poughkeepsie, between a Laundromat and a beer distributor, but it was only open at odd and unpredictable times, and nobody there spoke any English, so it did no good to call them. For the occasions when I found them open, I carried a sheet of paper with whatever

I needed written in Chinese by the chef at the Culinary Institute, which worked pretty well, though once again it was easier to buy things in the city. The produce on Broadway looked a lot fresher than it did at the Chinese grocery store in Poughkeepsie, where everything looked as if it had been shipped from China by slow boat, but once again the downside was that it had to be added to the load packed into the car every Friday afternoon.

Once Paul Kovi, then co-owner with his friend Tom Margittai of New York's famous Four Seasons restaurant, came up for the weekend and insisted on cooking for us, but he too brought everything he needed up with him, including his own set of knives. All day long—with a break so he and his longtime companion Eva Puszta could look at a nearby country property they were thinking of buying—Paul labored in the kitchen, chopping, baking, frying. There was something boiling or simmering on every burner of the stove, the oven was full to overwhelming, even the toaster oven was going full steam. While he cooked, the rest of us washed and cleaned every pot, pan, and utensil we owned a dozen times over in a vain effort to keep up with him. Occasionally he would pause and come up for breath so that I could drive him in search of something he had forgotten to bring, or had suddenly decided he needed at the last moment. By the time the magnificent meal was ready, we were all so tired that we could hardly keep our eyes open to eat it. Kovi, much as he liked the country, did not become a neighbor, he too having noticed the absence of all those things he associated with country living: red-cheeked, cheerful farmers selling fresh vegetables, plump geese and chickens, exotic herbs plucked straight from the garden, baskets of fruit at its prime. His visit to the Grand Union produce section in Pleasant Valley in pursuit of shallots and red peppers had left him shaking his head with deep Magyar gloom. This was not the country, as he had imagined it gastronomically.

We ourselves had grown more or less used to this state of affairs; as the center of our lives tilted toward the country and away from the city, we inevitably began to find it more difficult to bring everything we needed up with us, and became more dependent on what we could buy locally. This led to a certain lowering of our standards, perhaps reaching its low ebb with a period in which we lived on Weight Watchers frozen meals, and when the only vegetable we could find that looked edible was broccoli, which we ate with every meal.

I have lived places where the local supermarket is a place of pride and wonder (Santa Fe is one of them; Camden, Maine, another), but Pleasant Valley was not among them. A one-supermarket town is at the mercy of what it's got, and while the local Grand Union was better than supermarkets in East Germany or the Soviet Union, it was run in pretty much the same spirit, as is the A&P, which eventually opened more or less across the street from it. You bought what there was, and if you didn't like it—too bad, comrade!

It wasn't just a tendency to keep food on the shelves long past its sell-by date (even *milk*, in a part of the country in which dairy farming is a staple of the economy, and where hardly anybody lives very far away from real live dairy cattle), it was also, apparently, the land of the frozen TV dinner. Friends in New York City might express their envy of our living in the country, surrounded by fresh produce, but in fact our neighbors mostly seemed to be living on Wonder Bread, Stouffer's frozen macaroni and cheese, and bologna in various forms, with the occasional pizza or hamburger at one of the local diners to liven the palate up. Vegetables in the local supermarket were scarce, and of a quality that would have been unacceptable in New York (in midtown Manhattan, anyway)—in fact, it occurred to me that the supermarket chains probably shipped up to the country the produce they couldn't sell in the city. Fruit, except for apples, which grow locally, was either rock-hard or rotten, nothing in between, and the look (and smell) of meat and fish was seldom encouraging. Far from there being scads of talented local bakers around us, as our city friends imagined, everybody bought supermarket bread, and even supermarket cakes—the local bakers had gone out of business at the end of World War II.

Of course there were people who kept vegetable gardens—at the right seasons it was easy to be inundated by gifts of tomatoes and squashes from your neighbors (and, in our case, the Bacons), but nobody seemed interested in growing peas, or string beans, or even lettuce. Superb farmers the Vandenkamps might be—visibly *were*—but like most of the local farmers, they weren't interested in small stuff. Farmers devoted themselves to dairy cattle, or to growing apples on a big scale, and that was that. Once a week Gertrude was driven down to the GU by one of her brothers to buy, among other things, frozen vegetables—it did not seem to have occurred to the Vandenkamps that they might have grown their own. Nor did they seem to miss that kind of thing much. Things might be different elsewhere in rural America, but around here the supermarket, the prepackaged frozen dinner, and the invention of the microwave had changed everything.

Eventually this would change, and the first sign of it was the growth of so-called farmers' markets. This was something of a new phenomenon for the area. There had always been farm stands by the road, where you could buy pumpkins or apples in the autumn, or tomatoes in the summer, but these were usually modest affairs, with a stack of paper bags and a tin box to leave the money in. The more prosperous farmers looked down on that kind of thing. The farmers' markets, however, were more ambitious, and tended to be the concern of a younger breed of farmers, many of them amateurs or even transplanted city folk.

I FIRST BECAME AWARE of all this when a friend brought me a small container of tapenade, which he had purchased on Saturday morning at the Millbrook Farmers' Market. Tapenade? I asked myself. In Dutchess County? I had to see this with my own eyes.

"Who makes this?" I asked my friend, and was told that he had bought it off a French monk. It turned out there was a small Benedictine monastery hidden away among the trailers and tract houses not far from us, where the tiny contingent of monks cultivated their garden, grew their own herbs, and raised sheep. *This*, I thought, has to be worth seeing.

In the parking lot opposite the satellite office of the New York State Motor Vehicles Department in Millbrook I found a colorful assortment of tents and awnings, like a gypsy encampment, as well as a small corral full of goats. The Mediterranean flavor of all this was easily explained once I had introduced myself to Brother Victor-Antoine d'Avila-Latourrette, the prior of Our Lady of the Resurrection, and also its cook, shepherd, gardener in chief, and founder. Brother Victor, wearing an apron over his robe and a large straw hat of the kind worn by Impressionist painters, was seated at a folding picnic table under a beach umbrella, reading a small book. His demeanor was affable. He did not make any attempt to sell his wares, which included plastic containers of the tapenade I had enjoyed so much, homemade aioli, aluminum-foil plates of tomatoes Provençal ready for reheating, and tiny pots of herbs. When he founded his monastery, his homemade specialties were of interest only to those who came there to make a retreat. Now, he said, hands raised gracefully as if to cast a blessing over the adjacent DMV building, the local liquor store, and the yoga institute, there was a greater demand for the monastery's wares—greater than he could meet, sadly. People wanted variety, *nouveauté*, gourmet food in a place where there had been little, or none. "Look around us," he said, "who would have believed it possible! A miracle."

Indeed. A change was taking place, all over the Northeast, as wealthy city people moved up to buy farms, and those farmers who didn't sell out and move to Florida struggled to meet the newcomers' needs. A new breed of farmers had been moving back up to the country from the city to get into farming—not the old-style farming, which in our neck of the woods was pretty much limited to dairy cattle or apples. As more and more of the old dairy farmers gave up, people from the city began moving in, planting miniature vegetables—the kind of tiny turnips and squash that Marie Antoinette would have loved—and generally trying to grow their crops in an organic way (unlike the old-timers, who believed that a day without spraying pesticides was a day wasted).

As I looked around me, I saw what Brother Victor meant by miracles, and after all, he would know. There was a farm stand selling arugula, leeks, exotic lettuces, premixed mesclun salad; another displaying home-made goat cheese and goat's milk yogurt; a stout Slavic woman with homemade kielbasa sausage and fruit; a lady whose home-baked raisin-pumpernickel bread put Zabar's to shame; a mother-and-daughter team selling prepared Mexican foods; even a former New York City art director and book jacket designer giving out samples of his own locally made wine and champagne.

The customers too were a departure from the rural norm. Imperious, ruddy-faced men with the bustling air of success, wearing carefully chosen ensembles of country clothes, picking over the produce as if they were panning for diamonds; trim, attractive, well-dressed, forceful women, some of them carrying the kind of string shopping bags favored by French city dwellers, which fetched fancy prices in Manhattan food boutiques—the whole scene could have been contrived for the cover of the Barbour catalog. Jack Russell terriers proliferated, yapping fiercely at the goats. The John Deere tractor cap had been replaced by the artfully aged fishing hat, complete with fishing flies stuck in the hatband, never mind that the nearest decent trout stream is at least fifty miles away, even had this been the season. It was suddenly Range Rover country.

The changes brought about by the demand for more sophisticated produce soon spread. One of our neighbors, up until then content to raise Holsteins (the preferred local breed of dairy cattle) and sell milk, began to put acreage aside for vegetables. He began with arugula (there is still some local confusion about whether it should be cooked or eaten raw), then moved on to become the local asparagus king. Growing asparagus is a lot easier than getting up at three in the morning to milk cows, so he constructed greenhouses, upgraded and enlarged his stand, and phased out his cows.

"I could see the writing on the wall," he said. "Milk used to be right up there with motherhood and the flag, but once the goddamn government starting telling people milk is bad for them, it was all over for the dairy farmer. Hell, nobody thinks asparagus is bad for you." He himself, however, was not an enthusiast for his own asparagus. "I guess it's okay, if you like the stuff," he allowed, "but I hate the smell when I take a piss."

Paul Wigsten, who farms a hundred acres or so down the road from us, moved back from New York City to his grandfather's dairy farm a few years ago and became one of the local farmers' market pioneers. Though born on the farm, he has a natural understanding of his weekender customers from his years of living in the city. They want the best, he says, but they don't always know what they're looking at.

"I had some beautiful yellow tomatoes last year, same price as the red ones, but I couldn't sell them at all. Red ones were selling like hotcakes, but not the yellow. Couldn't figure it—they were delicious. I was giving away free samples on toothpicks, still people weren't buying. So I put a sign on them that read GOURMET, ORGANIC, LOW ACID, which is true enough of any good tomato, raised the price a dollar a pound over the reds, and sold out by the middle of the morning." He shrugged. He employs ten people, hires cheerful, good-looking youngsters to man his stand at the market, sells to restaurants, but it's still a marginal business. You need to have half a million dollars' worth of liability insurance just to set up a stand—people don't think about that kind of thing when they're shopping for scallions or leeks.

"It's a changing world out there," Wigsten said ruefully. There were two pet goats on his lawn, and a bunch of chickens. "I think we shook things up here when we started the whole concept of a farmers' market, got people looking at vegetables in a whole new way, but now you've got the kids at the 4-H club raising llamas, believe it or not . . . llamas here in the Hudson Valley." Wigsten shook his head. "I mean they used to raise pigs, rabbits, now it's llamas. . . . What the hell do you do with a llama?"

In fact, you sell them, at $5,000 apiece and up, although they can neither be ridden (by most people) nor eaten (certainly not by the kind of people who are raising them). The only people who *have* found a use for them are those who keep sheep. Llamas turn out to be better than sheepdogs, and only eat grass. Alpacas have become popular too, as have exotic Kashmiri goats. One of my friends from New York, a famous publisher, actually drove up from his faux French château in Westchester to buy a pair of exotic goats for his children (God forbid they should have ordinary goats as pets!) from the herd of a wealthy New York newspaper executive who not only raises them but scandalized the local gentry (what little remains of it) by turning up at the opening meet of the hunt dressed in a black riding coat, velvet hard hat, and white breeches and riding a llama. Even trendier and more expensive than llamas are imported Highland cattle, the favorite livestock of the new rich, since they can't be milked and aren't usually slaughtered, being bred mostly to look pretty in the distance while you're serving cocktails on the porch—the four-footed equivalent of a Ferrari in the driveway.

Brother Victor, whose newfound international success as a cookbook author may soon be carrying him away from the more modest demands of a stand in the Millbrook farmers' market, and who is giving serious thought to his own website, nonetheless sees in the farmers' market an experience that is at once earthly and religious. The work binds him to nature and to God; the act of selling his produce connects him to his fellow farmers. We are having tea in his monastery kitchen, with Irish biscuits sent over by a fellow Benedictine, while he explains how he took up gardening as a way of keeping the monastery solvent. Through the window we can see Brother Victor's goats and his chickens going about their business. Inside the abbey, it is peaceful, quiet, smelling of furniture polish and good soup. The kitchen in which we sit is that of a professional chef's, with every pot and pan in use, and on the shelves devotional works jostle cookbooks and folders full of Brother Victor's meticulously handwritten personal recipes. He sighs as he looks out the window—it is a rainy afternoon, with a lot of mud visible, and more to come, the kind of day on which even a monk might regard looking after the animals and tending the fields as a penance.

With a shy smile, he puts into my hand a small jar, as if offering me a blessing. It is labeled, rather handsomely, "Our Lady of the Resurrection Monastery Corn Salsa." I haven't seen it on Brother Victor's stand before. "A new product," he says shyly.

I ate it that night, and it was delicious.

OF COURSE it isn't just a question of produce—it's also a question of restaurants. When people talk about coming up to the country to visit us, often to our dismay, they invariably suggest dinner out at a great country inn, of which they expect there to be dozens to choose from. They usually have in mind some beautifully preserved and restored eighteenth-century hostelry, richly furnished with antiques, with huge stone fireplaces and wide-plank floors, and of course a true artist in the kitchen whipping up meals that would make a Parisian gourmet smile. . . .

Of course such places *do* exist—the Beekman Arms Tavern in Rhinebeck comes to mind, as does the Old Drover's Inn in Dover Plains—but generally, the deeper you go into the country (i.e., the farther from New York City) the fewer they are, and the less likely to live up to their facade, however pretentious. After all, in our neck of the woods, once the tourists have seen the autumn leaves turn and have gone home to the city, who is going to eat *raie au beurre blanc* or try any of those interesting California varietals? Certainly not the locals.

The truth is that outside those few big cities in America that have a truly cosmopolitan spirit, foreign cooking exists in a kind of spurious limbo. There is no shortage of Italian restaurants, but they tend to be the kind of places where pizza is the specialty and everything else—

meat, fish, chicken, even lobster—comes slathered under layers of glutinous cheese and spiced tomato sauce, and where everything comes with an automatic side of spaghetti bolognese. Quantity, not quality, is the definition of a good meal.

Chinese restaurants, with a few exceptions (in our part of the world, notably, the excellent China Rose in Rhinecliff), are usually lightly upmarket take-out places, with a few sad tables under glaring fluorescent lighting and the same food you could get in a cardboard take-out carton. French restaurants, even though they may have been opened once upon a time by honest-to-God French persons, eventually develop a menu that is safe and foolproof, and in the process become a sad caricature of the real thing. German restaurants reduce themselves to the repetition of two or three simple dishes, apparently designed to prove that Germans can absorb an unlimited amount of cholesterol and eat red cabbage with everything under the sun. Of Indian restaurants, by and large, the less said, the better.

The problem is that most of our neighbors don't really *like* foreign food, or have ideas about it that are immutable, such as that bread in Italian restaurants has to be totally tasteless, and if possible weightless, unless it is toasted, slathered with melted butter and garlic powder, then passed under the grill until it is charred and stiff, or that no French meal is really French unless it includes salad of damp iceberg lettuce served as a separate course. To survive, restaurateurs give in, and in the process start down the ever-steepening path that leads to bankruptcy, followed by reopening the restaurant as a hero-sandwich place or a video rental store.

All this may perhaps explain why one form of foreign cooking seems to be flourishing *chez nous*—it is, of all things, *English* food.

Long despised by everybody, even Americans, and treated with complete contempt and derision by Common Market Europeans, English cooking—and English staples—have been making a comeback here, of all places. After all, we live surrounded by traces of the Revolutionary War, in which Americans fought to free themselves once and for all from Mother Country, including, presumably, her cooking. Still, the great advantage that English food has over the cuisines of other cultures, albeit more glamorous and exciting, is that at heart it isn't really foreign. You may like it or not, but it doesn't ask you to learn to stomach odd and pungent spices, or develop a taste for snails, or burn your mouth on an overenthusiastic vindaloo curry. The ingredients are familiar and easy to identify (lamb, beef, mashed or boiled potatoes, brussels sprouts), and the menu is written in English. To many people this seems like a step ahead, after puzzling over the menu of a Vietnamese restaurant.

"Authentic English cooking served here" would hardly seem like a hearty selling phrase, even in England, evoking as it does childhood memories of shepherd's pie, fish and chips, bubble and squeak, Cornish pasties, and any number of desserts featuring large quantities of lukewarm yellow custard—in short, a national cuisine in which the ketchup bottle, the vinegar cruet, and HP Sauce play crucial roles—but as it happens English cooking is alive, well, and thriving, and attracting people from hundreds of miles away, many of whom—most of whom, in fact—aren't even English.

Yes, a certain *nostalgie de la boue* might explain this phenomenon. For those of us who are English, Horlicks, Smarties (a UK precursor of M&Ms), Cadbury's Flake Chocolate, trifle, treacle tart—all those oversweetened nursery foods—might remind us of Nanny, or simply bring back a world that once seemed comforting and safe; and certain things—teatime, English sausages ("bangers" or "chippolatas") for breakfast, kippers, kedgeree, Twiglets served with drinks—might reassure us that there will "always be an England." But at the thought that this trend now extends to people who *didn't* grow up in England, for whom all of this must surely be *exotic*, the mind boggles.

Nostalgia is a powerful emotion, to be sure. Once, years ago, when I was proposing to visit my friend and author, the distinguished writer Graham Greene, in Antibes when he was depressed and suffering from what he called "the incurable sickness of old age," I asked if there was anything I could bring him from London. He wrote back expressing a deep longing for bangers and mashed potatoes, and thought, if I wanted to be kind, that I might bring him some Maltesers, small chocolate-covered malt balls very popular among English schoolboys, which he later used, to sinister effect, in one of his spy novels. My wife, Margaret, can be cheered up on even the most loathsome day in the country (rain, fog, mud, lame horses, sick cat) by milk-chocolate-coated Hobnobs (a crunchy digestive biscuit) served with tea.

In fact, it was precisely, in the spirit of Proust's madeleine, in pursuit of the milk-chocolate-covered Hobnobs for Margaret, that I first ventured timidly, some years ago, into the village of Clinton Corners, in Dutchess County, just off the Taconic Parkway, having heard on the local grapevine that there was "an English store" newly opened there. At the time this caused derision and a certain amount of suspicion among our neighbors, since except for ourselves and our goddaughter Tamzin (and the visit King George VI and Queen Elizabeth paid to the Roosevelts in Hyde Park, in 1939), the last major intrusion from England in these parts had been in the form of redcoats burning barns and stabling their horses in Quaker meetinghouses—events that, in the local consciousness, might have happened yesterday.

One might therefore have expected the cry "The British are coming!" accompanied by a warning ringing of church bells, to greet the opening of an English store in Clinton Corners, but in fact it had caused no such sensation, even though, as I discovered, it was flying a conspicuous Union Jack above the porch, as if General Burgoyne had finally arrived to meet up with General Howe and placed his headquarters here.

Of course Clinton Corners is not exactly Paris, or even neighboring Millbrook. It turned out to be a small, sleepy cluster of houses, with rather more churches than seemed necessary for the number of people who lived there, a video store, and, on the outskirts, an Agway. The English store was the largest commercial establishment in town, and certainly the most visible. It must once have been, in fact, the town's only store, with rockers on the porch and a cat or two sleeping in the window, and it was still in the process of transition when I first entered it. In the back, shelves were full of the usual products carried by any small country store—canned soup, toilet paper, potato chips, and so on. Like most country stores, it catered to locals who had forgotten something on their shopping list when they were at the supermarket, a twenty-minute drive away, and didn't want to go all the way back, or were simply too old or too lazy to drive twenty minutes in the first place. There were farm-fresh eggs, a sparse display of local vegetables, copies of the *Poughkeepsie Journal* and the *Rhinebeck Freeman*, a bulletin board with notices about grange meetings, garage sales, and missing dogs.

Up front, the atmosphere was dramatically different—a positive cornucopia of British goods, some of which I hadn't seen or tasted since my childhood, the need for many of which seemed to me doubtful. Bottles of English Heinz ketchup I could understand, since to the connoisseur it tastes different from the American version, but why Dettol (a liquid antiseptic, of which innumerable American equivalents must exist)? It was as if a regular delivery to a small English village store had been mistakenly rerouted to America. Could anybody in this country want Heinz's Salad Cream, a uniquely English combination of mayonnaise and salad dressing, or chutney sauce, guaranteed to neutralize the taste of any meal, or English laundry soap?

For those with a sweet tooth there was a dazzling array of all those childhood things that make the English a nation of people with bad teeth—Fry's Turkish Delight, Jelly Babies, Aero Milk Chocolate, C&B Treacle Toffees, and the kind of glucose barley sugar sweets that the queen is reputed to carry in her handbag instead of money.

All the same, there was clearly a theme struggling for expression here, an attempt to create a certain English—or perhaps British, for there were many touches of Scotland visible—reality, far from home, down to the smallest authentic detail. Carefully hand-lettered signs taped to the glassed-in deli counter, which held the usual cold cuts and salads, advertised the availability of bangers, chippolatas, Scotch eggs (those doughy, fried cannonballs at the center of which is a hard-boiled egg), homemade steak-and-kidney pie, sausage rolls.

Sausage rolls brought me up with a start. If there was one thing guaranteed to please Margaret (apart from milk-chocolate-covered Hobnobs) it was a sausage roll, which, for those who don't know, is a piece of pastry stuffed with sausage meat—*English* sausage meat, which tastes entirely different from American sausage.

I made my way to the counter—the store was not crowded, but pleasantly full—and asked for half a dozen sausage rolls, which looked and smelled exactly the way they should, the pastry flaky, the sausage meat clearly English, and nicely browned at the ends. Two of these, with a dollop of Coleman's English mustard (the sharp kind, in tiny bottles) and a cup of tea, would, I felt sure, restore Margaret's *hozho,* as the Navajo call the perfect balance between a human being and the world, and maybe even mine, for I am partial to a good sausage roll myself. I remember stopping to buy one on Saturday nights, returning to camp as a young RAF recruit, from a stall just outside the camp gates. One stood there in the fog and drizzle, after a night out on the town in Birmingham or Walsall, drinking tea out of a thick, chipped china mug and wolfing down a sausage roll, trying to put off to the last minute the time to button up one's greatcoat, straighten one's cap, and report in at the guardhouse, where one of our lot, on sentry duty, eyed us enviously from the other side of the gate.

All of this—and more—came back to me as I stood before the counter, while a redheaded man carefully wrapped my sausage rolls in waxed butcher's paper and tied the package up with a string, just as if we were in England. "Do you sell a lot of these?" I asked.

He nodded. "All we can make." His accent was not English. American, with a slight trace of Scotland, I thought—enough perhaps to explain the racks of tea towels with a Scottish theme, the tinned haggis and freshly baked scones, and the many ribald Scottish bumper stickers on display.

"To people in Clinton Corners?"

He looked pained. "They haven't caught on in Clinton Corners yet, no. People drive up from the city, Westchester, and so on. And we sell them by mail, frozen. Sausage rolls freeze very nicely." He handed me a flyer, with a long list of items that could be ordered and mailed, and we fell to chatting, as one does in the country, where time is not of the essence. David Bean, it turned out, was a former child actor, a Californian and amateur aviator who had appeared in *Peter Pan* with Cyril Ritchard (an oil painting of whom graces the shop) and Mary Martin. When he met, and soon married, Jeanie Deeks of Greenwood, Middlesex (near Ealing), a dancer, they were both in the UK production of *West Side Story*. The young couple soon tried, in succession, an art gallery, a gift shop, caretaking country homes, teaching ballet (Jeanie), and selling real estate (David) before buying the Clinton Corners country store. Even then, it took them quite a while before the notion of turning it into an *English* country store occurred to them.

Once it had, there was no stopping them. In twenty years (with one interruption), the store has gradually become more and more English, until the local deli/grocery side of it has vanished from sight, buried under English artifacts, trade goods, and a small but thriving restaurant business. Indeed, Jeanie expresses a slight regret for having chosen Clinton Corners in the first place. Short, plump, energetic, and resourceful, she is a dynamo, cooking, telling ribald stories in stage Cockney, even singing as she dishes up the food. Her first sight of Clinton Corners did not thrill her. One look at the country store, and she said to David, "I want to go home," and started crying. "I didn't think this was for us," she says. "I mean, you're not considered a native here unless you have family buried in the graveyard."

Eventually, however, she saw beyond the immediate possibilities of what was in fact the local farmer's deli and coffee place, and settled down to transform it. It wasn't the ideal location, to be sure, but in the end that doesn't seem to have mattered. For those whose idea of heaven is a choice of dozens of brands of English beer and stout, or a nice slice of veal-and-ham pie, this is the place, maybe the *only* place of its kind on this side of the Atlantic. "It's still Clinton Corners," she says, "not Rhinebeck. If we'd started in Fishkill, nearer the city, we'd have set the world on fire."

Set the world on fire with bottles of Robinson's Barley Water or Ribena, and Jeanie's mother's recipe for bread pudding? But why not? Never underestimate the world's hunger for comfort food. Every Saturday and Sunday from 10:30 A.M. on, the little store, now arranged as a combination shop and restaurant, is packed with people consuming shepherd's pie (the menu boasts, "You'll need a nap after this dish," and indeed there are several large, plump sofas and easy chairs for those who are overcome), Scotch pie, Jeanie's version of the traditional English ploughman's lunch (a Mowberry pork pie, fresh greens, cucumbers, tomatoes, Spanish onions, bread and butter, pickle, and a piece of English cheese), Jeanie's own very English version of chicken curry, fish and chips, and, for those who have room left for dessert, scones with fresh cream or bread pudding. This is not food for the faint of heart (or those on a diet), but it is pretty much guaranteed to stick to the ribs, all the way back to New York City, or farther.

The heart of the business, however, is mail order, with a dizzying array for Anglophiles, from Batchelor's Mushy Peas (don't ask) and Paxo Sage and Onion Stuffing to such hard-to-find staples of English cooking as kippers, Yorkshire pudding mix, and Marmite. There are two and half pages of small print listing enough items to keep a fan of *Masterpiece Theatre* happy all year round.

Celebrities are regulars here (including Liam Neeson, who lives nearby), but everybody gets treated the same—as in an English pub, the atmosphere is friendly, easygoing, and devoted to the serious wolfing down of whatever it is that makes England still seem like home to people whose ancestors revolted against English rule more than two centuries ago (or in the case of Liam Neeson, are still disputing it). It is a measure of the shop's determined Englishness that Jeanie does not serve fancy teas. Her menu proudly boasts that "our tea of the day is

Lyons Quick Brew"—you can't get more English than that! No Earl Grey here, and indeed the tea on sale in packets is the kind of thing our nannies used to drink, PJ Tips and Ty-Phoo.

Indeed, it occurred to me, sitting on one of the sofas reading through old English magazines (many customers while away the afternoons doing this), that what Jeanie and David have created in Clinton Corners, perhaps not intentionally, is the quintessential English comfort zone, a place where the cozy side of English life can be tasted, perhaps more easily than in England itself, which is fast becoming part of Europe. Hence the slightly raffish, defiantly unposh classlessness of the place—a stroke of genius—with none of those fancy goods that you might find in, say, the Fortnum & Mason catalog, or at self-conscious corners in the lobbies of big hotels where they serve an English "tea" consisting of little iced cakes and fancy teas that nobody in England would touch. This is an England where you can put your feet up, drink Lyon's tea out of a mug, and eat yourself into a stupor, where everything in sight has too many calories, too much sugar, or unhealthy amounts of cholesterol, and where late breakfast runs seamlessly into lunch and on into tea, leaving just enough time to buy a few chockies and bikkies and jars of jam and toddle on home for supper, then to bed with a last cup of tea or perhaps even a soothing mug of Horlicks—the England, in short, that most people are thinking about when they express an envy of the English lifestyle. It is ironic, yet somehow comforting, that it has been re-created so lovingly here deep in the American countryside, so effectively that even some of the locals, stern-looking men with mud on their boots who raise Holstein cattle and their solidly built ladies, have gradually become customers, popping in to pick up the odd bar of Cadbury's Fruit and Nut chocolate or try one of the luncheon specials, even the sausage rolls, at first regarded with considerable suspicion.

I walked out of the store, whistling the old music hall song—
I like a nice cup of tea in the morning,
For it starts the day, you see.

At half-past eleven, my idea of heaven
Is a nice cup of tea.

I like a nice cup of tea with my dinner,
And a nice cup of tea with my tea,
And when it's time for bed, there's a lot to be said,
For a nice cup of tea.

Come to think of it, on a cold, crispy day, a sausage roll popped in the microwave might not be so bad to go with that cup of tea, I said to myself.

CHAPTER TWENTY-ONE

"Make That a Dozen Barbarian Kremes"

OF COURSE when it comes to socializing, particularly at the beginning of the day, the Dunkin' Donuts on Pleasant Valley's Main Street is a lot closer to home than the English store. I'm a regular at Dunkin' Donuts, though, I hasten to add, I don't have a regular *table,* unlike, say, Frank Zanchelli, a former IBMer who now details cars and likes to begin the day at the Dunkin' Donuts, seated at the table next to the side door with the *Poughkeepsie Journal,* where he can see his customers *and* their cars. I usually stop off there to pick up coffee for Margaret's barn help, one of those things that seemed like a nice thing to do on a cold winter's morning and quickly turned into a daily ritual. Well, there's nothing wrong with a ritual. If you don't like rituals, don't live in the country.

I'm not a doughnut man myself, but I feel the same way about

Dunkin' Donuts that my friend Larry McMurtry feels about the Dairy Queen in Archer City, Texas, his hometown. It's as close as Pleasant Valley, a utilitarian place if ever there was one, is ever going to get to having an agora like ancient Greek towns, or even to the shaded square with a war memorial in front of the courthouse of most small Southern towns. This is where citizens meet, chat, exchange greetings and information, and catch up with each other. The ladies behind the counter of the Pleasant Valley Dunkin' Donuts probably know more about what's going on in town than anyone else. It's at the Dunkin' Donuts, if you hang around a little, that you can hear the town gossip, such as it is, and pick up on local doings, the very occasional murder, the more frequent fires and automobile accidents, the funeral service for one of the Black Roses—for Sister Sabrina, as a matter of fact, founder of the local Black Rose chapter of Sisters in the Wind, an all-woman motorcycle club, who was killed on her bike in an accident with a car—to be held in the parking lot of Sawmill Plaza in front of a semi-defunct biker bar and a completely defunct slot-car racing salon, to be followed by a solemn memorial motorcycle run through town.

Some things about the Dunkin' Donuts I cherish, among them the fact that a lot of the customers refer to Bavarian kreme doughnuts—a local favorite, involving large amounts of whipped cream and powdered sugar—as "barbarian kreme" doughnuts, including one of my local motorcycling acquaintances, whose regular breakfast order (more likely post-breakfast) is for a large French vanilla, light and sweet, and two barbarian kremes, and perhaps as a result has had to trade his way up to bigger and bigger bikes as his weight increases, until he now rides a monster Japanese full-dresser that looks like a ship of the line in full sail coming down the road, if you can imagine a ship of the line painted candy-apple metallic red and equipped with a reverse gear, an intercom, a full stereo sound system for rider and passenger, and enough lights for an oil rig.

As a matter of fact, the Dunkin' Donuts is a pretty good place to go whenever you have a mechanical problem—it's right next to the service station, so there's usually a mechanic there, as well as the guys from the service department at Pleasant Valley Ford, who get their coffee there, as do their colleagues from the two tractor service places on Route 44, so there's no shortage of expertise. Well, perhaps "expertise" is putting it a bit strongly, but there's no shortage of strongly held opinion on whatever might seem to be ailing your machinery, anyway.

None of this mattered much to us so long as we were limited to one or two cars and a motorcycle, but as our country weekend house turned into our home, then metamorphosed into Stonegate Farm, our fleet of vehicles and machines grew apace. To Harold Roe's concern, we added a Yamaha "Terra-Pro" four-wheeler so Margaret could zip around the property, checking out fences and so on—not to speak of checking up on Harold himself—and soon found that it could tow either a bush-hog mower or a small cart, giving Margaret a chance to mow those areas of her fields that weren't big enough for Harold to bother with. The Terra-Pro was the thin end of the wedge, leading eventually to three cars, one seriously big Ford pickup truck, two trailers, three tractors, and two four-wheelers, not to speak of a snowblower, a couple of leaf blowers, and any number of gasoline-powered hedge trimmers, Weedwackers, and so on.

At that, most of our neighbors had collections of vehicles and equipment that dwarfed ours, Dutchess County, like most of rural America, being devoted to the belief that every imaginable task can be performed better with the right piece of machinery, and that no vehicle is ever so tired, rusty, and clapped-out that you need to get rid of it, with the result that people's garages, driveways, barns, and lawns are one big parking lot, jammed wheel-to-wheel, occasionally with objects that prompt the visitor to ask, "What the hell is *that?*" Harold Roe himself had two big garages behind his house—each much bigger than the house—packed with enough agricultural machinery for a collective farm, and kept himself busy at night maintaining it all with a grease gun and a spray can of WD-40, emerging only for supper and the evening news. On occasions when I went to visit him—to drop off a Christmas present or beard him in his den when he was trying to avoid a summons from Margaret—you could tell he was at home by the bright, purplish glare of his welder's torch out there behind the house.

The country is no place for those who doubt the wisdom of the internal combustion engine, or have environmental concerns about gasoline or diesel fuel. Older people up here remember what it was like—or at least recall their parents and grandparents remembering—when farming was done by teams of horses and sheer human muscle power, and nobody has any nostalgia for the good old days before the first Ford Model T chugged through the old wooden covered bridge that connected Pleasant Valley to the rest of the world.

Those memories contribute to a certain caution and thriftiness too—it isn't a place where people rush out to exchange a perfectly good car for a shiny new one every couple of years, except for the thin layer of professional people at the top. Then too, plenty of people in rural America need lots of cheap transportation—a family with three teenage kids is likely to own the husband's truck, the wife's van, and three beat-up but serviceable old cars for the kids, not to speak of motorcycles, trail bikes, four-wheelers, mowers, and snowmobiles. People who buy cars cheaply from the classified ads in the *Pennysaver* aren't looking for a miracle. If they find something that can be kept running for a while, great; when it stops running, it ends up on the lawn, to be cannibalized for spare parts to keep other vehicles running. Thus a family that needs, say, six vehicles in running condition may have a dozen or more cars scattered around the house, in various stages of repair or decrepitude, until they reach the final stage in which they are abandoned, jacked up on cinder blocks, and used for target practice. What seems, to a suburban- or city-bred person, like waste or sheer environmental irresponsibility is in fact the only way people who can't just go on down to a dealer and lease a new car when they want one can provide transport for every member of the family. Of course the easy way, if you've got the money and/or the credit rating, is to buy a new car; the hard way is to buy a lot of cheap used vehicles in the hope that you can keep some of them, at least, on the road. Safety lies in numbers—the more vehicles you have, the more likely you are to find something that can be jump-started when you absolutely need to go somewhere, not to speak of a source of spare parts right at your doorstep.

We had often joked about those of our neighbors whose driveway and lawn were littered with wrecked and rusty vehicles, but from the moment that Richard Bacon persuaded Margaret to buy our first tractor, I began to develop a fellow feeling for them. Margaret's Terra-Pro could at least be serviced by the local Yamaha dealer—and it was no great trick to load it into the bed of a pickup truck with a couple of planks—but our first tractor was something of an antique.

I had supposed that when Margaret talked about buying a tractor of her own to use around the farm that it would be something neat and modern, like Harold's Kubota—an expensive bright orange Japanese machine that represented the current state of the art in small tractors—but it turned out that Richard had in mind something less expensive.

Down on Route 44, out past the Masonic lodge, the firehouse, and the old mill, was a sprawling former dairy farm where two rather silent brothers ran a farm-implement repair place. They also sold vintage tractors—much too old to be called merely "used"—and here Richard found for Margaret a Ford tractor from the early 1940s that he felt was a real bargain.

At first I was doubtful at the idea of turning Margaret loose on the land at the wheel of a tractor that had been manufactured about the time of World War II, but that, I was assured, was not a problem. Tractor technology had hardly changed at all in the last thirty or forty years, and there was almost nothing in one that could wear out or break—they were just about as indestructible as a piece of machinery could be. The one Richard had in mind was a good specimen, old but solid, and would give us, he promised, years of service.

I wrote out a check, and a few days later an object appeared that looked as if it belonged in one of the Smithsonian Institution's collections—early twentieth-century American agriculture, perhaps. One look at it was enough to make me feel I should run, not walk to, Jack Haverty's Auto Parts on Main Street and stock up on motor oil, WD-40, and Loctite. The tractor had been resprayed a cheerful light blue, but all the paint in the world couldn't conceal its age, or altogether cover the many layers of rust, grime, and oil. Richard pressed the starter, and it roared to life instantly. Promising to show Margaret how to use it at the earliest opportunity, he took it off behind the studio barn, next to the gas tank. It was a lot bigger than I had imagined, with huge rear wheels and tiny front ones set close together, like a child's toy tractor, and an uncomfortable-looking metal seat, mounted on a single curved spring.

One afternoon he taught Margaret to drive it, then me. There was a long, springy gearshift that came up between your legs and required major two-handed force to move; a foot brake that seemed to produce no perceptible slowing down of the tractor, not at any rate for what felt like a very long time; and a stiff hand throttle set inside the steering wheel. No amount of WD-40 ever loosened the throttle handle—the nut holding it had apparently been torqued down by Thor. The steering was slow, like that of a ship—you moved the wheel, waited, and eventually, in its own sweet time, the tractor changed direction. It would be an exaggeration to say that I took to it like a duck to water, but then it was Margaret's tractor, not mine. It had a big, flat bush-hog mower behind, and a complicated hydraulic system to raise or lower it as needed. The hydraulics were iffy, at least for me. I would pull the lever decisively, and the whole bush hog, which seemed to weigh a ton, would come up behind me until it was several feet off the ground, which is where you wanted it to be while you were driving along the road, say. Then, once I was out onto the road, steering like crazy, there would be a tremendous crash behind me as the bush hog descended onto the road surface of its own weight. You had to keep your hand on the lever, Richard said, so you could feel when the hydraulic pressure was slackening off, then give her another tweak or two to keep it up. I could feel nothing, and the bush hog was always down when I wanted it to be up, and vice versa. Margaret took to it much better, maybe because she was the one who really saw herself mowing, a farmer's daughter blossoming late.

Right from scratch the tractor was temperamental. There is nothing complicated about tractors—"If you've got gas and a spark, she'll start," we were told, over and over again, as if it were a mantra—but getting a spark wasn't always easy, and sometimes getting gas wasn't either. Some days you could just sit there on the high, cold, uncomfortable metal seat, cranking the engine time after time, and nothing happened. Richard would come over, fiddle about with it for a bit, then start it up. It was the choke, he said. Or dirt in the fuel filter. Or maybe dirt in the fuel filter *and* the choke. But mostly it was the choke. You had to have the right feel for the choke, pull it all the way out for the first couple of tries, then lay off it before she flooded. Once she flooded, you were a gone goose.

In Richard's absence one of the two brothers who had sold us the tractor would come over when there was a problem and start it up for us. They agreed that we were probably giving her too much or too little choke, but thought there might be a problem with the spark too. That was such a common problem that they carried spare alternators wrapped in old newspapers in their pickup truck, but no matter how many times the alternator was changed, the tractor remained surly and unreliable. Sometimes it would burst into life with the first push on the starter, sometimes it wouldn't start for either of us at all. "You're giving her too much choke," the older brother would say. "Go easy with that there choke." The younger brother would shake his head, next time I called. I should pay no attention to his brother. "You're not giving her enough choke," he'd say. "Pull that choke out all the way before you crank her." There was no happy medium, apparently.

My own interest in the Ford tractor came to an abrupt end when I was asked to put it away behind the garage one afternoon. I swung myself into the seat, got it started, for once without trouble, steered it toward the right place, then laboriously put it in reverse to do what I hoped would be a successful job of parking. Right behind the tractor's parking space was a low-hanging limb of a substantial hemlock tree. I let out the clutch and advanced the throttle and with a sudden backward leap the tractor carried me into the overhanging branch, knocking me right off the seat. As the branch hit my neck, my arm caught the handle for the hydraulic system, and the bush hog dropped to the ground with an almighty crash. Fortunately, the tractor had stalled before I could break my neck. From a distance, I could see Richard Bacon shaking his head as he watched. He walked over to inspect the damage. "You might want to let that clutch out a bit more slowly," he said gravely.

I nodded, and made a vow to keep off the tractor in future. Margaret, however, persisted, and obviously enjoyed doing the odd bit of mowing when the opportunity presented itself, although on her first solo attempt the tractor chugged on at a steady rate straight into the fencing of one her paddocks, carrying her right through it. It was a scene to remember—Margaret high on the seat of this huge, bright blue tractor, steering and braking like crazy while it moved forward inexorably and unstoppably into a section of Eddie McDonald's expensive Secretariat fencing.

She too commented on the alarming nature of the experience. The tractor didn't move fast, unlike, say, a car, but it was hard to stop once it got going. Even moving no faster than a man can walk, it could knock down a pretty substantial chunk of fencing.

As our vehicle count rose, I got more used to the presence of mechanics around the place. Like old-fashioned doctors, they still made house calls, and also like old-fashioned doctors they clung firmly to their opinions and operated on the principle of "by guess and by gosh." I would come out of the house to find a solid, broad-beamed figure in blue overalls bent over one or other of the tractors, who would straighten up slowly and stretch his back as I hove into view. "The alternator again?" I say cheerfully, usually a fairly safe bet.

A mournful shake of the head in reply. "Nope, her alternator is fine." He wipes his hands on an oily rag before shaking mine.

A pause while we stand on opposite sides of the tractor, looking down at the engine, like doctors examining a patient on the operating table.

"See, you've got your spark," Steve, or Ed, or Jim will say, touching a wire with a wrench and producing an alarming avalanche of sparks, like a fireworks display.

"Richard thought it might be the battery, but I guess not," I say.

"That was first thing we did, was put a new battery in her."

"Ah. Good. So we've got spark?"

"Yup."

"How about gas? Have we got gas?"

"Yup. Filter's clean. I checked her fuel pump."

"That leaves us with?"

"Could be spark plugs. They might have oiled up on her."

"Ah."

Knowing that further conversation will lead nowhere—as well as exposing the depths of my ignorance—I walk off, leaving the mechanic to his work. When I come back, he is gone. There is a scrap of oily paper attached to the seat—his bill. Scrawled at the top, written with a thick, blunt pencil, is a note: "Runs fine." Nowhere does it say what the problem was, which means that next time we have to start from scratch, leaving to one side the possibility that although the tractor started up okay for the mechanic, it may not start up for Margaret or for me.

Again, like old-fashioned doctors, while our mechanics never agreed with each other, they refused to criticize a colleague. If we weren't able to get Jim—there were apparently tractors on farms all over Dutchess County waiting for a mechanic to turn up—Ed might come and shake his head gravely on being told that the plugs might have been the problem last time.

"You must have got that wrong," he would say, in a tone of mild accusation.

"That's what Jim seemed to think—"

Quick to cut off criticism of a colleague: "Well, he knows his tractors, Jim does. But me, I think it's your alternator."

"But we just had another one put in."

"Yes, but she could be shorting on you." He bends over the tractor, ducking out of sight, and stays there uncomfortably, loosening wires and banging a wrench against solid chunks of iron to show he's working on the problem. Every once in a while, he touches a screwdriver to a wire and creates a shower of sparks. It's clear that my presence is neither helpful nor required—that in fact no serious work will be done until I'm gone—so I go off about my business, such as it is, and by the time I get back, there's a bill on the seat of the tractor, with a penciled note that reads, "She runs O.K. now." No indication of what the problem was. Naturally.

Of course we live in a world where the old verities of the internal combustion engine no longer count for much, and shade-tree mechanics like this are something of a dying breed. Everything automotive is electronic, computerized, and has to be taken back to the dealer to be fixed, and in fact in most new cars the engine is covered by sheets of molded plastic in streamlined forms precisely to discourage the average person from getting in there with a box wrench or a pair of pliers to screw things up. There's a plug on board the car somewhere, into which "an authorized factory-trained technician" inserts a handheld computer that supposedly identifies the problem and suggests what needs to be replaced. Cars being cars, there are still plenty of things on which to scrape your knuckles, or ways to drench yourself in hot oil, or burn yourself badly, but by and large the diagnostic side of automotive repair has been removed from the hands of two guys in oil-stained overalls peering under the hood looking for a loose wire or a leaking hose, and placed in the hands of a guy with clean overalls and a computer.

When it comes to old farm equipment (and old cars), however, the old ways still hold good. You open the hood, test for a spark, see if she's getting gas, and try cranking her. A degree in computer science and freshly pressed clean white overalls aren't called for.

If you have enough equipment, you soon get to know a cross section of the area's mechanics, and learn which ones are reliable, which ones are likely to come in a hurry, and which ones seem to have stumbled into their profession by mistake, or learned their trade from one of those mail-order schools that advertise on the cover of giveaway books of matches—*"Learn auto repair at home in six weeks! Make good money! No experience needed!"*

Since there's hardly a moment when something mechanical doesn't need attention somewhere on the premises—and that's just *outside* we're talking about, we're not even going to get into the guys who come around to service appliances, or to revive the cable box after a storm, or to look after the well-being of the fax machine and the copier—it's a rare day when there aren't at least a couple of vans parked in the driveway and the sound of somebody hammering hard on metal in the background.

Perhaps it's why it always takes me a while to shop at the Dunkin' Donuts. There's nearly always somebody in the line wearing overalls whose face I recognize, and who clearly recognizes me, so I'm obliged to stop and think who it is who's smiling at me, and scan mentally through a list of machinery until I come up with the answer—Ah, the guy who couldn't figure out why Margaret's International Harvester wouldn't start! Ah, the guy who crossed the wires on the Ford so the ammeter kept draining the battery!—and make the connection, then wish him a good day as he collects his barbarian kremes and his coffee.

CHAPTER TWENTY-TWO

The Sporting Instinct

GOING EVENTING IS ONE THING; giving a cross-country trials on your own property is quite another.

In the first place, when you go eventing, it's somebody else's fields that are being torn up by horses' hooves when it rains on the day, and of course it's *their* fences, not yours, that are being knocked down, and *their* fields and lawns that are being turned into mud puddles as people park trailers and cars there. The food concession, the Porta Pottis, the PA system, all that is their problem, and good luck to them.

Still, with all the land we had at our disposal, it seemed like a generous idea for Margaret to put on her own trials. I didn't give too much thought it to it, except to ask if we needed special insurance, which, it soon turned out, we most certainly did. It would be fair to say, in fact, that I seriously underestimated what we were getting involved in.

Certainly I couldn't have guessed that eleven years later we would still be doing it.

Perhaps the initial benefactor was Harold Roe, who was happy enough to take up a new profession as a builder of fences and jumps and obstacles for the cross-country phase of a combined training event. Harold's hours—and hourly rate—soared as he puzzled over drawings and photographs of oxers and log jumps and stone walls from *Chronicle of the Horse* and *Horse and Hound*, not to speak of the fact that he and Margaret went off on field trips to look at other people's cross-country courses. Harold had a sweet tooth as well developed as that of a bear, and he would travel almost anywhere if there was a big bar of Cadbury's Fruit and Nut chocolate in the glove compartment. Argumentative, difficult, and opinionated Harold might be, but he dearly loved a challenge.

Of course holding a big sporting event of any kind on your own property is one of those things you either yearn to do or you don't, and this was clearly a yearning that Margaret had been feeling for many years—perhaps going back to her childhood foxhunting days in England. Not having grown up in the country, it wasn't among my fantasies, but I've always been a great respecter of other people's—besides which, there's a certain lord-of-the-manor appeal to the idea that is hard to resist. I saw myself, tweed-jacketed and benevolent, in the role of Bertie Wooster's uncle in the novels of P. G. Wodehouse, dispensing hospitality and sage advice on the subject of horses and pigs, a country gentleman of the old school, transported to the new world.

In any event, the whole idea of the big sporting event on one's own land was a well-established tradition among the Dutchess County gentry, or what passed for gentry since the Depression and World War II. There was undoubtedly a certain noblesse oblige aspect to the whole business, perhaps stemming from the simple fact of owning (or renting) enough land to have a lot of people ride over it, or whatever. Some people open their land to pheasant hunters (as we did, for a while, until we decided we preferred the birds to the hunters); some people yearn to have the local hunt meet on their front lawn and serve stirrup cups to mounted neighbors in scarlet coats; some people host balloon meets—there's just no saying what fantasies lurk in people's minds, waiting to emerge once they own a country place. I have a friend who has a flagpole on his lawn, and a working cannon, and fires off a salute every evening as he lowers the flag—something his neighbors can hardly object to without seeming unpatriotic—and another who hosts clay pigeon shoots from behind his pool house.

Running more than a hundred horses cross-country over big fences twice in one day is not something that can be done, or prepared for, without attracting attention, not that we were exactly trying to keep it secret. Down in Pleasant Valley, those who had noticed all the preparations as they drove along our road to and from Hyde Park and Rhinebeck would ask what we were doing up at the old Hewlett farm, and when I explained, would shake their head in wonder, as if to say, "Well, what else can you expect from city people?" I was reminded of a dinner party one evening many years before at the country home in Katonah, New York, of Mollie Parniss, the famous dress designer and wealthy Democratic hostess, to which I had been invited because her son, Bob Livingston, was a friend of mine at Oxford. At some point during the dinner Mollie Parniss asked me what my hobbies were, and I told her briefly, I thought, how much I enjoyed riding horses. Her eyes glazed over as I spoke, and as soon as she could she interrupted me firmly. "Listen to me," she said, in the tone of one offering frank and useful social advice to a young person, "everything to do with horses is *goyische nachess,* and don't you ever forget it."*

Goyische nachess was not a phrase that would have come to the lips of most people in Pleasant Valley, but the thought, or its equivalent, was

**Goyische nachess* is a Yiddish phrase best translated as "gentile nonsense," or perhaps more accurately as, "The kind of trouble and nonsense on which only a goy would waste time."

certainly there, at the sight of fences going up and being numbered and flagged, trails mowed, and parking lots for trailers prepared and fenced off by the road. It was, I could see from the expressions of people at the bar in Cady's, or at the GU, or at Mrs. Cotter's liquor store, just the kind of thing you'd expect from people who had spent a lot of money to put up a huge building just to ride horses in.

On the other hand, we were employing Harold Roe and creating business, which was all to the good, no doubt; besides which there's a tendency in small towns like Pleasant Valley, which find themselves too close for comfort to the nearest big city (if only Poughkeepsie) and look with some envy toward places only a few miles away where the property values are a little higher and there's less pressure from developers, to cling to the community's original rural roots. Although on the one hand a natural greed makes people want to line Route 44 with as many car washes, mini-malls, convenience stores (read self-serve gas stations that sell milk and groceries), and two-story apartment complexes with misleading rural names ("Fox Run Estates," and so on) as possible, there's also a need to emphasize the country life, to demonstrate that while this may not be as rural a place as backwoodsy Pine Plains, or Millerton, or Copake, on the other hand, it's not just another vinyl-sided suburb where people can have a tree in their backyard or a sight of wooded hills (flawed by the crisscrossing of power lines, admittedly) from their upstairs window, and still commute to a job in White Plains or Wappingers Falls; in short, that it has a soul of sorts.

The old men and young kids fishing from the highway bridge as you come into town are part of that, as is Paul Wigsten's farm, with its farm stand, goats, and resident pig, as is Jerry and Alta Conklin's organic vegetable farm, right smack in the center of town (self-service on Sundays because the Conklins are Christians as well as firm believers in the health benefits of organic food, and pillars of the Millbrook Farmers' Market and Pleasant Valley's own, held next to the parking lot of the GU on Friday afternoons). Take away that sense of being linked to a rural, agricultural world, and Pleasant Valley might be seen as a suburb of Poughkeepsie (it certainly looks that way on the map), a place with rather more small animal hospitals and nail and hair salons than a town of eight thousand souls would really seem to need—which perhaps explains why at the very epicenter of the town, right at its heart, at the crossroad, there still remains an old-fashioned family-owned feed store, housed in a traditional red barn, directly across from the cemetery and the town hall, squeezed between the Ford dealership and a bicycle shop. *S'il n'existait pas, il fallait l'inventer.*

Seen in this context, our event—though cross-country trials are hardly a spectator sport except at the very highest levels—might have been seen as a blow for Pleasant Valley's rural identity, right up there with turkey shoots and the opening of deer season, were it not that anything to do with horses tends to have an elitist ring to it. In any event, Margaret persevered, astonishing me with the sheer volume of work and attention to detail necessary to bring it off. My contribution, apart from signing checks, was to draw up detailed course maps for three divisions (in order of difficulty, beginner-novice, novice, and training) and to help scour the list of our friends for fence judges. Each fence requires a fence judge, who must observe whether or not a horse and rider has cleared the fence, and the fence judge must stick to his or her post faithfully, despite bad weather, biting insects, nearby clumps of poison ivy, boredom, arguments with competitors (or worse yet, in the case of children, their mothers), and the need to go to the bathroom. Every fence judge has to be equipped with a two-way radio, a clipboard, a Bic pen, and printed score sheets that are picked up by regular intervals, as well as a large clear plastic Ziploc bag to put the clipboard and score sheet in, in case of rain. A folding chair, an umbrella, and a hat are strongly recommended.

Needless to say, the event is not just a test of horsemanship but also, for the organizer, a test of friendship. If there are, say, eighteen fences, then you need at least eighteen fence judges in the morning, and another eighteen after lunch, since for most people four hours of fence judging is enough. Some people take to this kind of thing like a duck to water, others don't. We knew we could rely on such stalwarts as our friends Dick and Meryl Olpe, for example. True, they were both city dwellers, but they were also retired police officers, used to the idea of standing outdoors in bad weather and telling people what to do, and with a certain matter-of-fact toughness that comes handy in country matters.

Once, when they were staying with us for a dinner party, Roxie Bacon appeared from the barn in tears just as we were about to sit down to dinner to announce that one of Margaret's horses had been wounded by a hunter. We all trouped out to the barn, and found that the horse had indeed been wounded, in the shoulder, by a hunting arrow—presumably the kind that has an arrowhead that expands on entry, which the horse had managed to dislodge, but which had left a wound big enough and deep enough to put your fist into. It is hard to imagine how anybody could mistake a horse for a deer—a horse weighs about ten times as much, to begin with—which is one of the many reasons why deer hunters make me nervous, but harder still to imagine wounding an animal and just walking away from the situation, leaving it in pain and possibly to bleed to death. Roxie had stanched the wound as best she could, and Mike Murphy, who was then one of our horse vets, arrived quickly and took charge as we stood around and watched.

Dick Olpe is a big man, built in the tradition of the old-fashioned kind of New York City cop, from back when sheer size was thought to be essential to the job. Though he is in fact the gentlest and kindest of men, it is hard to imagine anybody *not* surrendering at the sight of Dick getting out of a police car, or circumstances in which he would need to draw his revolver. He towered above Mike by a head and watched the proceedings with keen interest, and without flinching.

Mike asked Dick if he was upset by the sight of blood, and Dick said he wasn't, no, so Mike asked him if he'd mind holding down two flaps of muscle, deep in the wound, while he sutured them. Dick reached in with strong fingers and did as he was told.

When Mike was done, he complimented Dick on his strong stomach. Most people, he said, just went to pieces when it came to dealing with deep wounds. What, he asked, was Dick's profession?

Dick rinsed his hands and shrugged. "I'm a cop," he said. "All things considered, this wasn't too bad. When I was in command of a detective squad, out in Brooklyn, some of the guys found a severed head under the Verrazano and left it in my desk drawer as a joke." He paused reflectively. "That was a lot worse than this."

I felt sure that whatever happened, the Olpes would make good fence judges, and would know how to deal with even the most difficult of competitors, and so it proved over many years. Others I was less sure of. Margaret's horse people were safe enough, of course, but about many of our friends from the city I was more doubtful. As the day neared, however, the sheer logistics of it all gradually had a numbing effect—*"Qué sera, sera"* might as well have been our motto. There was an EMT man with his truck, in case of a serious injury, the blacksmith, a vet, two competing photographers, the man with the food concession truck (who also produced box lunches for all the fence judges), the couple who ran the local tack shop to serve as starters and timekeepers, a young woman with a computer to handle scoring, Detlef Juerss, an upcoming local builder who became our friend, with a tractor, to tow trucks and trailers out in case it rained and they got stuck, Harold to repair damaged fences, Richard Bacon to install and maintain a generator-powered PA system, not to speak of people to look after the warm-up area and to pick up the fence judges' scoring sheets—in short, a cast of what seemed like thousands.

I felt a certain déjà vu that was hard to identify until the day before the event. I was sitting out in the field with Margaret on folding chairs as contestants arrived to pick up their maps and numbered "pinnies" and walk the course, when it came to me that it was exactly like an outdoor location in the movie business—the same need to keep a thousand things in mind, the same concern about the weather, the same difficulties in mediating between the performers and the technicians. Margaret and I sat side by side on canvas chairs, trying to look calm, in control, and confident of the weather, just as I had often seen my uncle Alex and my father sit in identical chairs, surrounded by the expensive chaos they had summoned up, smoking and talking from time to time in Hungarian. I remembered seeing Alex, Vincent, and Cecil Beaton sitting in front of a life-size plaster replica of the arch at Hyde Park Corner at Shepperton Studios during the making of *Lady Windermere's Fan,* while a prop man held a big umbrella over them to shield them from the pouring rain and a huge crowd of extras, riders on horses, and horse-drawn carriages milled about waiting for a break in the clouds. I remembered seeing my father and John Huston in Venice during the making of *Summertime,* seated under an umbrella in front of the Grand Canal while prop men in boats and the Venice Fire Police poured disinfectant into the water before Katharine Hepburn fell in. I remembered countless other outdoors locations, with my father peering from under the brim of his battered hat at the sky and muttering, "Ach, vat a silly bloody business this is!" I don't think I ever admired Margaret's determination, sangfroid, and sheer organizing skill more than I did that day, as Richard struggled with the balky rented generator in the background and competitors stopped to complain or simply to say, a few of them, how much they liked the course.

My role on the day was to go around the course on Zapata, keeping out of the competitors' way and picking up the score sheets at regular intervals to bring back to "the secretary's booth," in one of Margaret's trailers, parked near the finish line. It did not seem likely to tax my abilities, nor Zapata's, I thought, but then I woke at 5:00 A.M. to a gray, rainy day—not just rainy but pouring, the ultimate nightmare for any outdoor event.

Margaret and I looked at each other, but we both knew that there was nothing to be done. I had been to plenty of events where it rained, and the competition went on. If it rained for days beforehand, you might cancel an event because the ground became so slippery that it was dangerous to ride on, but if it rained on the day, the show invariably went on—there was no turning back.

We roused our reluctant houseguests and splashed out to Margaret's truck in the unappetizing dawn, with sheets of rain coming down, driven by a high wind and a low temperature that promised a day of acute, bone-chilling misery. I was reminded of the NATO maneuvers of 1952, which, together with the Hungarian Revolution of 1956, had seemed until now among the more memorably uncomfortable experiences of my life—heavy rain alternating with light snow for three days and nights, the latter spent in a leaky tent pitched on the slope of a drenched Alpine meadow in the Hartz Mountains and shared with three near-mutinous airmen and a drunken Australian company sergeant-major. The face of a horse is not necessarily expressive of any easily discernible emotion, but as Zapata was tacked up for me, he seemed to be saying to himself, "You've *got* to be kidding!"

I thought he might have a point. No rain gear made in the world was going to keep me dry in this, so I donned rubber boots, chaps, a voluminous rain poncho, and, on top of that, a big black garbage bag with holes cut into the bottom of it for my head and arms. On my head I wore an old Stetson with the brim artfully curled so as to provide a steady, cold spout of rain down my neck. Thus equipped, Zapata and I squelched off toward the event grounds by the back way as Margaret delivered the fence judges to their posts in the truck. They looked like troops about to be sent over the top into no-man's-land in World War I, milling around in the downpour, feet sinking into the mud, unable to believe that cruel fate had placed them here, but apparently resigned to it. I gave them a cheery wave and rode on to the secretary's booth—Margaret's trailer—where everybody was staring into the leaden sky and saying things like, "Well, one good thing—when it's coming down as hard as this, it can't last long."

I took Margaret to one side. "Are you sure we shouldn't cancel this?" I asked, trying to get as much of Zapata as I could under the awning.

She gave me a fierce look. "We can't."

"The show has to go on?"

"You know it has to." I knew it. I had been to plenty of events to watch Margaret compete in similar weather. At Gladstone, New Jersey, the headquarters of the United States Equestrian Olympic Team, I had once watched her ride her dressage test in a downpour so strong that I couldn't see her through the viewfinder of my camera—in the dressage ring the mud was so deep and liquid that it looked as if she was riding in brown soup. If it rained "on the day," that was it—you went on with the competition until somebody had won it, or drowned.

The amazing thing, I thought, was that people were still willing, even eager, to compete in this weather—which, as we watched them, was in fact getting worse, not better, proving unnecessarily that no matter how hard it rains, it can always rain harder. Eventually enough of them had competed that I had to mount Zapata and ride off to pick up the score sheets from the fence judges. At each fence I had to take the damp sheet of paper and fold it as carefully as I could into a waterproof canvas military haversack so that the ink didn't run. Some of the judges asked if there was any chance it would all be called off soon. "Not much," I told them. Others wondered if I could bring round a thermos of hot coffee next time. I said there was not much chance of that either. They didn't seem surprised. One or two of them offered me their pocket flask, and I was sorely tempted.

By midmorning there was no sign of improvement. From below, by the road, we could hear the roar of Detlef Juerss's diesel tractor as he freed trucks and trailers from the mud. Even people with four-wheel-drive vehicles were sinking into the mud and getting hopelessly stuck. And yet the competitors still went off at regular intervals, cantering away into the impenetrable rain and mist to reappear, eventually, covered in mud. Zapata and I plodded out to the fence judges at regular intervals, and plodded back with our sodden cargo of score sheets.

Eventually Margaret looked up sharply and said, "That horse is all tucked up. He ought to be taken in and dried before he gets sick." It was on the tip of my tongue to say that he wasn't any wetter than the rest of us, but I knew better. The person who was wettest—and suffering most—was Margaret. This was *her* event, carefully planned and prepared for, down to the last detail, and it was turning into a nightmare. One of the fence judges, an old friend from New York, had actually walked off and deserted his post (the Olpes, needless to say, stayed to the bitter end), and as the day progressed even some of the competitors failed to turn up.

Still, the day gradually drew to a sodden end, with the rain coming down heavier than ever. I had been moved to the secretary's booth to do the announcing over the PA system now that Zapata had been reprieved and sent home, but even so I was waterlogged. I cursed myself for not having been clever enough to bring along a pocket flask myself. By the time the day finally sloshed to an end—the rain was still coming down in solid sheets; the ground looked like a nineteenth-century field of battle, Waterloo perhaps, where it rained similarly, with disastrous effects on Napoleon's cavalry and artillery; the task of picking up the sodden, overflowing garbage cans and emptying the secretary's booth seemed daunting—all I could think about, all *anybody* could think about, was getting it all over with, then plunging into a hot bath with a stiff drink.

I made Margaret an Absolut tonic with lime. "I'm *never* going to do this again," she said vehemently. I nodded skeptically—correctly, for we have been doing it ever since, except for one year when it rained for a week beforehand, turning the course into a quagmire that would not only have made it impossible to compete but, worse yet, impossible to get even a four-wheel-drive vehicle anywhere near the fences to reach anybody who was injured.

One thing, though, was that the disastrous weather drew more attention to us than if the competition had been held successfully under bright, sunny skies. Disaster strikes a sympathetic chord among our neighbors, and people we hardly even knew stopped us in the street (well, in the parking lot of the GU, really, since Pleasant Valley doesn't run to much in the way of sidewalk traffic or even sidewalks), to say how sorry they were, as if we'd had a death in the family. This was no expression of Schadenfreude—it was genuine, well-meant, and sincere, a sign that we were at last becoming part of the community. Besides, going ahead with it in the face of the elements was a sign of true grit, an edifying example of the local determination to get on with whatever it is even in the face of a blizzard or a nor'easter. Total strangers would haul their shopping cart to a halt to say, "Aren't you the folks who live up at the old Hewlett farm? Had that big horse thing on that Sunday it just rained and poured?"

When we admitted that we were indeed those people, they would shake their head and nod as if to say, "What next?" One old person did say, but sotto voce, to her friend, "The Hewletts never had no sense either," but the general consensus was favorable. After all, Dutchess County gets more than its fair share of bad weather—it's not exactly Tuscany—and if you waited for good weather to do something, you'd never get it done. Mud, rain, wind, it's all part of country living, and if you can't put up with them, the general feeling goes, you might as well give up and go live in New York City or Florida.

CHAPTER TWENTY-THREE

Free Kittens!

In memory of Queenie and Jake

It wouldn't be a home without cats, some people say, Margaret among them—admittedly we don't have a dozen or so like our neighbors the Lynns, all of them strictly indoor cats (the Lynns buy kitty litter by the *truck*load), but I like to think that Margaret does her fair share.

Of course it's hard to avoid cats in the country, where the plaintive hand-lettered sign FREE KITTENS! seems to sprout on every other mailbox, but even without free kittens, cats tend to simply turn up at the door when they've had enough of living wild and somehow stake a claim to a dish of food and a place in the household, or at least on the porch.

Not that there aren't plenty of dogs and dog lovers—there's hardly a household around us without at least one dog—but much as Margaret likes dogs, she's really a cat person to the bone, though in the best of all possible worlds she'd probably have both.

Except for the two cats with which we originally started our life in the country, which were city-bred and obtained from the pound, all of our cats have adopted us by turning up on the doorstep. Well, some of them, actually, have had to be tempted to do so, after living wild for so long that they were almost feral, but most cats retain a firm memory of domesticity, involving regular meals, central heating, and varying degrees of affection, and aren't living out in the woods and fields by choice. Their hunting instinct never atrophies, so they have a reasonable chance of surviving, except in the dead of winter, but they never look as if they're enjoying the experience much, and I don't suppose it's ever a purely voluntary one. Cats don't run away from home as a rule, unless they're severely mistreated. They don't set out for the wilds with adventure in mind; they are, on the contrary, usually thrown out, or abandoned by their owners, and face the wilds resentfully, timidly, and without enthusiasm.

I suspect that the difficulty of capturing cats when they're living in the woods or fields is not that they're necessarily unwilling to be caught, but rather that they've come to fear and mistrust humans; they haven't forgiven the owner who got rid of them or treated them harshly, or the children who harassed them. Cats may not be famous for their memory the way elephants are, but they don't forgive easily, and certainly don't forget insults, injury, or assaults on their natural dignity.

When we first moved up to the country, we put out food for the animals most nights, and were rewarded by frequent glimpses of raccoons and possums, and even the occasional fox or two. Surprising numbers of cats turned up under the red floodlight. Cats, it appeared, were divided into two separate categories, those that showed up ready for a meal and hoping to move in, and those who wouldn't come near the house and approached even food that was left for them far away from it with deep caution.

I gradually came to the conclusion that those who had been mistreated fit into the latter category—they just didn't want anything to do with humans, thank you—and those who had been abandoned into the former—they were basically looking for a new home, like prospective home buyers going through the neighborhood with the real-estate section of the Sunday paper in hand.

Over the years, quite a few turned up and decided to stay, and for a long time we dated other events by the arrival and the death of cats, rather as English history is conveniently, if arbitrarily, divided up into the reigns of kings and queens. Margaret will occasionally ask about some happening we're discussing, "Wasn't that when we still had Bigfoot?" or, "Was that before or after Jake had to be taken to the emergency animal hospital with a broken tooth?" but for her the major dividing lines in our life up here remain the death of Irving—world traveler and as much a gentleman as a cat can be, with whom she had lived (Does one ever "own" a cat?) since he was a kitten, and back in the days when she was married to Burt Glinn, the Magnum photographer, and still modeling for him—and Chutney, also an orange-and-white male of distinguished appearance, prodigiously long whiskers, and great dignity, who had to be coaxed patiently for months before he would enter the house, but once there stayed to great old age.

For some reason we are not big on pet cemeteries—perhaps it's something alien to the English soul, as witness Evelyn Waugh's comic masterpiece *The Loved One* on the subject. On the other hand, Queen Victoria was almost as dotty about memorializing dead pets as she was about Albert, and even the dour and eminently practical duke of Wellington buried his favorite charger Copenhagen (named after one of Nelson's great naval victories) under a life-size bronze statue with the date of the battle of Waterloo inscribed on the marble base, and the lines:

Man's noblest friend,
Though born of baser clay,
Did share the glory
Of that glorious day.

(Copenhagen, for those who care, may also be seen in bigger-than-life bronze with the duke in the saddle, as he was at Waterloo, on Hyde Park Corner, facing the park.)

So perhaps it's just a modern phenomenon, this shying away from the idea of pet memorials. The vast reach of Victorian sensibility certainly included animals, and most of Queen Victoria's contemporaries would have approved of one neighbor's neat little graveyard for her boxers, each with its own headstone, whereas I can't remember what we did with poor Irving's ashes, which seems a shame, since I think he preferred me to Burt (which is not saying much—basically, he resented any male who came between himself and Margaret).

When Queenie died, our friend Thom von Buelow thoughtfully provided us with a bronze statue of a cat, which sits right below the birdbath outside our kitchen windows and contains her ashes, though poor Queenie, with her missing left front paw, was never allowed outside and could only sit on the windowsill and dream about killing birds as they swooped in for a drink or a bath. Chutney's ashes—he died in the garden on a cold winter's evening—are still upstairs in the bedroom, in a cardboard box, while Margaret considers where to put them and how to mark the place. Chutney was never an enthusiast for the great outdoors, once he had been tempted in from it, so the bedroom may be the right place for his remains, in fact—he was always perfectly happy there.

Eventually, we ended up with "barn cats," who lived in the tack room or the barn laundry room when we finally built one, and "house cats," who formed a rather more privileged elite. The role of barn cat was purely nominal—very little mousing or ratting was done by whoever happened to be barn cat at the time, but barns, like ships, are not thought to be fully staffed without a resident cat. The barn cat has one of those plastic pet doors so as to be able to get in and out of the laundry room when the door is locked, but curiously enough the house cats have never learned how to use it, despite many attempts to push them through it headfirst until they get the idea. Perhaps it's a question of class, somehow—the house cats feel that the right way to go in or out is to sit by the door until a human being comes along to open it, though they are not above speeding the process up a bit by yowling or, if inside, tearing at the piece of furniture nearest to the door. In a pinch, those who enjoy climbing will get onto the roof of the house by way of trees and bushes and make their way to the bedroom window, then scratch at the screen until somebody opens it, but none of them seems to get the whole idea of the pet door, or to have learned how to use it by observing the barn cat go in and out at will.

When the pet door was first installed, I was apprehensive that a raccoon or a possum, tempted by the plate of food inside, might get into the laundry room and wreak havoc, but that hasn't happened. Either they haven't figured it out, or the fact that the barn cat is likely to be inside, grumbling and spitting, acts as an effective deterrent—after all, what animal wants to push a plastic panel aside with its nose in pursuit of a bowl of dried cat food, only to meet an angry cat defending its turf on the other side?

In any event, if there's one thing the country provides, it's an endless supply of cats. Whenever Margaret starts talking about a stray cat living out on our fields somewhere, I can expect a new addition to the family before too long. Within the past few years two cats have been abandoned in the white house up the road—when people move out, they often leave their cats behind—one of which became our current barn cat, Hooligan, while a home was found for the other; and a large black-and-white male cat (soon named McTavish, or Mr. McT.), which Margaret spent weeks enticing out of the woods, where he was starving, eventually moved into the house, from which he clearly never again intends to set foot, if he can help it.

Our white cat, named Mumsy by Leslie Sant, who then worked in our barn, simply turned up at the house one day, scouting for a new home, no doubt. Once a quick meal was offered to her, off she went, to return shortly with two tiny, identical white kittens. Unlike some strays (Mr. McT. for one) who are afraid to come near the house and distrustful of human beings, Mumsy's approach was bold and confident, like that of somebody who has made her plans and expects everybody else to fall in with them without argument. She had surveyed the neighborhood for a new home for herself and her kittens, and ours had met with her approval. She was not foolish, either—she didn't bring the kittens with her on the first visit, just in case we might be frightened off at the prospect of adopting a whole family.

Over my protests—Do we need *three* more cats? Where will they live? Is our house going to become like that of the Lynns? What about our furniture, which Thom von Buelow had re-covered in many yards of wildly expensive fabric?—Margaret moved Mumsy and her kittens onto the big porch at the back of the house, where striped canvas curtains can be lowered to provide some degree of shelter. There, Mumsy and her kittens proceeded to make themselves at home by creating an incredible mess, combining cat litter, food, spilled water, and ripped-up newspapers. That they were healthy and happy, there was no doubt. Many strays are malnourished, wasted, near death, sometimes after many weeks or months of exposure—Chutney had been, Jake was near that state when he arrived, so was Mr. McT.—but Mumsy, though thin, seemed in reasonably good shape for a stray cat, perhaps because, as is so often the case, it was the kittens that got her ejected from her home. Somebody, I was sure, had gathered the lot of them up, driven them a good long way from their home, and dumped them in our fields to fend for themselves. In any event, fend Mumsy did, arriving like a heat-seeking missile right smack at the one house where nobody was going to turn her away from the door.

Shortly after the arrival of Mumsy and her brood, Margaret was scheduled to go away for the weekend to an event. I was planning to stay home to work, while a young Englishwoman named Trina French was to look after the barn. Together we were given strict and detailed instructions on caring for Mumsy and her kittens. At this point they were being allowed off the porch from time to time for a little supervised exercise in the garden, which the kittens usually spent by climbing as high as they could in the nearest tree, then getting stuck, while their mother studiously ignored them (her attitude, if there were humans present, was basically: if you think kittens are such a lot of fun, then *you* look after them). Mumsy was "a big-picture thinker," as somebody once described my friend Richard E. Snyder, the former president of Simon and Schuster; while she was an excellent mother in a crisis, and had kept her family alive and found them a good home, she didn't see it as her role in life to sweat the details or act as their nanny. Once they were released from the porch, she went off about her own business, while the rest of us worried about getting the kittens out of a tree or off the roof and eventually went off to bring a ladder and a stout pair of leather work gloves, the basic tools of cat rescue.

Once Trina and I had ridden, we popped round to the porch to deal with Mumsy and her family. Needless to say, the kittens were out the screen door the moment it was opened, which was unfortunate, since it was pouring rain—not your ordinary heavy rainstorm, but the kind of monsoonlike (but cold) rain that sends waterfalls cascading over the gutters, starts the streams and creeks flooding over their banks, and makes whole stretches of the Taconic Parkway resemble a swimming pool. The dreaded flash-flood warning for parts of Dutchess County—*this* part—had already been reported, and CNN was showing our neck of the woods in that bilious, swirling, fluorescent bright green that means "Don't even think about going here!" Trina and I were dressed ineffectually in a whole tack shop display's worth of English and Australian outdoor oilskin clothing—hats, ankle-length riding slickers with layers of flaps and straps and mysterious zippered pieces, rubber boots, you name it—not that it made the slightest difference, except to render movement more difficult. We spent a minute or so tightening buckles and draining the water off our hat brims while the kittens played, indifferent to the rain.

Our attention was diverted for a second or two by a gust of wind; when we looked back, the kittens were gone. Usually, if you looked hard enough, you saw a flash of white as they rolled and played on the lawn or in the branches of an evergreen—they never went very far from the porch—but this time there was nothing. Well, not quite nothing—Mumsy herself had taken refuge under one of the canvas awnings and was busy drying herself. She did not look concerned at the absence of her kittens, and if she had any idea where they were, she wasn't saying. "You guys are in charge," she seemed to be saying, "So you go find them." Besides, she might have added, we were the ones with all the fancy rain gear, not her.

Together Trina and I made our way from tree to tree, shaking the lower branches, but no cats fell out of them. We looked behind hedges, bushes, and shrubs—nothing. There was a large stone urn outside the porch, in which they might have fallen, or—God forbid!—drowned. We upended it, and got a lot of dirty water and green slime on our boots for our pains. We poked around in the ivy. Zip.

Trina made noises calculated to attract the attention of a kitten and called out, "Here, kitty, kitty," over and over again, to no effect. Mumsy looked on for a while with a certain interest, then, bored with the spectacle, went inside the porch, curled up, and fell asleep. So much for concerned motherhood, I thought.

I went off and came back with a cat dish and a spoon, and walked around in the rain banging the spoon against the dish enticingly, feeling a bit like the man on old-fashioned European luxury trains like Le Train Bleu or the Simplon Orient Express who used to go from coach to coach before mealtimes ringing a little silver bell and calling out, *"Première service, Messieurs, Mesdames, s'il vous plaît."* To this day, the sound of a little bell is enough to make my mouth water with foretaste of all those things you eat only on trains in Europe—*les hors-d'oeuvre variés*, thick soups, roast veal, the great plate of cheeses, the stupendous desserts that put you to sleep for the rest of the afternoon—but the noise had no effect on the kittens, who remained invisible.

Perhaps they were hiding under the porch, Trina suggested. That seemed possible—there were plenty of holes big enough for them to squeeze through, indeed a whole family of raccoons had once lived there before we made a determined effort to evict them. I went for a flashlight and got down on my hands and knees to point it into whatever holes I could reach, but no little eyes reflected the light back to me. Of course the kittens might have made their way farther back under the porch, it occurred to me, in which case the only way to get at them was to pull up hundreds of dollars' worth of brand-new tongue-and-groove floorboards.

Then it dawned on me that they might have made their way from under the porch into the cellar. Reluctantly I opened the door to the cellar and wedged myself into the crawl spaces, making little cooing noises that might, I thought—though who knows why—soothe and attract the kittens. Some of the crawl spaces were indeed aptly named—I could just get through them on my elbows and my knees, with the pipes and wires above me scraping the top of my head. I saw no kittens. I searched in dim, dark, warm places, like behind the hot water heater or the furnace. *Nada*, I reported to Trina when I emerged, covered head to foot in dirt and mud and wheezing from the dust.

Trina rolled her eyes. "I don't know *what* we're going to tell Margaret," she said, a thought that had already occurred to me. I allowed that this had been on my mind too, but said that whatever we were going to tell Margaret, it would have to wait for her return—there was no point in giving her the bad news when she was a hundred miles away and about to compete. That made sense to Trina too, particularly since she would not be here when Margaret got back. She stared at the house, rain pouring down her face. Might they have climbed into the water spouts, did I think? I frankly couldn't imagine why, but then again, who knows why cats and kittens do anything? We banged and thumped on the sheet-metal pipes leading from the gutters, dislodging several of them in process, but no kittens tumbled out.

Then Trina's attention was caught by an open culvert in the lawn, about twenty yards away. This was the far end of a complicated underground system of pipes that had once served to drain water coming down from the gutters via the water spouts out onto the lawn, away from the house. The pipes were the old-fashioned kind, heavy porcelain, and the Dutchess County winters had cracked most of them—another of old Mr. Hubner's bright do-it-yourself ideas gone wrong. The system had been disconnected long before we bought the house, but removing it would have meant digging up the entire lawn, so we had simply left it in place. Harold Roe had long nurtured hopes of getting the whole thing up with his backhoe, but I couldn't see the point, since it was causing no trouble.

"That's *exactly* where they must have gone," Trina exclaimed. "They were playing very near it when we lost sight of them." It did seem plausible—and was in fact the one and only place where we hadn't looked. I could imagine that they might have crawled in there to get dry, or perhaps just out of curiosity and mischief, then wandered up the pipe a bit, or perhaps followed a branch into another pipe, and got lost or stuck. The thing about kittens is that they're not afraid of much—they are born pretty much without common sense and caution, which explains how they so often manage to climb up a tree until they've reached a point from which they can't figure out how to climb down. "How on *earth* did this happen?" seems to be, after food, their most frequent thought.

Trina crouched on her hands and knees in front of the exit from the pipe and made enticing sounds, while I tried to imagine how far the entire system might extend. One thing was sure—this was no job for a backhoe. They would have to be removed the old-fashioned way, with a pick and shovel. I did not look forward to the task.

Since by this time we were soaked to the skin, I suggested that a cup of tea might be a good idea before we did anything else. It's the English tradition anyway—a nice cup of tea and a biscuit was always the first thing offered to victims of the Blitz. After a brief pause, we made our way out into the rain to beat through the bushes again—I was busy racking my brain for how to break the news to Margaret—when I happened to look up and noticed, fast asleep beside their mother on the porch, the two kittens, looking as if they had never been missing in the first place.

Of course that's the way it is with cats. Many a time I have searched the house late at night when Margaret is away at an event, desperately looking for a missing cat—under chairs, behind drapes, under beds, in closets and cupboards and even inside the washing machine or the clothes dryer—only to find the cat I'm looking for sitting at the top of the stairs looking down at me with mild curiosity. Where had it been? Where was it hiding? There is no answering such questions. Cats, when they want to, can and do simply vanish, only to show up unexpectedly just as you've abandoned hope of ever seeing them again.

I have combed the gardens with a flashlight late at night searching for a cat that's gone AWOL, only to find it sitting on the doormat when I've given up looking for it. Perhaps it's a game, a feline form of hide-and-seek? But I don't think so—cats don't seem to have a highly developed sense of humor. I think it's simply that they're natural hunters and camouflage experts, and can squeeze themselves into spaces (and through holes) much smaller than most of us imagine. When you've searched a room from top to bottom looking for a cat, without success, but convinced it's there, odds are, you're right—it's simply pushed itself behind a pillow or found its way into a cupboard and fallen asleep. After all, though you are frantically looking for the cat, the cat doesn't necessarily know or care—it's not really *hiding*, it's very likely simply doing what it wants to do, without reference to you at all. Hence, no doubt, the look of surprise blended with a slight touch of superiority on the cat's face when you finally "find" it.

Of course there's always another candidate out there in the woods somewhere. As I write this, Margaret has reported on an orange-and-white cat, very shy, that's been hanging about the fields and the house but doesn't dare to come close yet. I nod. The odds are that it will be joining us one day soon, perhaps as the barn cat, while Hooligan, the present holder of that office, gets promoted to house-cat status.

After all, why not? It's a big old house.

Chutney

CHAPTER TWENTY-FOUR

"Change and Decay . . ."

Margaret and Mrs. Thatcher

NOTHING LASTS FOREVER, of course—or lives forever, either.

It was a sad day indeed when old Tabasco, the big chestnut Thoroughbred that Margaret bought when she was still married to Burt Glinn and riding in Central Park in the mornings, finally had to be put down and buried in a sloping field between the barn and the woods. Tabasco, like Irving the cat, was a connection to the past; it almost seemed that he would go on forever, despite all his minor aches and pains, but one winter he just started to fade, and it was clear enough that he wouldn't last through another.

Poor Hustle, everybody's favorite horse, went through a long bout with cancer. He lost one eye, which had to be removed, though to everybody's amazement he was as sensible and reliable as ever at taking a jump, the only sign of his disability being the way he swung his head to one side so he could see the jump clearly and figure out the best approach. But then the cancer returned, and eventually he had to be put down.

The pigs eventually had to go too, to everybody's sadness. One of them, George, who in fact belonged to the Bacons, had to be put down early on, but the others lived on, growing bigger and bigger and becoming something of a wonder to the community, since everybody else's pigs were slaughtered at about two hundred pounds. They never quite grew to the size of Buzzy the Boar, but they got big enough so their trotters would hardly even carry their weight during the winter, when there was ice in their field, and it seemed very likely that they would fall and break a leg. Eventually a local farmer, Ritch Pulver, took them off our hands, and Margaret never forgave herself for letting them go.

Occasionally, she makes plans to replace them—she has her eye on a likely candidate at present named Mrs. Thatcher, a splendid black pig down the road at Paul Wigsten's farm who forms part of an informal summertime petting zoo. Whenever Margaret goes to the Dunkin' Donuts in Pleasant Valley for coffee, she brings back a couple of doughnuts for Mrs. Thatcher (who is very partial to maple-frosted doughnuts with sprinkles), and it would not surprise anyone if Mrs. Thatcher ended up enjoying a well-earned retirement *chez nous*—Mrs. Thatcher's heart, I would have to say, isn't really into being petted by children, unless the kiddies happen to have brought bags of maple-frosted doughnuts with them, in which case she is quite amenable to having her ears scratched, and shuts her eyes in ecstasy if you scratch hard enough.

Animals and people die, things change, and yet—which is surely part of the reason for living in the country in the first place—there remains a great sense of continuity and stability, as if just enough farming were still being done around us to anchor life to the seasons. Up here, for instance, Thanksgiving isn't just a question of eating turkey on the day, or going down to the mall to get started on your Christmas shopping. It's still a harvest festival, a celebration of the end of summer and fall abundance, and the beginning of preparing for the winter. The harvest, such as it may be, is in, the leaves are red and gold and about to fall, the pumpkins are in the fields, or stacked up in mounds for sale by the side of the roads, the wild turkeys are appearing close to the house; the curtain is about to rise on a new season, winter, and it seems perfectly appropriate to mark the occasion with a feast, even if the Pilgrims and the Indians hadn't invented it in its present form.

Of course the countryside changes—inexorably, the pressure for living space means more houses, more traffic, higher school taxes, more drive-in fast-food places and drive-in banks and video stores and liquor stores. Some places hold back the tide, at least for the present, by manipulating zoning laws to favor big estates; others are too remote and forbiddingly rural to interest commuters as yet; still others, like Pleasant Valley, are right in the path of development and eager for the promise of prosperity and jobs that invariably accompanies it.

And it's hard to criticize that. Ever since IBM downsized its workforce drastically, people in this part of the world have been waiting for something—anything, frankly—to jump-start the local economy. It's been, for most, a long, hard wait, and if the good news is going to come in the shape of lots of housing where there used to be farms, or jobs in fast-food outlets or video stores, so be it—nobody is about to turn their nose up at progress, or try to deflect it toward Millerton or Amenia.

Besides, everybody has different standards in this kind of thing. Only the other day I met an elderly lady, watching a riding clinic on our land, who told me that she had moved up to northern Vermont after thirty-five years in Litchfield County, Connecticut, because Litchfield was getting too crowded, too full of "bedroom" communities and commuters, too "trendy," with antique shops and gourmet food shops where there had once been honest, God-fearing feed stores and groceries. All of that may be so, but whenever I drive through that part of Connecticut I come home saying how beautiful it is, how well looked after (no garbage on the roads, no billboards, no visible trailers on cinder blocks) compared to our own fairly slovenly countryside. The banks and liquor stores across the state line in Connecticut look like Quaker meetinghouses, there is a distinct absence of vinyl siding, it all looks very civilized and prim-and-proper as compared to Dutchess County—Ralph Lauren country as opposed to red-and-black-plaid hats with earflaps and insulated bib-front overalls country. On the other hand, it drove this woman to move about as near to the Canadian border as you can get without meeting a Mountie, so who knows?

Everybody in the country always thinks that the place where they live is going to hell in a handbasket and that the next place north is an untouched rural paradise, where you can find help who are happy to scrub and iron all day long for five dollars an hour, and where the diners still serve homemade apple pie made from their own apples and topped with a slice of cheddar cheese an inch thick, and meat loaf to die for.

This is part of the American national character—in the eighteenth and early nineteenth centuries, Americans moved (then, mostly westward) at the first sight of smoke from another chimney, always in the conviction that in the next county or beyond the next river they would find someplace to live without neighbors, or what we would now call "development," without recognizing that the mere fact of moving there sets off the process irrevocably.

This is not England, after all, where perfect little rural villages are lovingly preserved over the centuries, with their Norman churches and their medieval inns and manor houses. Actually, the first residents came here from England precisely to escape all that in the first place, rejecting, along with established religion, the whole social structure that has preserved for so long in England the relationship between the manor and the village, between gentry and peasantry, and kept things as they had always been: quaint, tidy, polite, and resistant to change.

In England in the eighteenth century (and well into the nineteenth), people could be (and frequently were) hanged for poaching a pheasant or a rabbit, whereas in America game was plentiful and belonged to nobody. Change, progress, "development," was seen as beneficial; preserving the old—what there was of it—seemed backward, fussy, undemocratic, a form of turning one's back on the firm, upward march of progress that was taken to be the whole purpose of American life. Hardly anybody in America wants to live in the past, whereas in England there are a great many people who still yearn to do exactly that. Hence whatever remains of the appeal of the royal family, which lives firmly and unapologetically in the past, and indeed can be said to incarnate it.

Not so on this side of the Atlantic. No matter how far north you go in Vermont, you are only buying yourself a little time before the rest of America—developers, teenagers on dirt bikes, yuppie Internet millionaires building huge, tasteless houses too close to yours for comfort, and faux-eighteenth-century outlet shopping malls and retirement homes—follows you. You can leave Litchfield County, all right—it's a free country—but you can be sure that whatever you're getting away from will be coming after you, the way abandoned pets are said to follow their owners to their new homes, showing up at the front door days or weeks later. Like the early settlers who had no sooner cleared a few acres around their cabin of trees and rocks than they saw the smoke from somebody else's chimney rising above the trees on the horizon and decided to move on, it's a mug's game. You can move as fast and as far as you please, but the culture will catch up with you. There's no "unspoiled paradise" because it's in our nature to spoil it the moment we set foot there.

And so it is with the country—not just our bit of it, in rural Dutchess County, but everywhere. "Change and decay in all around I see," sure, in spades, but change and decay are nothing new. People used that phrase way back when the English arrived to lord it over the Dutch; they felt it in the early nineteenth century, when the steamboat made the river towns along the Hudson prosperous—rural Sodom and Gomorrahs Newburgh and Poughkeepsie and Kingston no doubt seemed then to the doughty farmers farther inland—they felt it when Commodore Vanderbilt drove his railway up along the river, drenching the riverside mansions of the old patroons with soot and cinders; and they felt it when the New Deal drove the Taconic Parkway up through rolling farmland and dense forests to make it easier for tourists from the hated Big City to drive up and look at the autumn leaves.

Change is inevitable and inescapable, and decay is relative. Was life better before the steamboat, or the railway, or the parkway? Who can say? And what does it matter, since we can't go back and find out? One thing we *do* know—moving to the country to escape change is an illusion, and people who try break their hearts. You treasure what you *can* keep—a certain way of life, a view of trees instead of buildings, the relatively greater closeness of wild things, and the more direct impact of seasons and weather—without trying to turn what's around you into a rural theme park or a museum, and say good-bye when you must. Life goes on.

Around here, people tend to cling to reminders of the past for as long as they can. Often, riding along the trails through the woods, we come out behind houses where the old outdoor privy has been carefully, even lovingly preserved, sometimes with flowering vines and ivy artfully softening the stark, simple lines of that familiar piece of American folk history. It isn't that these houses don't *have* indoor plumbing or that the people who own them are poor—some of them have swimming pools, satellite television antennas, hot tubs, a gas-fired barbecue on the lawn, you name it. The people living there just don't want to tear down a symbol of country living—besides which, in a crunch, if the electricity or the plumbing fails, I guess it can probably come in handy to have the old privy out there in the garden, where it always was. House after house, as we ride past them, looking at the side away from the road that most people don't ever see, still has the old privy behind it, like some kind of monument to the rural past, the way people will keep old farm tools and implements hanging in their original places in the barn to remind themselves, or perhaps their children, of the way it used to be.

Nowadays there are more new houses around us (chimney smoke on the horizon), there is more (and more aggressive) traffic—the days when you could exercise horses by riding them down our road, even ponying another one alongside, are long gone—there are fewer dairy farms—indeed, the *Poughkeepsie Journal* recently ran a front-page story lamenting their decline, but then people were lamenting on that subject way back when Franklin Delano Roosevelt was still alive and spending the summer at Hyde Park—but the *feel* of the place, its Zeitgeist, remains predominantly rural, and the price and availability of hay (scarce and about $3.95 a bale, as I write this) is still a subject of interest almost everywhere, if you're at a loss for ways to start a conversation. It's not so much that most people here *need* hay or straw anymore (except for putting the latter on top of newly laid grass seed), but hay is a local commodity, like apples and milk, and forms a part of people's sense of themselves, one of those million and one small things that makes them country dwellers instead of suburbanites (or, horrid word, *ex*-urbanites). Granted, a lot of the houses going up around here look like suburban houses, and some even have conventional lawns and pools, but then in the suburbs their neighbors probably wouldn't be raising their own chickens. Or pigs.

Perhaps the biggest and saddest change in our lives was one we never saw coming. One winter afternoon, while I was at my desk in New York City, I got a call from Leslie Sant, a young woman who was working in our barn. She sounded shaken and upset. I asked her what was wrong. "Margaret's not here," she said, "but something's happened to Harold."

I sighed. Harold was Margaret's favorite, her big gray Canadian coach horse, a real sweetheart who looked like an amiable total klutz at first sight but won blue ribbon after blue ribbon, as if he lived to jump fences. Anything happening to Harold was bad news indeed. "What happened?" I asked.

Leslie paused to catch her breath. It sounded to me as if she had been crying, which wasn't something Leslie did a lot of, so I steeled myself for the worst. "He's dead," she said. "He simply fell over, in the barn, right there in the aisle."

"Dead?"

"Dead."

I knew Margaret would be heartbroken. Harold was one of those horses who didn't have a mean bone in his body—he didn't bite, he didn't kick, he was about as affectionate as a horse can be, and if you put him at a fence he would do his damnedest to get you over it every time; in short, "a real gentleman," as they still say of horses.

"Was it quick?" I asked.

Leslie said it had been instantaneous. One moment he had been standing there in the aisle between the stalls in the barn, the next moment she looked around, and he was on the floor, dead.

"Margaret will be really upset," I said.

There was a slight pause. "Well, sure," Leslie said. She sounded a little puzzled, I thought, and decided that she was probably spacey from the shock.

"Were you alone? Is anyone there to help?"

"The guy was here servicing the generator when it happened. He's a volunteer fireman, so he gave Harold CPR, but it was too late, I guess."

There was a moment of silence while I pondered this. It didn't seem to make any sense. "He gave *Harold* CPR?" I asked.

"Yes," Leslie said matter-of-factly. "Then the ambulance came, and took him to Vassar Hospital, but he was DOA—"

"Wait a minute," I interrupted. "Are we talking about Harold the *horse?*"

Leslie gave a slightly hysterical laugh. "No, no," she said. "I'm talking about Mr. Roe. Harold *Roe*. Harold *the horse* is okay."

HAROLD ROE, it turned out, had come into the barn to warm up a bit and chat with Leslie. One minute he had been standing there talking to her, then when she looked back up from whatever she was doing, there he was, stretched out on the concrete aisle, dead. It was probably the way he would have wanted to go, quickly and in the middle of exchanging gossip with somebody, but nevertheless, as I put down the telephone, having done my best to calm Leslie, it felt like the end of an era, and of course it was.

It wasn't just that Harold was one of the last of the old-timers who knew everybody and could do just about anything, or even that Harold, infuriating as he could be, was a friend, somebody you could rely upon absolutely—Harold had shown up on our first day here, had taken us under his wing, had made us feel a part of the place, in a way we could never otherwise have been, and had come to seem, frankly, immortal. I had suffered a fleeting moment of relief at the thought that it might be easier to break the news to Margaret about Harold Roe than about Harold the horse, but on reflection, I realized that losing Harold Roe would touch her deeply. He was her link to the farm of her childhood, a countryman to the bone, to use the English word, like so many of the men she had grown up around, indeed like her own father, though no two people could have been less alike than Margaret's father, an elegant, gentlemanly figure of a man who managed what was, for England, a huge farm, and Harold Roe. Still, in their love of the soil, their understanding of nature, and their solid common sense about all those country things that puzzle the rest of us when it comes time to undertake some large outdoors project, swales and drainage and so forth, they shared a certain knowledge and point of view, and on the one occasion when they had met, Margaret's father came away saying that while Harold was "a bit of a character," he seemed like the kind of chap who knew what he was doing, which was true enough—and high praise too, coming from an English farmer.

Harold's funeral was private—country people don't make a big fuss of these things as a rule—but we went to Harold's house in Salt Point after the funeral to pay our respects to Birdie Roe. It occurred to me as we were driving over there that I'd never been in the house before—on the few occasions when I'd needed to see Harold, I'd always found him in his garage workshop behind the house, busy welding or servicing his tractor or sharpening his mower blades. On a couple of occasions I'd knocked at the front door of the house to deliver a Christmas present, or, on one occasion, a glamour photo autographed to him by Joan Collins, whom Margaret and I had been visiting in L.A., but Mrs. Roe was seldom home; if she was, she opened the back door and called out from there, from which I derived the impression that the Roes' front door was probably only used for ceremonious occasions, if at all, and perhaps hadn't been opened since Harold carried Birdie across the threshold, hard as it was to imagine Harold doing that, or Birdie letting herself be carried. In any case, the front door was in use for the day—we didn't have to skulk around the house rapping on the kitchen windows to attract Birdie's attention as had been the case when Harold was still alive.

Salt Point is what city dwellers have in mind when they think of a small country village. Except for the absence of an old-fashioned village pub, it is more English-looking than, say, Pleasant Valley, which, fifteen minutes distant, seems like a veritable urban center by comparison. There is no supermarket in Salt Point, just a convenience store with a deli counter, a tiny post office, a rather handsome church, a flourishing auto-body repair shop (the local prejudice against snow tires, makes body repairing a winter bonanza), a bar-restaurant that burned down, and another that hasn't, but that changes hands all the time, so that you never know whether the house specialty is going to be a burrito or corned beef and cabbage, and one of the few old-fashioned hardware stores still left around here, usually full of large, slow-spoken men in bib-front overalls and manure-covered boots looking for things I don't even know the use of—men who look a good deal like Harold Roe, now that I think of it, and whose hands are witness to a lifetime of manual labor.

The approach to the village is marked by a strong smell of silage from a dairy farm, which is appropriate, and generally regarded hereabouts as healthy—the powerful odor of fermenting silage, used to feed cattle during the winter, is thought to prevent colds and keep the nasal passages and lungs clear. Harold Roe was a great believer in it, and it certainly kept him healthy long enough—his heart gave out after a lifetime diet of steak and fried bologna, but his lungs and nasal passages were in pretty good shape for a man his age, and he seldom had a cold, so perhaps there's something in it. Another example of the wisdom of those old-time dairy farmers?

In any event, Salt Point is small and rural, and Harold owned a surprising amount of it. Just about the whole population was crowded into his house, along with the members of the widespread Roe and Daley clans, and of course Harold's golden-oldie snowmobilers, come to say good-bye to their leader. Many of these people we had met a few years back, in happier circumstances, at Harold and Birdie's anniversary party, held in the back room at Cady's, in Pleasant Valley, with steaks the size of tennis rackets and enough hash-brown potatoes to sink a battleship. The atmosphere here was nostalgic and jolly rather than grim, the snowmobilers exchanging stories of Harold's superhuman indifference to cold, others praising his knowledge of machinery, his firm belief in sticking to a job until he'd finished it (rare in a part of the country where most people leave a job half-finished to go off and start on another one), his unrivaled work ethic. I told the story of Harold's finger, which he cut off in an accident with some piece of machinery while working at our place. He had wrapped the missing part of his finger up in a handkerchief, and Margaret urged him to go down to Vassar Hospital and have it sewn on again—at the time, regrafting severed body parts was in the news. Harold was persuaded to go to the hospital, over his strident protests. A couple of hours later he was back, the stump of his finger wrapped up, ready to resume work. When Margaret asked what had happened, he shook his head and grinned. "They said I was too old to have it sewn back on again," he shouted cheerfully. "Not worth the bother."

This story, though rather lugubrious, went down very well. Everybody shook their head solemnly and said, "That's Harold for you all right." And so it was—the stubborn determination to get back to work, the stoic ability to withstand pain, the underlying cheerfulness . . . As we left, Mrs. Roe promised to send us Harold's last bill, which showed a nice touch of practicality, even in grief, of which Harold himself would certainly have approved.

On the way home I couldn't help thinking how lucky we had been to have encountered Harold, who gave us a kind of place in the community, an identity we would have been hard put to establish for ourselves. From Pleasant Valley to Staatsburg, Clinton Corners, Salt Point, and points beyond, people said to us, from the very beginning, "Oh sure, you're the people bought the place Harold Roe looks after, aren't you?" as if that was all they needed to know about us. There was never a problem about opening up a charge account at the Clinton Corners Agway or the feed store in Pleasant Valley—at the mention of our name, the man or woman behind the desk would smile cheerfully and say, "Why you're the people who bought the old Hubner place, right? Harold Roe works for you?" and let us start charging right away—none of that nonsense about bank account numbers or credit ratings, no filling out of forms. Harold's name was as good as gold, and gave people a certain sense of stability where we were concerned. If Harold worked for us—and had good things to say about us—then we must be okay, and that was that.

His death was a kind of watershed in our lives, coinciding as it did with the beginning of a push to make Pleasant Valley a more up-to-date commercial center for the many even smaller towns and villages around us. A new shopping plaza was inaugurated, and proved to be an instant failure, the tenants dwindling down to a nondescript Chinese take-out place and a slot-car racing track; an A&P was built right opposite the Grand Union, in a white stone shopping-mall complex the rest of which remains mostly untenanted, replacing one of the town's few authentic early nineteenth-century inns; the firehouse was replaced by a bigger, more modern one; the bank acquired a drive-in window; the old mill was finally torn down (after a fire ended years of discussions about turning it into some kind of a museum or cultural center), and a McDonald's went up on part of the site; a new, wider bridge replaced the old one to relieve traffic congestion; and plans were made to build a town park—all changes Harold would have greeted with a healthy dose of skepticism, and a searing disquisition on how politicians and bureaucrats wasted the taxpayers' money, while developers made their fortunes replacing perfectly sound old buildings with new ones that nobody needed.

It wasn't that Harold looked backward, necessarily, and he certainly wasn't sentimental about the past—or anything else, come to that. He simply understood better than any politician, or planner, or developer—in the gut, rather than the head—that a place like this exists because it's on the borderline between urban and rural America, and that if you let the urban or the suburban side of it get out of hand, eventually nobody will want to live here at all. One shopping mall too many, one or two more farms turned into housing or trailer parks, a few more roads widened by the state, and it's all over. It's why Harold, though God knows he was no tree-hugger, would sometimes put his trusty Kubota into neutral and dismount to pick up a bit of garbage or straighten a stone wall, his expression somewhat sheepish, as if he were afraid of being caught doing a good deed. He didn't care much for cows himself unless they were on a plate, well done and served with ketchup and a side of home fries, but he understood that if you take away the cows and all that goes with them, pretty soon you'll just have rows of houses, gas stations, and video stores from Yonkers to the Canadian border, and who would want to live here then?

And so he would have shaken his head at the sight of the new homes going up too close to each other at the bottom of the road, or the decay of the apple orchard up the road from us a bit, which was once a profitable business and kept as neat as a pin and has now been allowed to decline into a ruin of brambles and dead and unpruned apple trees. Then again, he would have slowed down to look farther up the road, where a local doctor with a passion for old dairy farms has taken over the old Vandenkamp farm, now that only one of the Vandenkamps is still alive, and is running it just the way the Vandenkamps would have wanted it run. Indeed, Cornelius Vandenkamp, the surviving brother, who now lives in a brand-new house with a wishing well out front, still comes out from time to time to supervise and help, and can sometimes be seen hunched over the wheel of a tractor chugging down one of the big fields beside the road, doing what's he always done all his life, getting in his hay before it rains on everybody else's. Near us, Jeff and Sue Lynn, he a business executive in the computer industry, she an airline flight attendant, they of the dozen cats, have bought Sheila Melville's horse farm and are rebuilding the barns, the house, the fences, pouring their savings and his stock options into the place, and gradually, all over Dutchess County, similar things are happening, though whether they're happening fast enough to make the difference remains to be seen. The old Frank's Dairy Farm on Route 44 is now a huge, modern old-age home; on the other hand Sinon Farm, down the road a bit from us, still survives, benefiting, no doubt, from the fact that its owner is a successful ice cream distributor.

On the one hand, developers, parking lots, drive-through fast-food outlets; on the other, people who have made their money doing something else pouring it (no other word will do) into the preservation of open space, trees, land. We'll see.

In America nothing lasts forever, as Harold would have been the first to acknowledge. The great mansions on the Hudson, a few miles from here, built in the mid-nineteenth century with the thought that children and grandchildren would live in them, that they'd be the equivalent of the manor houses and castles of the English gentry, were mostly untenanted and neglected by the time of World War II (a few were saved by becoming national historical sites). The open land around Franklin Delano Roosevelt's home has given way to shopping malls, a movie theater, even a drive-in; even some of the big estates in Millbrook are being subdivided, while out toward Amenia one of the most attractive dairy farms in the county has become, God help us, a golf course.

Well, better a golf course than a field full of mobile homes, of course, but there it is—even money, old families, and landmarking can't hold back progress forever, so you just have to fight like hell to keep your little piece of the country intact.

With or without Harold.

CHAPTER TWENTY-FIVE

No Place Like Home

Mid pleasures and palaces, though we may roam,
Be it ever so humble, there's no place like home.

—John Howard Payn,
1791–1852

As I WRITE THIS, the Pleasant Valley Farmers' Market has just reopened, though it's early days yet, and there are only a few vendors. It's too early for the tidal wave of tomatoes that will come our way by midsummer, but neighborly Jerry and Alta Conklin have got fresh organic salad mix and arugula and two kinds of parsley, plus a new mix of strange-looking oriental greens—they look rather like weeds, to tell the truth—that I'm looking forward to trying. Several people are selling from folding card tables under awnings freshly baked bread, red potatoes dug this morning, homegrown garlic, and home-baked pies, not to speak of a man who has three different grades of hot pepper jam, the hottest being a green jalapeño jam, which tastes fairly harmless at first but then builds to a crescendo in your mouth, and proved to be a sensation on roast pork. (The jalapeño, like the cowboy hat and cowboy boots, has moved east to become part of the local culture, and now appears in dishes where you wouldn't normally expect to find it, jalapeño turkey stuffing being one of my favorites, along with jalapeño corn pudding.)

Of course the Millbrook Farmers' Market is much bigger, and the Rhinebeck Farmers' Market too, but we're happy to see the big banner stretched across one end of the GU parking lot, as a sign not only that summer is here at last but also that Pleasant Valley agriculture is still alive and well, albeit on this fairly modest scale.

I've come to enjoy that sense of belonging that comes over me when I walk through the farmers' market and see people I know, perhaps only vaguely—by face, sometimes, rather than by name. I feel the same way when I go to the gym (which, oddly enough, is situated right next to a deli, where people can undo all the good they've done on the treadmill with a bacon, egg, and sausage sandwich to go), or when I go for a walk, which, if I time it right, will usually bring me the company of one or two agreeable men of my age.

It took me a long time to develop this sense of belonging to a community, probably because for most of the years I lived up here, my attention was still fixed on New York City, where my job was, and a lot of my time was spent driving back and forth on the Taconic Parkway in a hurry to get where I was going, or to come home.

Then, in 1994, I discovered that I had prostate cancer, underwent a radical prostatectomy at Johns Hopkins, Baltimore, and came home to recuperate. Not unexpectedly, my life, which had hitherto been lived at a fairly rapid pace, slowed down considerably for a while—the big moment of my day was a half-mile walk, usually taken with Margaret and a male nurse supporting me at first. Then, as I began to recover, I joined the local prostate cancer support group, and eventually wrote a book about the whole experience, and toured the country speaking about prostate cancer.

I was careful not to portray myself as an expert on the subject—after all, I'm not a doctor—but inevitably, as I appeared on television and the radio, I became a sort of spokesman for prostate cancer patients for a time, if not quite a poster boy for the disease.

This had two unexpected consequences. First, large numbers of worried middle-aged and elderly men sought me out; second, I suddenly and unexpectedly tapped into the deep layers of concern that lie buried in any small community. Total strangers offered their help and their advice when I was sick, and when I started to get better, equally total strangers would stop me in the street, at the supermarket, at the bar in Mackey's Pub to get my take on *their* prostate problems, or that of their husbands.

My telephone rang day and night with people in need of counseling, advice, the name of a good surgeon, some hint of what to do and expect now that disaster had hit them. I was the person who knew—or at any rate had strong opinions about—such matters as what kind of adult diaper to wear postsurgery, who to see if incontinence didn't diminish, what to expect on the subject of sex, and I was available locally and in person every time I went to town. I became friends with the retired principal of a Christian school who lived a bit up the road from us and seemed to be going through the various stages of prostate cancer at the same rate that I was, developed a relationship to a number of middle-aged men about whose health problems I learned more than I really wanted to; in short, I began to feel that, at last, I fit in. Some years later, when I suffered (*le mot juste*) a cardiac arrest while running in Central Park, and recovered from being in a coma with a defibrillator/pacemaker installed in my chest and a neurologist asking me to spell "world" backward, I tapped in to any number of people in the community with heart problems of one kind or another. As important, unlike New Yorkers, people cared, reached out, asked after me, stopped me in parking lots to see how I was doing, occasionally shouting out their symptoms (or asking after mine in a loud voice) in public places. There's nothing like a conversation about incontinence or arrhythmia shouted out loud from one checkout counter of the A&P to another three slots away to make one feel a part of the community. It's hard to know what kind of secret might be worth keeping once people have heard how many times you had to change your Depends adult diaper yesterday.

Or perhaps it's part of the aging process—after all, we've lived here for more than twenty years. There's no way to pretend that it's a weekend home at this point, or that any really important part of our lives (except my job) takes place elsewhere. For better or for worse, this is it, home, where some of Margaret's animals are buried, where our possessions are, where the best and sometimes the worst of our lives has taken place.

At various times we have tried to put subsidiary roots down elsewhere. At one point we bought a *casita* in an exclusive development at Wellington, near West Palm Beach, Florida, with the notion that it would be nice to have a place to go to when the winter became unbearable, sometime around February, but we didn't take to it, or perhaps we weren't ready for it. More ambitiously, we actually built a house in Tesuque, in northern New Mexico, near Santa Fe, with a view to die for from every window, but it was too far to go, and we never came to think of it as home.

Home, it seems, is here, where even the smallest of storms invariably knocks out the electricity for hours or days, where it's hot and humid in the summer and like the snow-and-ice scenes from *Doctor Zhivago* during the endless winter; there's never a happy medium, so far as the weather is concerned.

"Well," we say to each other as we look out the windows, "at least it's not as bad as the winter we had to have Detlef Juerss clear the snow off the roof of the indoor ring with snowblowers before the roof collapsed." Or not as bad as the summer when it rained so hard that it was impossible to mow the grass, mildew formed on all the porches, and frogs appeared like a biblical plague. Or not as bad as the year of the ice storms, when I rolled my car into a ditch, upside down, on Wigsten Road, and neither the state troopers nor the flatbed guys could stand upright on the road surface, it was so slick. Or not as bad as the year of the drought, when everything turned brown and the trees lost their leaves in midsummer, and the water table dropped so low that our well ran dry. Or not as bad as the year of the tent moths, or gypsy moths, or whatever they were, that devoured acre after acre of woodlands—at night you could actually *hear* them, chewing away at the leaves by the millions like something out of a horror movie.

Other places seem tame by comparison. In Santa Fe it gets hot in the summer and cold in the winter, but the weather is pretty predictable most of the time, and Florida is always warm and muggy, except for the occasional excitement when a major hurricane hits, but up here we live in the middle of a constant weather drama, where people can get as much excitement as they want (or more) simply by watching the Weather Channel all day long.

Partly it's a question of geography—the Hudson Valley and the Catskills seem to trap and intensify weather disturbances as they move north toward Boston or east from the Canadian border and the Great Lakes to the sea; partly it's that this is still rural America, and there are plenty of people around whose livelihoods depend on the weather, and for whom a bad storm means more than just remembering to take an umbrella to the office. Except for England, where if you took away the subject of the weather there would be hardly any conversation at all, I've seldom lived any place where the weather consumed as much attention, or formed such a large part of social discourse.

Even when the weather is good, people approach the subject cautiously. Tom Kirchhoff will stop his car to chat for a few minutes if he sees me walking on the road while he's driving by (this is still one of those places where people don't hesitate to block the road while they exchange a few words, and where it's considered bad manners not to stop if you see somebody you know on foot). "It's a beautiful day, isn't it?" he will say expansively, but his eyes are wandering toward the blue line of the Catskills, looming on the far horizon across the Hudson and above the Vandenkamp barn. If you can't see the Catskills, bad weather is either here or on its way; if you *can* see them, it still doesn't count for much, since they have a way of disappearing while you're looking at them on even the clearest of days. "I thought I might get in a round of golf this afternoon," he says.

I nod. "It's the perfect day to play hooky."

"You'd think so. Heard the weather report in the car, man says it will be like this for the next couple of days."

"Great!"

"Of course he's down there in New York City. What the hell does he know?"

"Good point, but still, it's only—what?—ninety miles away."

"It can be sunny down there, pouring rain up here. I'd say it's going to rain this afternoon, in fact."

I look up. The sky is clear, blue, cloudless. I look skeptical.

Tom stares at the Catskills, doesn't like whatever he sees there, and decides against golf. "You'll see," he says. "Don't bother watering your flowers, or paying your gardening lady to do it."

I ignore his warning—the Catskills are so clear they look as if they'd been cut out of blue paper and pasted there on the horizon—and by four o'clock, just after we've finished dragging a hundred pounds of garden hose around to water the flowers, the Catskills vanish, the sky darkens, and rain pours down. On the evening news, the weatherman down in Rockefeller Center is still announcing sunshine now and for the foreseeable future.

Of course we all know that there are weather signs—Margaret, as a farmer's daughter, knows dozens of them, from cows lying down at midday to the leaves curling up or the geese all firmly seated on the ground looking in the same direction (either toward or away from approaching bad weather—the latter seems to make more sense, but nobody is quite sure)—but reading them correctly is quite another question. On the other hand, everybody has their own. If I stop to pick up my prescriptions at John's Apothecary, John the pharmacist can reel off dozens of ways in which various bodily aches and pains predict the weather, and if any of his older customers are there chewing the fat (and they usually are; what else do they have to do?), they can come up with dozens more. Aching wrists, stiff knees, a sudden fit of sneezing, headaches, unusual behavior on the part of pets ranging from tropical fish to dogs, everything from flowers bending in a certain direction to the sight of a few stray seagulls, is harbinger to a change in the weather, and the change is seldom, if ever, for the good.

Up here, in Pleasant Valley, everybody is an expert on the weather. If I go to the doctor, the first thing she says is not "How are you?" but "What do you think it's going to do?" The dentist whom I use for emergencies has patients whose teeth are more accurate at forecasting than the National Weather Service. There's hardly anybody who doesn't start a conversation by looking up at the sky and shaking his or her head. Maybe it's being on the east coast of a big country where there are always plenty of weather problems building up and moving our way, not to speak of Canada, the national export of which seems to be arctic weather with high winds and heavy snowfalls starting, if possible, sometime just after Labor Day, or at any rate when you still have porch furniture out and the snow tires are still in storage. When is the last time you heard anybody announce on the Weather Channel, "And coming from Canada across the Great Lakes is a stream of nice warm air, bringing clear skies and bright sunshine, so break out those Bermuda shorts, folks, and say thanks to the Canadians." Every time the wind howls from the north I have an unfair urge to hum the theme music from the old James Bond movie, with a slight change in title: "From Canada, with love." I mean, I understand that the Canadians have lots of cold weather up there, but couldn't they keep it at home, *chez eux?*

In any event, it's always a safe bet to start a conversation in Pleasant Valley by looking out the window or, if you're outside, up at the sky, and saying, "Can you *believe* it?" Even when it's good weather, old habits die hard. Farmers are natural pessimists—Mother Nature gives them plenty about which to be pessimistic—and tend to view even the most perfect day with suspicion. Besides, they're superstitious. Anyone who deals with Mother Nature learns not to make rash or boastful predictions, or count on anything. If you can catch Cornelius Vandenkamp's eye long enough to say that it looks as if it's going to be a nice day tomorrow, he will rush to the nearest piece of wood and rap it with his knuckles before cautiously saying, "Well, I guess we'll see." And who can blame him? Anybody who has seen the horses put out in their fields to graze on a warm, sunny day, only to be standing ankle deep in mud a few hours later, trying to get them back in when a sudden storm has blown up out of nowhere bringing torrential rain, high winds that wrap your ankle-length Barbour rain gear around your face, and, if the local forecast on the Weather Channel is to be believed, hailstones the size of baseballs, knows that you'd better not take Mother Nature for granted or she'll teach you a lesson you won't forget.

That slight tinge of pessimism is part of the local Zeitgeist, a hand-me-down from the days when cows were driven through Pleasant Valley on their way to the slaughterhouse in Poughkeepsie, and when just about everybody who mattered around here was either a dairy farmer or an apple farmer and treated the weather with pretty much the same awed respect and fear with which Pacific Islanders treated King Kong. I don't know that too many virgins have been sacrificed to the weather gods in the Hudson Valley, but that's probably only because it never occurred to anybody to try. Or perhaps then, as now, they were in short supply.

Other towns, nearer to the river, or closer to New York City, trumpet their advantages or make a play for tourists—even Copake, hardly a town that's on every tourist's lips ("See Copake and die"?), has made a valiant effort to become the Holstein dairy cattle center of America, with everything in town painted black and white, including the mailboxes, and innumerable souvenirs for sale in the shape of Holstein cows—while Pleasant Valley still searches for that elusive, defining identity that might put it on the map.

The old wooden railway station building was saved when the tracks were torn up and moved behind the parking lot of the school, where it is not easy to find—tell the truth, not too many people are looking for it—but, as in a lot of other small American towns, not much of the past has been preserved. An aficionado of small rural cemeteries might find a few interesting gravestones, and somebody who cares about old barns might find one or two notable examples still standing, more or less, but the present has pretty much swallowed up the past.

Maybe it's just as well, really. We're spared a certain artificiality that comes along with the spirit of preservation, a coy smugness that comes from carefully elevating to landmark status things that for the most part weren't all that fascinating to begin with. One thing's for sure, we're never going to be inconvenienced by having our streets blocked with tourist buses or not being able to find a table at the Village Restaurant because of the influx of summer visitors. There are no reenactments of Revolutionary War battles to attract the visitors with fife-and-drum corps and the like (this may be because there were no battles around here, but that hasn't stopped other towns from celebrating what never happened), there's no harvest festival (unless you count pyramids of pumpkins in the aisles of the supermarket), and we don't have the draw of major historical figures boasted of by, say, nearby Hyde Park, only ten minutes from here, which has made a whole industry out of Franklin Delano Roosevelt (despite not having voted for him as a governor or a president), and is now doing likewise for Eleanor Roosevelt, in the hopes of becoming a shrine of sorts to feminists. (FDR reciprocated by building one of the ugliest small-town post offices in America in Hyde Park.) King George VI and Queen Mary (the present Queen Mum) came to Hyde Park and ate hot dogs on the lawn with the president; Winston Churchill came to Hyde Park and was given a cocktail he couldn't swallow instead of his usual whiskey and soda without ice. Ambassador Joseph P. Kennedy, father of JFK, came to Hyde Park and made FDR so angry that the president ordered Eleanor to throw Kennedy out of the house before lunch, and when told there wouldn't be a train to New York for several hours said, "Give the son-of-a-bitch a sandwich and drive him around town until the train comes, but get him out of this house." The great, the near-great, the famous, and the beautiful trooped up to Hyde Park by car or train from 1932 until 1945, but there is no record of any of them having driven down what was then Crumb Elbow Lane for fifteen minutes or so to visit Pleasant Valley—further proof that the town fathers probably shouldn't have been so quick to get rid of the covered bridge when the first automobiles reached here, thus losing what would surely have been a tourist attraction.

In the meantime, life goes on. We had intended to have the porches rebuilt this summer—dry rot, wet rot, process of dilapidation setting in—but we're having trouble building up the necessary sangfroid to undergo a large repair job, even if it is outdoors. It couldn't be as bad as replacing a roof, we tell ourselves, another of those landmarks around which we date other events ("Was that before or after the roof?"), but the thought of scaffolding, of hammering, of what may be found once parts of the porches have been torn up ("Looks like we've run into a little more than we bargained for here. . . ."), have combined to make us put it off from week to week, perhaps, if we're lucky, to the point when it's too cold to do outdoor work anymore. After all, it's not as if there aren't other things to do—we have plenty of other ways of supporting the local economy and keeping the workforce busy—windows to be stripped and rebuilt before the winter sets in, fences to be repaired, ancient and long-repressed plumbing problems to be solved that involve plaster and new tile and painting, work in the barn, a new run-in shed Detlef is putting in for Margaret's latest horse, a dark gray Irish youngster with white dapples named Dundee (after the marmalade).

We're hoping to put off having the blacktop people back this year, much as we liked the blacktopper-in-chief, with his flamboyant ash-blond punk hair, tattoos, and facial piercings, and we've got our eyes on one of our five septics, which might be going "kapooey," as Harold Roe used to say, meaning kaput, but—Knock wood!—the house hasn't produced any major surprises in quite a while, which is not to say that it might not do so at any moment.

Well, and why not? It's two hundred and sixteen years old, and now in its third century, and the people who built it weren't, after all, building for the ages like the pharaohs, even had they known how. Last year we had to have the whole front of the house pulled in, like an old lady having a face-lift—the weight of the electric and phone and cable lines had pulled it away from the house, leaving noticeable gaps through which the wind howled, particularly in Margaret's bathroom. We couldn't blame the builders for that, after all—they couldn't have imagined anybody would ever run heavy cables from the road to the house way back in 1785. A close examination by Detlef revealed that at any moment the entire front of the house might collapse onto the lawn, exposing Margaret's bathtub, the master bedroom, the library, and the living room to the elements—not to speak of anybody driving along the road who cared to slow down to look.

Margaret fought a spirited action to put off the day of reckoning, but eventually it had to be done, and needless to say proved to be traumatic, as well as uncovering all sorts of problems that one would have been happier not knowing about, but which would probably have led to the collapse of the house. We decided to use the opportunity to bury all the lines, which merely involved removing part of the white picket fence, carefully digging a trench to avoid damaging a septic tank and leach field, then covering it all up again—in short, however efficiently and quickly it was done, another big job, though not as bad (or as expensive) as the roof, or as difficult as getting a new "aboveground" oil tank into the cellar when the EPA made us fill in the buried one, or as messy as painting and wallpapering. . . . Come to that, replacing the furnace was no picnic either, now that I think of it.

Never mind. At some point we traded a modest degree of perfectionism for leaving well enough alone, and these days we're just about willing to settle for the promise that the whole place won't simply fall down on our heads before we're trundled off from here in wheelchairs for assisted living in one of the many nearby old-age homes, which have begun to replace the big state psychiatric institutions as a source of local employment.

Just last year Margaret came out of the barn to find a car idling in the driveway with two elderly women seated in it, staring at the house. They did not look to her like burglars sizing the place up—though these days, one never knows—and she assumed they were lost. Not at all, it turned out. They were on a pilgrimage of sorts, visiting the places where they had lived, and this had been their home, fifty or sixty years or more ago. They walked around the house, noting the changes, and pointed out that the big, moss-covered stone urn in the garden, by the porch, was upside down—I had always thought it was ugly and badly proportioned, but once it was turned right side up it looked a lot better.

They sent us a photograph of the house, taken before World War I, they guessed, maybe even earlier, I thought, on what looks like a nice day in the early summer. The house looks exactly the same; the same white picket fence can be seen, but the trees are noticeably smaller. A young woman is looking out the open parlor window. Over to the left, a boy in overalls holds a shiny, well-groomed horse, which is standing between the shafts of an elegant buggy. Behind the front gate stands a rather severe-looking woman in a long dress, and on either side of it are two men, one elegantly, even foppishly dressed, with a rakish hat and a neat little mustache, the other recognizably a farmer type, in baggy trousers, muddy calf-high boots, a long, old-fashioned coat, and a porkpie hat, full bearded, wearing a truculent expression, as if he were saying to himself, "When is all this nonsense going to be over and done with so I can get back to work?" A young boy in corduroy breeches and canvas-topped riding boots leans against the fence to the far right, next to his sister, who is sitting on the fence, tomboy style, and wears a pinafore. Between the two men is a dog, perhaps part collie, its tail blurred as it wags.

It's a nice scene, this, taken at our house back when the horse was still more common than the automobile, and no doubt when Pleasant Valley still had its covered bridge, when Main Street was lined with boardinghouses and small hotels for city people escaping the summer heat, and when the mill was still working, the center of the modest local economy. I note tiny Greek urns on top of the fence posts on either side of the gate, filled with flowers, or perhaps ivy, it's hard to tell. Farm life was hard, with none of the conveniences that we take for granted, but there was still apparently time to do something pretty for its own sake, as well as to dress up, or at least stand still, for a photograph. The house would have been considered old even when the photo was taken, a century and a quarter old, more or less, but it looks in pretty good shape, the paint fresh, the shutters hung the right way up (which is more than could be said of them when we bought it), the porch pleasantly shaded by a mulberry tree that has since, alas, died.

It looks like an idyllic scene, and—who knows?—perhaps one day in the future somebody will unearth a photograph of Margaret and myself, on horseback, with the house in the background, or sitting in front of the porch together, almost, by some strange coincidence, where these people were standing, and think that it all looks idyllic—a loving couple, the handsome old house, the big trees shading it all—and envy us our happiness, or perhaps the illusion of a simpler, better time in the past. . . .

Sometimes, when I need to walk out onto the rolling lawn that slopes unevenly down to the woods on one side of the house—usually because whoever is looking after the lawn has managed to get his mower stuck in the soft, wet patch in the center of it, and left deep tire tracks—I sigh, and stop, and turn, and look up at the house from where I'm standing, and feel a sense of surprise and wonder, as I did the day we bought it; this, I say to myself, *belongs* to us, it's ours.

At such times I feel not so much a sense of pride—after all, the house isn't a landmark, or even architecturally distinguished in any way; it's merely old and has a lot of "character," as they say—as a deep feeling of satisfaction, coupled with a fierce determination to protect it. People we know in Westchester have houses with far more beautiful grounds, or much larger houses, with a swimming pool and a tennis court, but this is *ours*, with all its problems, most of them having to do with sheer age, and the consequences of trying to correct them on the cheap in the decades since the photo was taken.

Not far from where I stand lies an old tombstone, disfigured and worn almost smooth with time. The lettering was carved by an unskilled hand, the stone chisel wielded by somebody to whom writing didn't come easily or naturally. The letters are really scraped into the stone rather than carved—there's no embellishment to them. In fact they look a little like Nordic runes, and it takes a while before you can make out that they're letters of our familiar alphabet. There's a failed effort at neatness, but after the first couple of lines the letters are all higgledy-piggledy, at wrong angles, squeezed together in clumps when whoever was making them realized that he was running out of space. At the top a lovely curved line attempts to suggest the shape of a more expensive formal gravestone; then the date "1771," framed by the initials "E.V." With much effort it is possible to read, "Elizabeth, 16 yrs. 11 months, the daughter of Elisa and Oliver V——, died April the 24th." The name beginning with a "V" might be Vaughan, it's hard to say.

The place was a farm long before our house was built. Probably there was a cabin here first, then a modest house, then after poor Elizabeth's death, some moment of prosperity and optimism led to building something larger and more elaborate in 1785. Long before then, somebody—the grieving father Oliver V—— of the tombstone? *his* father or grandfather?—cleared the land, uprooted the trees, dragged out the stumps with a team of oxen, and used the stones to build walls. I am standing, feet sinking in the wet, soggy patch at the center of this lawn, looking up toward the big porch and what used to be the front door in the eighteenth century. There would have been no porch on the house at all then, if only because nobody on an eighteenth-century farm at this latitude would have had the time or the inclination to sit on one.

Behind me are the remnants of a stone wall that dates back to the time of poor Elizabeth's tombstone, a time when, oddly enough in view of Margaret's nationality and my own, the people here still thought of themselves as English, those of them who weren't Dutch. From this angle the house has a certain substantial look to it, with many interesting angles, and despite its far too many windows and doors, it gives the impression of being good for another two hundred years or so.

I walk around the house, trying not to look at it too closely. Usually I do this in the company of Detlef and his two Labs, looking for things that need fixing, while Detlef writes them down on his clipboard, or occasionally reaches over to prod at some doubtful piece of wood and shake his head sadly in commiseration, but I don't want to spot any flaws or problems today for some reason. Two hundred years ago the house probably wasn't nearly as shaded; the big trees all around us would have been smaller then, some of them only saplings. Even today, people look at our trees with a certain amount of disapproval—trees close to the house mean, sooner or later, a big tree limb down on the roof, if you're lucky; if you're unlucky, a whole tree. Still, the trees are part of the charm, part of what makes the house special, the fact that it sits on a rise, surrounded by big, old trees into which it nestles artfully, like the hobbits' houses in J. R. R. Tolkien's *Lord of the Rings.* You see it through the trees, parts of a house, never—except in the depths of winter, and from a certain spot on the lawn, where I am standing now, with wet shoes—the whole.

In front of the door to my office are a pair of wonderfully lifelike reclining white marble lions, eighteenth-century Italian copies of Roman originals, which my father bought to decorate the fireplace of some set at my uncle Alex's studios in Denham before the war, then brought home to put in our garden, first in Hampstead, then in Chelsea. They survived the Blitz and thirty years of London fog and grime, and now, scrubbed clean, have settled in here in Pleasant Valley for good with us. I think my father would have approved. He would have enjoyed seeing them sitting at either end of the huge eighteenth-century slab of granite that serves as a step. He had a great contempt for the kind of collectors who kept things that were meant to be outdoors indoors, merely because they were valuable.

I continue around the house—there is the well house, close by, as it would have to have been in the days when you had to haul in the water in buckets, and securely protected with a gate to prevent children from playing there. A wise precaution. If you lift the wooden floor and drop a stone down, it's a moment before you hear a splash—a long way down. Nowadays, of course, we have a more modern well—though not necessarily more reliable—with a pump deep down that needs to be replaced every once in a while, usually at just the wrong moment, like the July Fourth weekend, when even the most dedicated plumber isn't likely to show up in a hurry.

I stand now where the photographer must have stood who took the picture the two old ladies showed us—and of which they sent us, very kindly, a copy. The window through which the young woman was looking out is sealed shut now, but otherwise nothing much has changed, except for our widening the front porch and screening it in, under the illusion that we would be sitting on it for drinks or dinner in the long summer evenings, looking out at the woods, instead of which, given the prevailing climate, our first instinct is to go inside and turn the air conditioner on full blast.

Besides, who has the leisure? What were we *thinking* of, back then? The day goes by in such a blur of activity—horses to be ridden and looked after, cars to be serviced and repaired, people to pick up at the station, workmen double-parking in the driveway to fix this or that in the house or the barn, the blacksmith or the hay man or the vet expected at any minute (which means making everybody move their cars)—that the idea of sitting down on the porch and doing nothing seems as hard to imagine for us as it would have been to those hard-working farmers of the eighteenth century.

We must have been out of our minds, or simply swayed by looking at too many photographs of elegant country living in *Vogue* or *The*

New York Times Sunday Magazine. Who *are* these people in their designer clothes sitting on their beautifully decorated porches, sipping Bellinis without a care in the world? Where is the plumber who has chosen this moment to tell them, on a Friday night with a house full of guests, that he won't be able to get the part he needs to fix the hot-water heater until Monday? Where is somebody from the barn bringing the news that Madam's horse has just thrown a shoe, and we need the blacksmith right away if he's going to be ridden tomorrow? Where are the guys who have been working on the truck to say that they're knocking off for the night now, and that they can't figure out what the problem is either? Where is the person who has just remembered that when the propane man came last week he filled up the tank by the barn but forgot to fill up the one by the house?

Every spring we unwrap the porch furniture, with the beautiful flowered cushions that Thom von Buelow had made for us, and set up the porch as if the photographer from *Vogue* were on the way, and every autumn we wrap it all up again, and say, for the umpteenth time, with a sigh, "My God, we never used it *once* this year!" as if that were a surprise. But when would we be using it? At just the time of day when the people in *Vogue* are drifting onto their porch to rest languidly and admire their own good taste, we are looking for that missing horseshoe in the high grass and the mud, or gathered in the driveway for a postmortem on the truck, or still upstairs, undressed and sweaty, wrestling with the fact that there's no hot water, or out in the garden trying to water all the flowers before they die. We live, in short, a different life, in a different part of the country.

There are compensations, of course. Only the other day, I was standing in one of the local hardware stores trying to replace a burned-out lightbulb—not as easy a task as you might suppose, since Thom, when he "redid" our house a few years ago, installed many wonderful and attractive lamps, most of which seem to use bulbs that nobody outside the specialty shops in New York City or some decorator's lighting place in Milan has ever heard of or seen.

The proprietor takes the burned-out bulb from my hand, looks at it suspiciously, and shakes his head. "We don't stock anything like that," he says, giving it back to me. "Never seen the like of it."

I am not astonished. Even to me it looks like a fairly unusual bulb. I pick up a few other things I need, and as the boy behind the counter looks at me, I hear the proprietor whisper, "That's Mr. Korda—from up at the Korda place."

"Up at the Korda place." My ears ring with pleasure, as if I were listening to Handel's *Messiah.* No doubt one day it will be "the *old* Korda place," when we've gone like the Hubners and the Hewitts, but that's all right. I have a brief epiphany, right there in the housewares aisle, at the thought that at last, after more than twenty-one years of living up here, the house is *ours* in the minds of our neighbors, no longer "the old Hubner place," or "the old Hewlett farm" to real old-timers, but *ours*—"the Korda place" finally, *home!*

I put the burned-out bulb into my pocket and get into the car, parked between the health food shop, run by Seventh Day Adventists (closed on Saturdays, open on Sundays, like Orthodox Jews), and a shop that sells radio-controlled model airplanes—Pleasant Valley is full of small businesses that seem to survive without any evidence of customers. I drive home, past Dunkin' Donuts, past the Methodist Church parking lot—scene of a recent love-triangle murder after choir practice—on past another new vinyl-sided apartment complex, then turn and pass Wigsten Farm, where Mrs. Thatcher is waiting wistfully in her pen for Margaret to appear with leftover mashed potatoes and crab cakes, or a maple-frosted doughnut with sprinkles from Dunkin' Donuts; the animal hospital, then trees, a flash of broad green lawns (looking better from a distance than up close), lots of fencing, red barns with white trim, the woods and fields just visible beyond the paddocks as I turn into the driveway past the big English pig sign, which I put up as a present to Margaret, to the great confusion of our neighbors and occasional passersby—home.

John Howard Payn got it right, I think.

Acknowledgments

FIRST, AND MOST IMPORTANT, my love and thanks to Margaret, who is both a major character in this book and the one who urged me to write it. It is a shared story—a major chunk of our lives.

My thanks also to my dear friend and agent, Lynn Nesbit, who never wavered from her initial enthusiasm, perhaps because she too has a house in the country, not an hour from ours. Lawrence Ashmead, my editor, also owns an old house about an hour north of us, which gave him a deep and instant feeling for this material—he too has heard the sound of freezing pipes at midnight. Tina Brown gave me the opportunity of first writing about "country matters" in *Talk* magazine, for which I am deeply grateful.

I am particularly indebted to the following people for all sorts of information: Peter and Joyce Banks, Libby Dowden, Richard and Roxanne Bacon, Olive C. Doty, Pleasant Valley's former librarian and now its historian, and our friend Detlef Juerss, whose peerless gifts, patience, and sound judgment as a builder and contractor set him apart from many of those described in this book, and to Judson D. Hale, Sr., and Yankee Publishing, Inc. for their kindness..

Finally, with affection and sadness, this book would not be complete without the mention of two indispensable figures and dear friends in our lives up here, Dot Burnett and Harold Roe, whom we still miss every day.

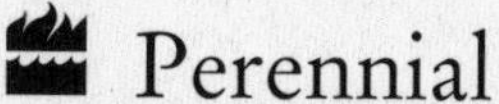

Perennial

Books by Michael Korda:

COUNTRY MATTERS

The Pleasures and Tribulations of Moving from a Big City to an Old Country Farmhouse

ISBN 0-06-095748-4 (paperback)

With his inimitable sense of humor and storytelling talent, *New York Times* best-selling author Michael Korda brings us this charming, hilarious, self-deprecating memoir of a city couple's new life in the country. Sure to have readers in stitches, this is a book that has universal appeal for all who have ever dreamed of owning that perfect little place to escape to up in the country.

"Korda's search for a rural paradise is easy, often hilarious, reading."
—Maxine Kumin, *New York Times Book Review*

CHARMED LIVES

A Family Romance

ISBN 0-06-008556-8 (paperback)

Rising from obscurity in the Hungarian countryside to the pinnacle of Hollywood society, Sir Alexander Korda was the embodiment of the Cinderella legend—but his darker impulses nearly brought his family to its knees. His brothers, Zoltan and Vincent led similarly charmed lives in circles that included H.G. Wells, Winston Churchill, and Alex's wife Merle Oberon. With a loving but undeceived eye, Michael Korda recounts the trials and successes that fame brought to the Korda brothers.

"A rags to riches fairytale...Rich in anecdote...In a word: Charming!"
—*Newsday*

Available wherever books are sold, or call 1-800-331-3761 to order.